Vincent van Gogh

1853 | 1890
| 1990

Vincent van Gogh

DRAWINGS

Rijksmuseum Kröller-Müller

Otterlo

PAINTINGS

Rijksmuseum Vincent van Gogh

Amsterdam

March 30th - July 29th

1990

DRAWINGS

Vincent van Gogh

Johannes van der Wolk

Ronald Pickvance

E.B.F. Pey

ARNOLDO MONDADORI ARTE

DE LUCA EDIZIONI D'ARTE

Contents

Vincent van Gogh
The Road to Tarascon with a Man Walking, 1888
Zurich, Kunsthaus (Graphische Sammlung)

Foreword

Few painters appeal to the imagination as much as Vincent van Gogh. In less than ten years, under very difficult circumstances and almost entirely through his own efforts, this inspired son of a parson grew from amateur into a mature master whose work has become renowned far beyond the borders of his native land.

He did not live to see his talent recognised. Nor could he possibly ever have dreamt that he would be an enduring source of inspiration for subsequent generations of artists.

Only a small circle of artists showed any interest in his work during his own lifetime. Now he is a household name and his paintings and drawings are admired throughout the world.

It is safe to say that his oeuvre is still best represented in his own native country. The Rijksmuseum Vincent van Gogh in Amsterdam and the Rijksmuseum Kröller-Müller in Otterlo contain the two largest Van Gogh collections in the world. The Amsterdam museum also has the fascinating letters which the painter wrote to his brother Theo.

Thanks to the efforts of both museums, this great artist is being honoured on the centenary of his death with a major retrospective of his work, which has lost none of its eloquence in the last one hundred years.

QUEEN OF THE NETHERLANDS

Van Gogh 1990

Patron

Her Majesty the Queen of The Netherlands

Committee of Honour

Otto M. von der Gablentz *Ambassador of the Federal Republic of Germany*
Dr Frantiseck Chlád *Ambassador of Czechoslovakia*
Tadashi Otaka *Ambassador of Japan*
M.R.H. Jenkins *Ambassador of the United Kingdom*
L. Ceyssens *Ambassador of Belgium*
K. Wildau *Ambassador of the German Democratic Republic*
A.D. Chikvaidze *Ambassador of the Soviet Union*
F.-Ch. Pictet *Ambassador of Switzerland*
C. Howard Wilkins Jr *Ambassador of the United States of America*
J.R. Bernard *Ambassador of France*
Antonello Pietromarchi *Ambassador of Italy*
R.F.M. Lubbers *Prime Minister*
W. Kok *Deputy Prime Minister, Minister of Finance*
H. van den Broek *Minister of Foreign Affairs*
H. d'Ancona *Minister of Welfare, Public Health and Cultural Affairs*
L.C. Brinkman *Ex-minister of Welfare, Public Health and Cultural Affairs*
J. Dondelinger *Commissioner for Cultural Affairs at the European Commission in Brussels*
R.J. de Wit *Queen's Commissioner in the Province of North Holland*
M. de Bruijne *Queen's Commissioner in the Province of Gelderland*
E. van Thijn *Burgomaster of Amsterdam*
W. Blanken *Burgomaster of Ede*
J. van Gogh *Chairman of the Vincent van Gogh Foundation*
Dr J. Bartels *Chairman of the Kröller-Müller Foundation*
H.J.L. Vonhoff *Chairman of the Executive Board of the Hoge Veluwe National Park*

Committee of Recommendation

C. Boonstra *Chairman of the Executive Board of Sara Lee / DE NV*
A.H. Heineken *Chairman and Delegate Member of the Supervisory Council of Heineken NV*
J.A.J. Janssen *Chairman of the Board of the Dutch Savings Banks Association*
J.F.A. de Soet *KLM Royal Dutch Airlines*
Toichiro Hitotsuyanagi *Special Advisor Asahi Shimbun*
Kikuo Tashiro *Corporate Advisor TV Asahi*
Noboyuki Nakashima *Former Ambassador of Japan*

Sponsors

Sara Lee/DE
Heineken NV
KLM Royal Dutch Airlines
Dutch Savings Banks Association

Lenders

Austria
Vienna Albertina

Belgium
Brussels Musée d'Art Moderne
Tournai Musée des Beaux-Arts de Tournai

Canada
Ottawa National Galleries of Canada/
Musée des Beaux-Arts du Canada
Toronto The Art Gallery of Ontario

Federal Republic of Germany
Essen Museum Folkwang
Frankfurt Städelsches Kunstinstitut
Karlsruhe Staatliche Kunsthalle (Kupferstichkabinett)
Munich Staatliche Graphische Sammlung
Stuttgart Staatsgalerie (Graphische Sammlung)

German Democratic Republic
Berlin Nationalgalerie der Staatlichen Museen zu Berlin

France
Paris Musée du Louvre

Great Britain
London The Trustees of the British Museum
London The Trustees of the Tate Gallery
Manchester Whitworth Art Gallery (University of Manchester)
Walsall, West Midlands Walsall Museum & Art Gallery

Hungary
Budapest Szépmüvészeti Múzeum

Italy
Milan Civica Galleria d'Arte Moderna

The Netherlands
Amsterdam Rijksmuseum Vincent van Gogh
Amsterdam Rijksmuseum Vincent van Gogh (Vincent van Gogh Stichting)

Amsterdam Rijksprentenkabinet (Rijksmuseum)
Amsterdam Stedelijk Museum
Amsterdam Stichting P. en N. de Boer
The Hague Haags Gemeentemuseum
The Hague Mevrouw W. Nieuwenhuizen Segaar
Groningen Groninger Museum
Otterlo Rijksmuseum Kröller-Müller
Rotterdam Museum Boymans-van Beuningen
Utrecht Centraal Museum

Norway
Oslo Nasjonalgalleriet

Switzerland
Winterthur Kunstmuseum
Zurich Kunsthaus (Graphische Sammlung)

United States of America
Baltimore The Baltimore Museum of Art
Boston Museum of Fine Arts
Chicago The Art Institute
Dallas The Dallas Museum of Art
Glenn Falls, New York The Hyde Collection
Houston The Menil Collection
Los Angeles The Los Angeles County Museum of Art
Malibu The J. Paul Getty Museum
New York The Brooklyn Museum
New York Cooper-Hewitt Museum
New York The Metropolitan Museum of Art
New York The Museum of Modern Art
New York The Pierpont Morgan Library
New York Mr. and Mrs. Eugene Thaw
Philadelphia The Philadelphia Museum of Art
Washington, D.C. The Phillips Collection
Worcester, Massachusetts Worcester Art Museum

and some private collectors who prefer to remain anonymous

The assistance of many was indispensable in organising this exhibition. We owe a major debt of gratitude to the people who played a vital role in obtaining the loans: William R. Acquavella (Acquavella Galleries, New York); Hofrat dr. Hubert Adolph (Österreichische Galerie, Vienna); Julian Andrews (The British Council, Amsterdam); Serge Baron Le Bailly de Tilleghem (Musée des Beaux-Arts de Tournai, Tournai); Pietro M. Bardi (Museu de Arte de São Paulo, São Paulo); Heinz Berggruen; J. Carter Brown (National Gallery Washington); Timothy Clifford (National Gallery of Scotland, Edinburgh); Roland Dorn (Kunsthalle Mannheim); Douglas W. Druick (The Art Insitute of Chicago); Elaine Evans-Dee (Cooper-Hewitt Museum, The Smithsonian Institution's National Museum of Design, New York); Sabine Fehlemann (Von der Heydt Museum, Wuppertal); Walter Feilchenfeldt; Mary Gardner Neill (Yale University Art Gallery, New Haven); Christian Geelhaar (Öffentliche Kunstsammlung, Basel); Mr L.H.J.B. van Gorkom (Dutch Ambassador in Vienna); Sir Lawrence Gowing; Margrit Hahnloser; Armand Hammer; C. Hasegawa (Galerie Nichido, Tokyo); Ay-Whang Hsia (Wildenstein and Co., New York); Nathan Kernan (Robert Miller Galleries, New York); Tsukasa Kōdera; Jirí Kotalík (Národní Galeri, Prague); Werner H. Kramarsky; Michel Laclotte (Louvre, Paris); Ellen W. Lee (Indianapolis Museum of Art); Arnold L. Lehman (Baltimore Museum of Art); Neil MacGregor (National Gallery, London); Gabriele Mazzotta; Th. Meijer (Netherlands Institute, Rome); Charles S. Moffett (National Gallery of Art, Washington); David Nash (Sotheby's New York); Martha Op de Coul (Rijksdienst voor Kunsthistorische Documentatie, The Hague); Laughlin Phillips (Phillips Collection, Washington); V.J. Popov (Minister of Housing and Communal Economy of the RSFSR); Eliza Rathbone (Phillips Collection Washington); John Rewald; Kathryn A. Ritchie; Joseph J. Rishel (Philadelphia Museum of Art); Samuel Sachs II (The Detroit Institute of Arts); S. Salzmann (Kunsthalle Bremen); Alan Shestack (Boston Museum of Fine Arts); Julian Spalding (Glasgow Art Gallery and Museum); Rudolf Staechelin (Rudolf Staechelin'sche Familienstiftung, Basel); Marja Supinen; Peter C. Sutton (Boston Museum of Fine Arts); Susan Alyson Stein (Metropolitan Museum of Art, New York); Michel Strauss (Sotheby's London); John L. Tancock (Sotheby's New York); Gary Tinterow (Metropolitan Museum of Art, New York); Kirk Varnedoe (Museum of Modern Art, New York); Charlotte Wiethoff (Museum Boymans-Van Beuningen, Rotterdam); Martha Wolff (Art Institute of Chicago); Kasumi Zenitani (Fujii Gallery, Tokyo); Marke Zervudachi. In restoring the works important assistance was given by: Mette Marie Bang; Centraal Laboratorium voor Onderzoek van Voorwerpen van Kunst en Wetenschap, Amsterdam; Carol Stringari (Museum of Modern Art, New York). The organisers of the exhibition and the makers of the catalogue are very grateful for the assistance of: Cécile Brunner (Kunsthaus Zurich); Martin Cleaver; Han van Crimpen (Rijksmuseum Vincent van Gogh, Amsterdam); Jacqueline van Ewijk; The Framing Sisters; Anne Göschel; Tom Haartsen; Michael Hoyle; Jan Hulsker ; Artemis Karagheusian; Monique Nonne (Musée d'Orsay, Paris); Thijs Quispel; Anne Roquebert (Musée d'Orsay, Paris); Drukkerij Mart. Spruijt, with special thanks to Jan Kohlmann; Han Veenenbos (Vincent van Gogh Stichting, Amsterdam). For the technical arrangements in the Rijksmuseum Vincent van Gogh we wish to express our gratitude to: E. Guidjaja; Ir. T.H.W. Horstmeijer (Technische Universiteit, Delft); E.J.F.B. van Huis (Ministry of Welfare, Public Health and Cultural Affairs, Rijswijk); F.J.P.M. Koopman; F.N. Kuyper; R. Maak; Prof. B.M. Polak (Technische Universiteit, Delft); Rijksgebouwendienst; C. van 't Veen (Ministry of Welfare, Public Health and Cultural Affairs, Rijswijk), and Frank Wintermans. For the technical arrangements in the Rijksmuseum Kröller-Müller we wish to express our gratitude to: Rijksgebouwendienst Directie Oost (Arnhem); W. Quist (architect Rotterdam); J.G. Verheul (Bureau W. Quist, Rotterdam); J.C. van Iperen (Ministry of Welfare, Public Health and Cultural Affairs, Rijswijk); Adviescentrum Beveiliging Rijksgebouwen (Rijksgebouwendienst, The Hague) and the Gemeentepolitie of Ede.

Preface

No more fitting tribute is imaginable on the centenary of Vincent van Gogh's death than an attempt to bring together that part of his work which the artist himself considered most important. Van Gogh, who produced about eleven hundred drawings and almost nine hundred paintings in a career that spanned barely ten years, was very critical toward his oeuvre. He regarded many of his products as no more than exercises for a mature work of art. Only the sum of these mature paintings and drawings did he consider his true *oeuvre*, the essence of his artistry, by which he wanted to be known by the public and remembered by posterity.

The Rijksmuseum Kröller-Müller in Otterlo and the Rijksmuseum Vincent van Gogh in Amsterdam naturally regarded the organisation of this exhibition as their own special responsibility, given that they house the two largest Van Gogh collections in the world. Otterlo provides a home for the former collection of Mrs Kröller-Müller, which has been kept in the Rijksmuseum Kröller-Müller since 1938. The works from the estate of the Van Gogh family are preserved in Amsterdam, having been kept for many years by Theo van Gogh's widow Mrs J. van Gogh-Bonger and her son ir dr V.W. van Gogh. They are now administered by the Vincent van Gogh Foundation.

In 1953 an exhibition was put together from these same two collections to mark the centenary of Vincent van Gogh's birth, but this time the aim is to bring to The Netherlands as many works as possible from abroad as well. Such an undertaking has not been attempted since the two Van Gogh exhibitions in 1905 and 1930, both held in Amsterdam. The current exhibition is presented as a unified whole, with a division by medium: the paintings are on show in Amsterdam, the drawings in Otterlo.

It would have been impossible to organise any exhibition without the willing cooperation of so many lenders throughout the world. We are grateful to all of them for the trust they have placed in us by lending their rare and valuable possessions.

The exhibition stretched the capacities of both museums to the limit and has only been possible thanks to the fundamental and substantial assistance of both government and business. We are, first and foremost, most grateful to Her Majesty the Queen of The Netherlands for her willingness to act as patron for the exhibition and the other events taking place in the Van Gogh Centenary Year 1990. This massive undertaking would not have been possible without the practical and moral support provided by the Minister of Welfare, Health and Cultural Affairs, Mr L. C. Brinkman and after him Mrs H. d'Ancona. For instance, it was partly because of the Van Gogh plans that a government-sponsored indemnity arrangement was introduced, which in turn made the exhibition feasible.

The world of industry and commerce has been most willing to help, and its generous financial support made it possible to organise not only the exhibition but also the whole Van Gogh Centenary Year. We are extremely grateful to all the many firms which have provided financial, moral and material assistance and mention here only the main sponsors: Sara Lee/DE; Heineken NV; KLM Royal Dutch Airlines; Dutch Savings Banks Association.

The Van Gogh 1990 Foundation was formed to assist with the exhibition and to coordinate the Van Gogh Centenary Year. It has been active in many ways organising and coordinating the exhibition. We are most grateful to the board of the foundation and its advisors chaired by S. Patijn and the bureau of the foundation and director F. Becht for all they have done for the exhibition. The Board of the Vincent van Gogh Foundation and the College of Regents of the Kröller-Müller Foundation have been closely involved all along in developing the plans. They have always been willing to provide sympathetic advice and support.

Louis van Tilborgh and Johannes van der Wolk were responsible for the selection of the paintings and drawings respectively and for editing the catalogues. In this regard we would also like to thank Professor Ronald Pickvance, who assisted us with the selection and with obtaining loans. Sjraar van Heugten, Ineke Pey, Professor Pickvance, and Professor Evert van Uitert also worked on the catalogue alongside the two editors. Professor Van Uitert's article about the concept of Van Gogh's oeuvre provided in many ways the starting point for the exhibition. Liesbeth Heenk provided indispensable assistance in putting together the volume of drawings. We are most grateful for their efforts.

Large teams in both museums have provided intensive and vital assistance to the technical and administrative organization of the exhibition for several years. The efforts of the restorers, who worked hard to make sure that Van Gogh's works from our own collections are in the best possible condition to be shown to the public, are also greatly appreciated. Finally, we would like to thank Walter Nikkels, the designer of the catalogues and the posters, and Marijke van der Wijst and Pieter Brattinga who designed the exhibitions in Amsterdam and Otterlo respectively.

Both museums regard it as a privelege that they have been able to bring together Van Gogh's *oeuvre* in order to reveal both the strongly individualistic quality of Vincent's work and its remarkable coherence.

RUDOLF W. OXENAAR
Director
Rijksmuseum Kröller-Müller

RONALD DE LEEUW
Director
Rijksmuseum Vincent van Gogh

JOHANNES VAN DER WOLK

Van Gogh the Draughtsman at his Best

THE ROOT OF EVERYTHING IS DRAWING

It is scarcely possible to imagine a finer motto for an exhibition such as the present one than 'the root of everything is drawing' [290]. Van Gogh explicitly and deliberately began his artistic career as a draughtsman and not as a painter. It is, of course, the obvious thing for a beginner in the field of art to start by exploring its problems and possibilities as a draughtsman. After all, a painter's materials are more expensive than a draughtsman's. Apart from a few early experiments, Van Gogh only really started painting in The Hague. But even at that time this still represented a big step for him. Van Gogh then wrote to his brother Theo: 'One day, when people begin to say that I can draw something, but cannot paint, then perhaps I will come up sometime with a painting just at the moment when they are not expecting it. But as long as it looks as though I must do it, and as though I could do nothing else, then I will certainly not do it' [184].

Van Gogh prefers to do things his own way. He thinks that 'the most practical road' is to practise drawing first, 'since one can go more easily from drawing to painting than the other way around, that is, making paintings without drawing the neces-sary studies for them' [188]. 'I have restrained myself greatly and confined myself to drawing, precisely because I know so many sad stories of people who threw themselves into it [i.e. into painting] rashly – sought the answer in the process and woke up disillusioned without having made any progress and had got up to their ears in debt because of the expensive items they had made a botch of. I was frightened and hesitant about that right from the start, I regarded drawing, and still regard it, as the only means of not sharing in the same fate. And I have fallen in love with drawing, instead of regarding it as a burden' [226].

In letters to his family and to his artist friends, Van Gogh often wrote in detail about individual drawings, but even more about the series, about the groups to which he assigned his drawings. He is not so much the artist of the single, indepen-dent drawing, as the artist who depicted subjects in a series of drawings in a planned manner. These groups of drawings constitute the backbone of the exhibition. They are presented in more or less chronological order. In one of his letters to

Theo [316] Van Gogh announced to his brother that he would write him a letter at his leisure in which he would summarise his own thoughts and intentions as an artist. Theo could then use this letter if he happened to meet a possible purchaser for Van Gogh's work. It is not known whether Van Gogh ever really wrote the letter mentioned. What we do know, however, is that in numerous letters he did inform the addressee – and the reader of today – bit by bit about his views. Van Gogh: 'My idea mainly being this: one of my drawings in itself will not be fully satisfactory even as time goes on, but a number of studies, however different they may be, will nevertheless complement each other. In short, for the art lovers themselves it is, in my opinion, better to take a number of them than just a single one. And if it comes to money, I would prefer to deal with an art lover who buys cheaply but constantly rather than with someone who buys only once, even though he then paid well' [316].

The exhibition opens with some drawings which were presumably created in Brussels early in 1881 and concludes with the drawings Van Gogh made nine years later, in 1890, at Auvers-sur-Oise. In the intervening period we follow him in The Netherlands, first to Etten, then to The Hague, Drenthe and Nuenen, to Antwerp in Belgium and finally in France to Paris, Arles and Saint-Rémy-de-Provence. The drawings are arranged in groups according to place as far as possible. In this way, the result of the drawing campaigns on which Van Gogh embarked throughout the years unfolds. Although, of course, there are the inevitable sidetracks and interruptions, one main, continuous line nevertheless becomes apparent. The decision to exhibit the groups which were of most essential importance to the artist himself and, within these groups, his most outstanding drawings, has resulted in an exhibition which shows Van Gogh 'at his best'.

The relationships between Van Gogh's paintings and his drawings are numerous and varied in nature. Taken together, they constitute a pattern which changes with the years, made up of preliminary studies, interim reports (letter sketches), colour notations, copies intended for others, and so on. This exhibition is primarily concerned with the drawings which, although links with paintings are of course discernible in virtually every case – and these relationships are sometimes intentionally suggested by the artist – had their own value and autonomous significance for Van Gogh precisely as drawings. Although the geographical distance between Otterlo and Amsterdam entails a certain degree of inconvenience for the exhibition visitor, the opportunity to concentrate on the paintings and drawings as two separate media, disregarding their mutual dependence, more than makes up for this negative aspect. 'Van Gogh the Draughtsman' cannot help but emerge from it more clearly and more strongly.

THE MIRACLE OF SPEED

While it was quite some time before Van Gogh got into his stride as a painter, the process of learning to be a draughtsman also involved some hard practice and perseverance on his part. This process of gradual development, of successes and setbacks, can, of course, be most clearly seen from the surviving drawings themselves. A few quotations from letters dating from his Hague period make it clear that Van Gogh, too, fully realised that fact. Van Gogh: 'Drawing is something like writing. When one learns to write as a child, one feels that it is impossible ever to master it, and it seems like a miracle when one sees the schoolmaster writing so quickly. That does not alter the fact that one gets the hang of it after all in due course. And I really believe that one must learn to draw in such a way that it goes just as easily as writing something down and that one must have the proportions so clearly in mind and must learn to see in such a way that one can reproduce at will what one sees on a larger or smaller scale' [232]. 'It always remains a cause of a kind of disappointment to me that in my drawings I still do not see that which I wanted to have in them. The difficulties are really many and great, and cannot be overcome at one go. Making progress is a kind of miner's work, which does not advance as quickly as one might wish oneself, and as others also probably expect, but when one is confronted with such work, the first thing one must preserve is patience and faith. Actually, I do not think about the difficulties much, precisely because if one started worrying about them one would become dizzy or confused. A weaver who has to manage a large number of threads and weave them through each other has no time to philosophise about how they hang together, but rather he becomes so lost in the work that he does not think, but does, and feels more how all of it can and must work out correctly, rather than being able to give an explanation of it' [274].

As regards the speed of drawing mentioned in the passage just quoted from *letter 232* it is useful to know that it was not until six years later, in the summer of 1888, that Van Gogh felt he had achieved the desired speed. At that time he was working in Les Saintes-Maries-de-la-Mer, the small fishing port on the Mediterranean not far from Arles. Earlier that year, he had moved from Paris to Provence, to that part of France which he sincerely believed resembled Japan as he had come to know it from the

Japanese woodcuts collected so assiduously by him in Paris. Van Gogh: 'As regards the question of staying in the south, even if it is more expensive, let me see: one loves Japanese painting, one has undergone its influence, all the impressionists have that in common, and one would not go to Japan, that is, to what is the equivalent of Japan, the South? So I still believe that, all things considered, the future of the new art lies in the South [...] I would like you [Theo] to spend some time here, you would feel what I mean after a while, your view of things changes, you see with a more Japanese eye, you feel colour much more intensely'. And then he comes right to the point: 'The Japanese draws quickly, very quickly, like a lightning flash, because his nerves are finer, his feelings simpler. I have only been here for a few months, but tell me, could I have made the drawing of the boats in an hour in Paris? Not even with the perspective frame, and this was done without measuring and just by letting the pen go its own way' [500].

Van Gogh was constantly aware of the conflict between the careful preparations for the construction of a composition, on the one hand, and the drawing speed he regarded as desirable, on the other hand. In his pointillist phase in Paris, for example, this quickly led him to replace the minute dots of colour in his paintings by much more rhythmical and longer, more briskly applied strokes of paint. Van Gogh was explicitly interested in the effect of colours placed side by side in the form of dots, but did not have the patience to accept the inevitable slowness this involved. He is the artist of the flowing movement. Concentration on minutiae was not in his nature.

The drawing of the boats referred to in the passage just quoted is probably F 1428. The perspective frame *(le cadre)* is an *fig. 2* instrument which was frequently used by Van Gogh. It gave him a basis for the mutual relationships and the course of the lines in a composition. So on the beach at Les Saintes-Maries-de-la-Mer Van Gogh – as he mentioned specially in his letter – did not use the frame. Oddly enough, Van Gogh once portrayed himself in action on the Scheveningen dunes with the perspective frame, in a sketch in *letter 222* to be precise. *fig. 1* Van Gogh on that perspective frame: 'The result is that on the beach or in a meadow or in a field one has a view as though through a window. The perpendicular lines and spirit level lines in the frame, in addition to the diagonals and the cross, or otherwise a division into squares, definitely give some main points which enable one to make a drawing with certainty which indicates the main lines and proportions. At least they do that if one has a feeling for perspective, and an understanding of the reason why and the way in which the perspective gives the lines an apparent change in direction, and the masses and planes a change in size. Without that, the frame gives little or no help and one becomes dizzy looking through it. I think you will certainly feel that it is a wonderful thing to train these sights on the sea, on the green fields or, in winter, on the snow-covered plain or, in autumn, on the irregular network of thin

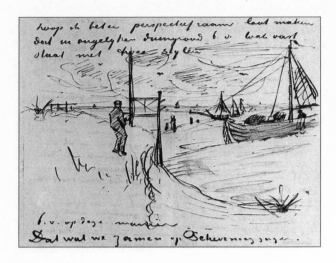

and thick trunks and branches, or a stormy sky. With a great deal of practice, and with long practice, it enables one to draw at lightning speed – and with the drawing completed, to paint at lightning speed' [223].

SOWING AND REAPING

Van Gogh always set his mind to practising over and over again so that when the time came he could build on routine and no longer needed to search. Van Gogh: 'I really am so happy that it has been arranged in such a way that I can work here [i.e. in Etten] for some time. I hope to make as many studies as I possibly can, for that is the seed from which drawings come later' [144]. In this way, Van Gogh made a distinction between (drawn) *studies* and *drawings* derived from them. In his later paintings, too, he made an explicit distinction between (painted) *studies* and *paintings*. For example, he wrote 'that studies which one makes out of doors are something different from paintings intended to go into the world. Which latter, in my view, stem from the studies but nevertheless may and even must differ greatly from them. For in a painting the artist gives more of a personal vision, and in a study his aim is simply to analyse a piece of nature. Whether it is to give his idea or conception correctness – or to get an idea. So studies belong more in the studio than in the shop, and must not be looked at from the same viewpoint as paintings. Now I think that you will probably also look at it in this way and automatically take these things into account [...] I regard making studies as sowing, and making paintings is reaping' [233].

Among other things, during his period in The Hague Van Gogh worked hard to develop a repertoire of figures in numerous attitudes intended for later use. At one moment, he regarded these 'repertoire figures' as being of only secondary importance, namely as elements to be used as he wished in a large composition. The next moment, he considered them as individual figures, but also thought they were suitable for duplication as lithographs. At one time, therefore, they were only suitable for use as and when required and, at another, also worth the respect and the trouble of printing as lithographs in their own right. As regards the combined compositions, Van Gogh was also faced with another problem 'like that of the chicken and the egg, must one make figures for a composition which has first been found, or combine figures which one makes individually so that the composition is the result of them? It will, I think, probably amount to the same thing, if only one works' [237].

SOMETHING NOBLE AND DIGNIFIED

Van Gogh remained primarily a doer, a pragmatist. On the theoretical plane, he was just as flexible as it suited him to be in practice. This does not mean that Van Gogh did not set himself any goals, but rather that these goals could be exchanged relatively spontaneously and were always located on a shifting horizon. For example, one of Van Gogh's goals was his idea of developing into a magazine illustrator. From childhood onwards he had shared the hobby of collecting illustrations with his brother Theo and his sister Wil. These were divided into two categories, namely illustrations specially made for magazines and reproductions of existing artworks, and he was interested in both. The pictures they cut out were first pasted into scrapbooks. Later, when the collection became too big for this and the need to put it into order became more strongly apparent, Van Gogh stuck the illustrations on to separate sheets.

fig. 3 - 4

In letters to his artist friend and fellow collector of magazine illustrations Anton van Rappard, Van Gogh has given us pointers which enable us to understand why he was so intensely interested in these. Van Gogh: 'And particularly while I myself am toiling to make something of these things which continually interest me more on the street, in the third class waiting room, on the beach, in a hospital, my respect for these great draughtsmen of the people [...] increases more' [R 12]. 'To me, the English draughtsmen are what Dickens is in the field of literature. It is one and the same sentiment, noble and healthy and to which one keeps on returning again and again. Sooner or later I would very much like you to have an opportunity of looking through my whole collection at your leisure. Precisely through seeing many of them together one gets an overview and it begins to speak for itself and one sees clearly what a magnificent whole this school of draughtsmen forms. Just as one must read Dickens or Balzac or Zola as a whole in order to know them individually' [R 13]. 'I assure you that in my collection of woodcuts, on every occasion when I am feeling less lively, I again find a new desire to set to work myself. In all these people I see an energy and a willpower and a free healthy lively mind which inspire me. And in their work there is something noble and dignified, even if they are drawing a dung heap' [R 16].

No subject was too humble for Van Gogh. Following in the footsteps of the illustrators he so greatly admired he developed a preference for everyday subjects. He did, however, endeavour to elevate these everyday subjects above the anecdotal level and give them a more universal validity. Van Gogh to Van Rappard: 'I assure you that the Graphics I now have are amazingly interesting. More than ten years ago in London I went every week to the display window of the works which printed the Graphic and London News to see the weekly editions. Impressions I obtained there on the spot were so strong that in spite of everything that has gone over my head since then the drawings have remained clear and bright. And now I sometimes feel as if there were nothing between these old days and now – at least the enthusiasm I felt for them then is now more, rather than less, than it was originally' [R 20]. 'On

fig. 3
H. Herkomer
Low Lodging House St. Giles
Amsterdam, Rijksmuseum Vincent van Gogh
(Vincent van Gogh Stichting)

fig. 4
Auguste Lançon
Une Equipe de Ramasseurs de Neige
Amsterdam, Rijksmuseum Vincent van Gogh
(Vincent van Gogh Stichting)

VAN GOGH THE DRAUGHTSMAN

looking through them, all the memories from the London of ten years ago came back to me, of when I saw them for the first time and they moved me so much that I have kept on thinking about them constantly since' [R 23]. 'To my mind, pages like these together constitute a kind of bible for an artist which he reads now and then in order to get into tune. It is good not only to know them, but also to have them in the studio once and for all, I think' [R 25].

In his letters to Theo, too, Van Gogh made no attempt to conceal his enthusiasm for magazine illustrations. Van Gogh: 'What I value in Herkomer, in Fildes, in Hol and the other founders of the Graphic, why they appeal to me even more than Gavarni and Daumier, and will continue to do so, is, that while the latter seem to look at society more with malice, the former, in keeping with men such as Millet, Breton, de Groux, Israels, choose subjects, just as true as those of Gavarni or Daumier, but which have something noble about them and in which there is a more serious sentiment. That above all must remain, I think. An artist need not be a minister or a church elder, but must nevertheless certainly have a warm heart for people, and I think, for example, it is something noble that no winter went past but the Graphic did something to keep sympathy for the poor alive' [240]. 'Theo, when you come to the studio sometime then I will be able to show you something which you most certainly cannot see everywhere gathered together in this way. I could show you something that might be called *les cent chefs d'oeuvres de la gravure sur bois moderne* [the hundred masterpieces of modern wood engraving]. Work by people whose names are completely unfamiliar even to most connoisseurs of art [...] Seen together, one is amazed at this firmness of drawing, that personal character, this seriousness of conception and that penetration and elevation of the most everyday figures found on the street, on the market place, in a hospital or orphanage' [297].

Magazine illustrations were a recurrent source of inspiration to Van Gogh not only because of their themes, but also because of the 'black & white' technique which greatly appealed to him. Van Gogh: 'In many cases Black & White is precisely a means which makes it possible to put down on the paper in relatively short times effects which in any other way lose something of what is called *spontané*. I doubt whether the fig. 3 London sketches such as *Low Lodginghouse St. Giles* by Herkomer, and *Casual Ward* by Fildes would not be slightly less moving and full of character if they were painted than in the rough Black & White. There is something manly in it, something rough which attracts me strongly' [R 20]. 'In these punchy, powerful, manly drawings there is something stimulating and strengthening just as there is in old wine' [R 23].

In the exhibition, the drawings are arranged by place and then, once again, by group. This has been done with the intention of placing the emphasis on the same aspects as Van Gogh did in setting his goals: figures as anatomical studies, figures as types, figures at rest, figures in action, the topography of the town, life in the town, but also the 'black and white' of the line drawing as against the colour of the watercolour drawing. Sometimes a group is dictated by the kind of paper on which Van Gogh drew, or by something practical such as the size of the sheet. Sometimes, too, by the function of the drawings – for example, in those cases where he made a drawn version for Theo or for his artist friends of one or more paintings he had completed.

At a certain moment Van Gogh intended to make albums with six, ten or twelve drawings for Paul Gauguin and Emile Bernard, among others. As the form for these albums, he thought of the type he had seen in use in Paris for Japanese drawings. In a letter to Theo [492] he clarified his intention with a small sketch of such an album which he planned to bind in an orange or lemon-yellow cover. As far as is known, however, Van Gogh never carried out his plan. He did, however, make loose-leaf series for Bernard and John Russell which are reasonably different from each other because of their difference in style. The point is that in this case Van Gogh took account of the artistic views of the person for whom he made the drawings. Everything points to the fact that Bernard did put the drawings he received from Van Gogh into an album. At a later date, however, the drawings were again removed from the album for at present they are in private and public collections in Europe and America.

Sometimes, too, inscriptions on the drawings help them to be recognised as belonging to a particular series. For example, in some but not all of the drawings which must be attributed to the first series Van Gogh made in The Hague for his uncle C.M. van Gogh (Uncle Cor) the locations depicted are mentioned in handwriting on the back. One problem in that case, however, is that the handwriting cannot be attributed with certainty to Van Gogh. It certainly does not look like the style of writing in which he usually wrote his letters. Nor does comparison of these titles with titles which can be attributed with certainty to Van Gogh, such as those on the drawing 'Sorrow' (F 929a) and on the lithograph 'At Eternity's Gate' cat.. 35 (F 1662), lead to a clear conclusion about the authorship of these fig. 16 inscriptions either for or against Van Gogh. Whether Van Gogh – or whoever else wrote them – was so consistent as to indicate the titles on the complete series remains an open question. That would probably be asking too much of an artist to whom the drawings themselves were naturally more important than recording where he had made them. That would, however, certainly have been very convenient for reconstructing the group a century later.

In Nuenen, Van Gogh gave some of his drawings of male and female peasants at work a title which was intended to clarify the nature of their labours. He did that in French, writing them on those drawings which he regarded as especially suitable for Theo to show to his acquaintances in the art trade and the publishing world. In Arles, it was particularly the topographically based compositions to which Van Gogh gave a title, sometimes bordered by a drawn cartouche. Then too, however, he certainly did not do this systematically and consistently. That simply was not part of Van Gogh's nature either, for he was always busy with the next work when he had scarcely finished the previous one.

SOUVENIRS DE PROVENCE

To conclude this introduction I cannot resist speculating on a series of etchings which he planned to make in Auvers-sur-Oise on the theme of 'Memories of Provence'. The sketchbook which Van Gogh used in Auvers-sur-Oise (SB 7) and his letters constitute the key to what could have been such a fine culmination of his work in the south of France. Van Gogh did not give himself the time for this. When he met Dr. Paul Gachet in Auvers-sur-Oise, he did not only come into contact with someone who had already been a good friend to numerous artists – including Cézanne, Pissarro and Guillaumin – but also someone who had an etching press at home and kept it regularly in use both for himself and for his artist friends. During his time in The Hague, Van Gogh had made eight lithographs and another one in Nuenen. After that, nothing more had come of it, either in Antwerp and Paris or in Arles and Saint-Rémy-de-Provence. And from the period when Van Gogh was living and working in Auvers-sur-Oise, only one etching has been preserved. It is the etching with the portrait of Gachet, which is also known as 'The man with the pipe' (F 1664).

Thanks to Gachet and his etching press, in Auvers-sur-Oise Van Gogh suddenly saw the opportunity within his reach to make a series of prints based on earlier work, only now these would not be lithographs but etchings. His enthusiasm for the printing process from the Hague period acquired a new impetus. Van Gogh was firmly convinced that Gachet would be willing to print the etchings for him free of charge, particularly if he were allowed to keep a number of copies for himself. Van Gogh expected that Paul Gauguin would also certainly be interested in such a plan. Surprisingly enough, however, he did not propose that any of Gauguin's recent work should be represented in the series of prints. Instead of this he thought mainly – or perhaps even exclusively – of work which Gauguin had produced much earlier, during his stay on Martinique. In view of the fact that Van Gogh himself chose subjects from Provence, Gauguin's production from the period when he was staying with Van Gogh in Arles would have been the most suitable works for a joint portfolio.

In *letter* 642 Van Gogh announced to Theo that Gachet would come to Paris to look at the paintings he had in store and that Gachet and he himself would then select the works which could serve as examples for the series of etchings. Sketchbook SB 7 can help us to discover the motifs which Van Gogh had in mind for his series of etchings. For example, it contains a drawing of 'The Olive Pickers' (SB 7|5), a theme which Van Gogh had already selected for this purpose in Saint-Rémy-de-Provence, although at that time he was still thinking of lithographs and not etchings. He had hit upon the idea because of the description Theo had given him of a portfolio with twenty lithographs printed by A.M. Lauzet in various colours, made after paintings by Adolphe Monticelli, who was very highly regarded by Van Gogh. Fired with enthusiasm, he immediately began to devise plans for producing a similar portfolio based on his own work. It seems justifiable to assume that in Auvers-sur-Oise, Van Gogh was practising in his sketchbook for the *Souvenirs de Provence* which he planned to start etching. Perhaps he also wanted to show Gachet the paintings to which the latter should pay particular attention in Paris.

Leafing through this sketchbook, we come across three subjects from Arles and three from Saint-Rémy-de-Provence. Those from Arles are 'Vase with Fourteen Sunflowers' (SB 7|90), 'Vase with Twelve Sunflowers' (SB 7|91) and 'Les Alyscamps' (SB 7|142). The subjects which can be traced back to Saint-Rémy are 'The Olive Pickers' (SB 7|5), 'Two Walkers in a Ravine' (SB 7|6) and 'A Vase with Irises (SB 7|92). *fig.* 6

The theme of 'Les Alyscamps' in Arles is also known from four paintings which are compositionally related to each other, two by two. Paintings F 486 and F 487 offer a view between the autumnal poplars which border Les Alyscamps, seen from a high vantage point. In the other two (F 568 and F 569) Van Gogh lets us look along Les Alyscamps. The sketchbook drawing SB 7|142 is closest to F 486. The vantage point selected, however, is now much lower. There are no walkers to be seen and the sarcophagus in the centre almost completely fills the picture. What has remained, however, is the slanting view between the trees. Van Gogh has relied on his memory and, in doing so, intended to concentrate on the most characteristic feature of the place: the trees and the sarcophagi.

That also applies to SB 7|6 in relation to paintings F 661 and F 662. While we first see the rocky landscape in the paintings *fig.* 5 and only discern the walkers on the little bridge after that, in the drawing the walkers are the first thing that strikes us. Paul *fig.* 6 Gauguin was very impressed by one of the two painted versions when he saw them at the Salon des Indépendants (March/April 1890), an exhibition at which Van Gogh was well represented with ten paintings. Gauguin reproduced it in a 'thumbnail sketch' in one of his letters to Van Gogh [GAC 40]. *fig.* 7 The difference between Gauguin's sketch in the letter and Van Gogh's sketchbook drawing is striking. It is almost incredible that both drawings refer to the same painting. It is note-

worthy that Gauguin, in his sketch, emphasised the landscape, and Van Gogh the human presence.

The history of the planned but unproduced etchings makes us realise that Van Gogh did not always manage to carry out all his plans and, in addition, that not all the work which was in fact created has been preserved. For what would be more obvious than to assume that Van Gogh, along with the sketchbook drawings in preparation for the etchings, would also have made larger drawings of the same pictures? That applies to the work Van Gogh produced in Auvers-sur-Oise and it will undoubtedly also be true of that from earlier periods. Nevertheless, I believe it may unreservedly be said that the present exhibition forms a framework showing what was important to Van Gogh as a draughtsman. To join Van Gogh [245] in quoting Herkomer: 'For you – the public – it is really done'.

fig. 5 (F 661)
Vincent van Gogh
Two Walkers in a Ravine, 1889
Otterlo, Rijksmuseum Kröller-Müller

fig. 6 (SB 7|6)
Vincent van Gogh
Two Walkers in a Ravine, 1890
Amsterdam, Rijksmuseum Vincent van Gogh
(Vincent van Gogh Stichting)

fig. 7
Paul Gauguin
Sketch in letter GAC 40
Amsterdam, Rijksmuseum Vincent van Gogh
(Vincent van Gogh Stichting)

RONALD PICKVANCE

Drawing and Painting:
the French Connection
(Post-Paris)

A comparatively slender dialogue exists between drawing and painting in Van Gogh's post-Paris *oeuvre*. One immediate reason for this is the scarcity of drawings from the model that so characterised his output in The Hague and Nuenen. Van Gogh's predicament was highlighted in the two attemps he made to paint 'Christ in the Garden of Olives'. On both occasions, in July and September 1888, he scraped them off because he felt he 'must not do figures of that importance without models' [505]. He even thought of a variation: a starry night 'with a group of living figures of artist-friends' [543], a democratized version, presumably, of Cézanne's 'Apotheosis of Delacroix'. But that, too, was never realised. And no trace of these compositions exists, no figure studies of Christ or the Angels, or the artist-friends. Perhaps they were rapidly indicated in a now lost sketchbook. Van Gogh made no ambitious figure compositions in his post-Paris period. Gauguin may have cajoled him into painting from memory, but the few imaginative compositions that followed were evidently done without preparatory drawings. The will to undertake a grand figure composition was occasionally there; but models failed him, or he felt discouraged, or he was seduced by the beauty of the Provencal landscape.

Thus, a large corpus of figure drawings that would occupy our attention in the drawn *oeuvre* of Watteau, Ingres, Degas, and Gauguin, simply does not exist. We are spared that investigation into the nature of the dialogue between the drawn studies and their counterparts in the finished paintings. For these artists, drawing had that vital primary function. Their drawings were precious objects, secretly and jealously hoarded in portfolios, private documents not to be shown publicly, as Gauguin coyly claimed.

Moreover, in the act of transference from drawn to painted image, these artists would often square-up their drawings, including their final compositional studies. Or they would use tracing paper to transfer a composition, even, in the case of Degas, reversing the tracing to evolve a mirror-image. And Gauguin utilized the Renaissance technique of pricking through his drawings in order to transfer the design to canvas.

Such instances of direct physical transference are extremely rare in Van Gogh's post-Paris work. There is one isolated example of his using tracing paper to transfer a drawn image of a death's head moth from paper to canvas (F 1523). Not one squared-up drawing exists: only in making his 'translations' from Millet, Daumier, Delacroix, and Doré, in Saint-Rémy, did Van Gogh square-up the prints for transfer to canvas. Even his use of a drawing annotated with notes on colour is rare: only one from his entire Arles period (F 1428), one in Saint-Rémy (F 1549 v), and two much more minor examples in Auvers-sur-Oise (F 1638 r and F 1640 v). (Paradoxically, the only two drawings in Paris that have colour annotations – F 1374 and F 1409 – have no painted equivalent.)

cat. 244

Unlike Ingres or Degas when working on a portrait, Van Gogh did not make any preparatory studies. The only possible exception is the small drawing of 'Mlle Gachet at the Piano' (F 1623 r), which may be a first idea for the painting (F 772). And what is also extraordinary, is the virtual absence of drawings from the model in Arles, Saint-Rémy, and Auvers-sur-Oise. The one exception is the large drawing of the Zouave (F 1443) which is quite altered in pose, costume, and setting from the two paintings that were done contemporaneously.

cat. 203

The vast majority of Van Gogh's post-Paris drawings are landscapes. It is the interaction of their relationship to his paintings that constitutes the slender dialogue between the two media. Four categories can be established. (i) Drawings that are quite independent of paintings, and often produced in distinct phases. (ii) Shared motifs, where drawing and painting are used to explore a new subject, but where ultimately the two remain distinct. (iii) Those paintings that are definitely made from drawings. (iv) The reversal of this last category – those drawings that are definitely made after paintings.

Drawing was not a continuous daily activity. Painting, after all, was Van Gogh's primary means of expression in his post-Paris period. But there were times when, for reasons of economy or lack of materials, he was unable to paint. In Arles, where his drawing activity can be followed in considerably more detail than in Saint-Rémy or Auvers-sur-Oise, three distinct drawing phases can be isolated. Van Gogh's first series of some twenty-four pen-and-ink drawings were made during the fortnight in late April and early May 1888 when he gave up painting. Later in May 1888, he drew a special series of seven views of the Abbey of Montmajour. And, above all, in early July 1888, he spent almost a week working exclusively on five large

fig. 8 (F 407)
Vincent van Gogh
Path through a Field with Willows, 1888
Private Collection, Switzerland

fig. 9 (F 1455)
Vincent van Gogh
A Garden in the Provence, 1888
Winterthur, Sammlung Oskar Reinhart 'Am Römerholz'

finished drawings of Montmajour that were intended as surrogate paintings. In Saint-Rémy, only one such all-encompassing phase can be isolated: a fortnight in May and June 1889, when he produced a series of large drawings in the garden of the asylum. In Auvers-sur-Oise, where his stay was brief – seventy days – and where documentary evidence is weakest, no clear-cut phases can be suggested.

The second category encompasses a different phenomenon. Van Gogh sometimes chose to attack a newly discovered motif in both drawing and painting. Such instances can often be observed in Arles, for example, a Provencal garden *fig. 9* (F 1455), a view of the Rhône (F 1462), a café in the centre of the *cat. 205* town (F 1519). These are joint explorations, in which the draw- *cat. 208* ing retains its independent status. In all cases, there are sufficient changes between the two media to suggest that each represents a separate recording. These drawings were not used directly in the making of the painting.

This phenomenon of the shared motif did not arise in Saint-Rémy. Even though Van Gogh spent the first month of his stay there confined to working in the asylum garden, the motifs of paintings and drawings never coincide. Immediately upon his arrival in Auvers-sur-Oise, however, Van Gogh made four drawings, three of which are closely related to paintings *cat. 241* (F 1640 r, F 1640 v, and F 1638 r). Yet in all three cases, they too *cat. 244* are separate recordings. Their fascination lies in comparing the variations that ensue from a slight shift in vantage-point and a differently proportioned format.

The third category concerns those drawings that were used directly as working guides to paintings. Apart from the two examples already cited of drawings annotated with colour (F 1428 and F 1549 v), there are three clearly documented instances of Van Gogh's direct use of a drawing in making a painting. The first is the early drawing 'Path through a Field *cat. 165* with Willows' (F 1499), which became the working model for the studio-made painting (F 407). The other two were on-the- *fig. 8* spot drawings done at Saintes-Maries-de-la-Mer (F 1434 and *cat. 180, 182* F 1438), which, a few days later, formed the basis of two studio-made paintings in Arles (F 419 and F 420). An undocumented pairing can also be suggested – that between the drawing of a 'Mas de Provence' (F 1478) and the subsequent studio-made *cat. 204* painting (F 565). No comparable instances occurred in Saint-Rémy or Auvers-sur-Oise.

The fourth category – drawings and watercolours after paintings – is very much Van Gogh's own. Other contemporary artists might reproduce their paintings as etchings (Manet), or in illustrated avant-garde periodicals, or in illustrated Salon catalogues (particularly prevalent in the 1880s), or have selected works reproduced by another hand (for example, Thornley's fifteen lithographs after Degas, published through the auspices of Theo van Gogh, by Boussod and Valadon in 1888). But only Van Gogh made entire series of drawings after his own paintings – and not for publication, but as progress reports for his brother, or exchanges with, or gifts to, two artist-friends, Emile Bernard and John Peter Russell. More than one third of Van Gogh's drawn *oeuvre* in Arles consists of drawings and watercolours after his own paintings. Their purpose was clear; and their stylistic characteristics overtly distinguishable from drawings from nature.

cat. 237 - 238
fig. 10

This process continued in Saint-Rémy, but for Theo alone. Ten drawings after May-June landscapes were despatched to Paris on 2 July 1889; two further ones after late autumn landscapes (F 1545 and F 1552) were done in late November or early December 1889, and a final one in February 1890 (F 1525a). The nature of the 'improvements', whether simplifications or elaborations, that occurred in these drawings, highlights their idiosyncratic place in the dialogue between drawing and painting.

So much for the dry mechanics. (These various elements are discussed more fully in the respective sections of the catalogue.) But apart from questions of segregation and categorisation, drawings have their complex graphic systems that send out different messages in coded analogues. These graphic systems, however, do not exist in a vacuum: they are adjusted to the purpose of the drawing and its intended destination. And Van Gogh always distinguished between a *croquis hâtif*, a quick sketch from nature, and a more deliberately conceived and executed drawing. He so divided the seven half-sheets of Montmajour, done in May 1888, from the five large drawings of July 1888. Such an application of the academy-based hierarchies to the act of drawing should not surprise us. He always maintained a comparable hierarchical distinction in his painting between *étude* and *tableau*.

cat. 187 - 188

Van Gogh rarely expressed a value-judgement on his drawings. From the excess of one hundred done in Arles, he only commented twice. Once was on the two 'cartouched' drawings of Montmajour (F 1424 and F 1420): 'the best things I have done in pen-and-ink'. The other occasion was when citing three large drawings of Provencal gardens he picked out

cat. 207

'the little cottage garden done vertically' (F 1456) as the best. He described the motif. It 'has in itself amazing colours: the dahlias are a rich and sombre purple; the double row of flowers is pink and green on one side, and orange with hardly any leaves on the other. In the midst a white dwarf dahlia, and a little pomegranate with flowers of the most vivid reddish-orange, with yellowish-green fruits. The ground grey, the tall reeds, 'cannes', blue-green, the fig trees emerald, the sky blue, the houses white with green windows and red roofs, in the morning full in the sunshine, in the evening drowned in the shadows thrown by the fig trees and the reeds' [519].

Words as substitute painting. Can a black-and-white drawing also be transformed into a substitute painting, not in containing all these *colours*, but in conveying *colour*? Colour as an abstract emanation from the intricate web of strokes of the sinuously used Provencal reed pen. Colour which evokes

fig. 10 (F 1525a)
Vincent van Gogh
Cypresses with Two Women, 1889
Otterlo, Rijksmuseum Kröller-Müller

fig. 11 (F 1540)
Vincent van Gogh
The Starry Night, 1889
Now lost, formerly Bremen, Kunsthalle

DRAWING AND PAINTING

intense Provencal heat; and that marvellously limpid atmosphere, that often peculiarly tangible air and amazing clarity, that constantly beguiled Van Gogh's Northern eye. All this he sought in his five large drawings of Montmajour, where 'colour' is accompanied by the repetitive sounds of the cicadas and the mixed perfumes of fig, pomegranate, oleander, pine and cypress.

Similar sensations are experienced in front of the ten Saint-Rémy drawings, especially those done after Van Gogh's June landscapes, emblems of early summer in Provence. For Theo, unaware of the landscape of the South, these drawings were difficult to comprehend. The wilful and arbitrary marks of the reed pen (graphs of a distorted nature, or of nature distorted?) might make sense, he thought, once he had seen the paintings. In 1990, eight of these nine June landscape paintings are on show in Amsterdam; while all nine surviving drawings are at fig. 11 Otterlo (only the drawing after the 'Starry Night' (F 1540), once in the museum of Bremen, is absent). The stylistic ricochets between painting and drawing, the immediate confrontation of impastoed brushstrokes with simplifying marks of the reed, the 'translation' of colour into pen-and-ink, the tenuous shifts in format and alignment that affect the compositional base, have to be experienced at forty miles distance. In September 1889, Theo was able to compare them in one place, at his own pace.

One of the most astonishing facets concerning Van Gogh's Arles drawings is the fact that they were so quickly despatched to Theo in Paris, sometimes the day after completion, at most a fortnight later, in pairs or small groups. Between April and mid-August 1888, Theo received some seventy drawings. From mid-August until May 1889, he received less than six, as Van Gogh's output declined to a trickle in the autumn and drawing was put into long hibernation from November 1888 to May 1889. Would Watteau or Ingres, Degas or Gauguin have deprived themselves of *all* their drawings so soon after their creation?

But Van Gogh had his special reasons. Part of his 'contract' with his brother was to send work to Paris from time to time. This not only proved that he was working, but it produced an encouraging and critical dialogue with Theo – and with others who saw it. Drawings were very much part of this process. The first series of some twenty-four pen-and-ink sketches introduced Theo to Provence, giving him a guide to Arles and its environs, however idiosyncratic and anti-picturesque. Seven others of Montmajour were intended for exhibition in Amsterdam. Five larger and more finished views of Montmajour were seen as potentially salable to a minor Paris dealer, to help settle Gauguin's debts in Brittany and pay for his journey to Arles. And the special category of watercolours and drawings after paintings was meant to give Theo an immediate indication of what he had done, as well as 'improving' in their more controlled touches some of the paintings.

'If the roll is not too big to be accepted by the post office, you will receive another large pen drawing, which I should very much like the Pissarros to see if they come on Sunday', Vincent told Theo on 28 June 1888 when sending his view of cat. 183 Arles from Montmajour (F 1452). This shows something of his predicament as an exile in the South, away from the mainstream, engaged in the conflict of country versus city, provinces versus Paris. And it underlines what has just been said: how his Arles, and subsequently his Saint-Rémy drawings (though we have much less precise details of their movements), left his Provencal hide-away and reached the centre of the European avant-garde. Van Gogh was not unwilling or shy about showing his drawings – at least not to Camille Pissarro, whose judgement he greatly respected, whose advice he would listen to as much as Cézanne and Gauguin had done in the past. Theo's Paris apartment became Vincent's studio; there his drawings, often grudgingly accepted by the post office, would be kept and shown to interested visitors.

That, too, has to be of some moment, some historical interest. Were these drawings appreciated as much as the paintings? The first two pen-and-ink drawings sent to Theo clearly impressed the young Dutch artist A.H. Koning, then staying with Theo, who offered to exchange one of his paintings for them. Theo himself must also have been impressed by what he saw of his brother's increasing ability with the reed pen, for he asked Vincent to make a set of drawings specially to send to the second exhibition of the Dutch Etching Society in Amsterdam. Van Gogh responded enthusiastically by making his seven *croquis hâtifs*, but then in sending them to Paris, wondered whether it was really worth the price of the frames to have them in the Amsterdam exhibition.

Some of these seven drawings might have been shown to other artists, Guillaumin, Toulouse-Lautrec, Signac and, in November, on his return from Brittany, Emile Bernard. As for Bernard, he had made an album of the fifteen drawings that Van Gogh had sent him in mid-July, showing the album to Gauguin and his circle of followers in Pont-Aven: another source of dissemination and appreciation.

Such encounters *chez Theo* can only be imagined, but others are documented. In July 1889, for example, Octave Maus, secretary of Les XX, the avant-garde exhibiting society in Brussels, visited Theo along with the Belgian painter Theo van Rysselberghe. The two were in Paris looking at the work of artists they might like to invite to their next annual exhibition, due to open in January 1890. Theo showed them paintings – mostly of Arles, but including some recently arrived Saint-Rémy canvases. But what especially fascinated Octave Maus were the drawings. Maus wanted to include some of them in the exhibition. As late as December 1889, Theo was still asking Vincent if he should frame two drawings and send them to Brussels with six paintings. In the event, because of Van Gogh's breakdown in the last week of December, no drawings were sent. Maus's lively interest suggests that he did not see the drawings as secondary to paintings, but admired them for their own sake.

An even warmer admirer of the drawings visited Theo in December 1889. This was A.M. Lauzet, a young artist from Marseilles who was engaged on an album of lithographs after Monticelli and who visited Theo's apartment to look at the six paintings owned by the Van Gogh brothers. 'But what pleased him most', wrote Theo on 22 December, 'were your canvases and drawings; oh, my dear fellow, that man understands them! [...] While going through the drawings he came across a gatherer of fallen apples which he liked very much, and I made him a present of it, for I think you would have done the same. Next day he came to see me again at the shop to ask me whether it was not possible to have another drawing which you did at the very beginning of your stay at Saint-Rémy. On the left there is a small cluster of sombre trees against a sky with a waxing moon, on the right a gate. He told me he could not get this drawing out of his mind, that it was even finer than the drawings by V. Hugo, which he liked very much, and so on. I proposed to him to exchange it for a copy of his Monticelli album, and he accepted immediately' [T 22].

In spite of Theo's efforts for Amsterdam in 1888 and Octave Maus's efforts for Brussels in 1890, Van Gogh's drawings were not exhibited during the artist's lifetime. But where Maus had failed in 1890, he succeeded in 1891. He then arranged a small memorial exhibition of Van Gogh's work as part of Les XX in Brussels. Eight paintings were shown; but they were almost balanced by seven drawings. It was the first time that Vincent's drawings were included in an exhibition. One of them 'Provence, Verger d'Oliviers' was bought by the prominent Belgian collector Henri-Emile van Cutsem. It is ironical that the very first drawing to be bought from an exhibition was then lost to Van Gogh's *oeuvre* for almost a century. 'Provence, Verger d'Oliviers' was one of the five large Montmajour drawings of July 1888: the long-lost drawing that had led to all kinds of ingenious speculation on the true identity of the 'missing' fifth drawing. Part of the generous bequest of Van Cutsem to the city of Tournai, the drawing was reunited with Van Gogh's *oeuvre* in New York in 1984.

cat. 185

For all his pains in making possible the exhibiting of these drawings in Brussels, Octave Maus was offered a drawing by Theo's widow – the 'Marine' (F 1430b), one of the five drawings after paintings sent to Theo in August 1888.

cat. 201

Van Gogh's post-Paris drawings had, in terms of influence, three central exemplars: Japanese woodblock prints, Delacroix and Daumier. Japanese prints provided his idealised vision of the South; he used them constantly in a whole range of analogies that he applied to the Provencal landscape, to his own paintings, and to his watercolours and drawings. They provided stylistic nourishment: he wanted to do watercolours 'in the manner of Japanese prints'. His two 'best'

drawings from the Montmajour series (F 1420 and F 1424) were said not to look Japanese, 'but which really are, perhaps more so than some others' [509]. And that perhaps is the clue. Van Gogh absorbed the influence, rather than slavishly copied the external effects. The same process had occured earlier in The Hague when he was so deeply under the spell of the English illustrators. In the end, there is no possibility of confusion between Van Gogh and his sources.

cat. 18

Delacroix was a constant beacon to Van Gogh from the moment in Nuenen in 1884 that he read about him in Blanc, Gigoux and Silvestre. And Delacroix's theory of drawing by oval masses rather than by contour was one that stayed with Van Gogh, not only as a practice always to be followed literally, but as a conscious expression of those dynamic and pulsating rhythms that infuse so many of his post-Paris drawings.

Daumier's presence was less profound than Delacroix's, but it did have one moment of intensity. In autumn 1888, Daumier invaded Van Gogh's conception of Arles. He wanted his simple, yeoman-like studio in the Yellow House to have 'a feeling of Daumier about it' [574]. In Arles itself, he assured Gauguin, 'you will see nothing more beautiful than Daumier; for very often the figures here are absolutely Daumier' [544a], a sentiment repeated to Theo: 'I am content with my lot, it isn't a superb, sublime country, this; it is only a Daumier come to life' [522]. And he wanted to emulate the lightening draughtsmanship of Daumier, catching a figure on the spur of the moment.

Of his contemporaries' drawings, Van Gogh said little. But then it is doubtful that he ever saw a drawing or a watercolour by Cézanne; doubtful, too, that he saw any of Seurat's conté crayon drawings (Theo acquired a Seurat *café-concert* drawing three weeks after Vincent's departure for Arles). Degas's charcoal and chalk drawings would also be unknown to Van Gogh, though he certainly saw the pastels of nudes and milliners at the last Impressionist Exhibition of 1886, and a smaller group of nudes at Theo's gallery in early 1888. But no influence is obvious on his post-Paris drawings.

Drawings he certainly did see were Emile Bernard's, sent to him in Arles from Brittany. These tended to be rather light-hearted sketches than seriously conceived drawings. And in any case, they were quickly sent on to Theo in Paris. In fact, the only drawings Van Gogh saw at first hand were Gauguin's during their two months together in the Yellow House. Yet neither artist said a word about drawing at the time, nothing of their activity, nothing about the primary function of drawing in the making of a painting. But Gauguin left behind a drawing of 'L'Arlésienne' (The Fine Arts Museums of San Francisco) from which Van Gogh later made five painted copies: four survive (F 540 - F 543). This was the only occasion in the whole of Van Gogh's post-Paris period that he used a preparatory drawing of a model to make a painted portrait. It is profoundly ironical that the drawing should have been by

Gauguin. But this emphasizes once more the main reason for the relatively slender dialogue that exists between painting and drawing in the post-Paris period: the absence of figure drawings. The exchanges are conducted about landscape. Often distinctions are clear-cut and decisive. The most intriguing aspect lies in those cases where there is not a one-to-one relationship, but where margins of deviation and difference, in composition, surface, and stroke, constitute the enigmatic centre of the painting-drawing dialectic.

E.B.F. PEY

Chalk the Colour
of Ploughed-up Land on
a Summer Evening[1]

WHAT WERE VAN GOGH'S DRAWING MATERIALS?

To draw, you use a pencil. Or chalk. Or ink. Or you use all three side by side with each other, perhaps even also supplemented by other materials, resulting in a mixed technique. But is that also true of Van Gogh? This is a question that confronts every attentive observer of Van Gogh's drawings. Not only curators and restorers, but also the interested museum visitor. Many other questions arise in addition to this. Did Van Gogh also use drawing materials other than those most familiar to us? Did he use them automatically, uncritically, because they were also employed by other artists or because they were readily available? Did Van Gogh have a preference for a particular material? If so, did he use it to achieve a special effect? Or was a particular effect perhaps created by using various materials side by side with each other?

Up to now questions such as this about Van Gogh's drawing technique have hardly ever been discussed in the literature.[2] We may wonder why this should be. Does this subject lack interest or is there little to be said about it? Nothing could be further from the truth. In the first place, Van Gogh himself was very interested in his drawing materials. His letters are frequently 'larded' with detailed comments on drawing techniques and materials. Secondly, Van Gogh approached his materials in a fascinating way. He was engaged in an endless search for new ways of creating the effect he wished to achieve.

The reason why Van Gogh's drawing techniques and materials have nevertheless hitherto been treated so much as a Cinderella in terms of the attention paid to them must probably mainly be sought in the fact that drawing materials are difficult to identify with the naked eye, and even with a normal magnifying glass (5 x to 10 x magnification). Here there is a very high probability of incorrect interpretations.[3] Careful observation of drawings at exhibitions makes this particularly apparent: inaccuracies repeatedly occur in the descriptions of the materials used. For example, black chalk is taken for charcoal, or for pencil, etc. Sometimes, too, drawings are linked with materials which were not (yet) available at the period in question (anachronisms).

During the research for the present article forty drawings displayed in the exhibition were examined. For the purposes of the description I had to confine myself to a selection from these which may be regarded as representative of Van Gogh's oeuvre in this field. In investigating the materials used in these drawings a microscope (maximum magnification 50 x) proved indispensable. The point is that under the microscope details can be seen which, in fact, make it possible to distinguish between apparently identical drawing materials. Greatly enlarged, they frequently display a characteristic picture (unfortunately impossible to record on film), besides which they are unexpectedly beautiful: for example, pencil lines gleam like metal, while Italian chalk contains a mass of dazzling crystals, dark, white and clear. Under the microscope charcoal lines look as if they have 'exploded', surrounded as they are by countless dazzling black needles which have flown off. The drawing materials on Van Gogh's drawings were compared with modern, similar materials, for to date it has proved impossible to find nineteenth century pencils and chalks as reference materials. Not all of Van Gogh's drawing materials could be recognised with this method. For instance, it did not succeed with lithographic chalk. Under the microscope a 'fresh' line has a scaly appearance, looking like soap shavings from grandmother's day. This characteristic is absent from, or no longer present in, Van Gogh's drawings. The problem would be solved if we had had a sketch (as reference material) on which Van Gogh had written 'This is lithographic chalk'. Sadly enough, we do not have that, though we do in the case of Italian chalk.

To enable the characteristic differences to be recognised, it was necessary to make a source study into the composition of drawing materials in the nineteenth century. To this end, patents, chemical literature and recipe books of the time were consulted. Supplemented by the information from Van Gogh's letters, this resulted in a picture of the materials we encounter in his drawings.

This article gives an overview of the drawing materials which Van Gogh used over the years. It is not possible to keep to a chronological sequence in this respect. The point is that from the very outset of his artistic career Van Gogh tried out various drawing materials and techniques and experimented with them interminably. In some drawings he worked with one or two materials, but in most cases he used several drawing materials, which are not always readily distinguishable from each other. In the latter case we speak of mixed techniques. The sequence of the materials discussed here is therefore inevitably relatively arbitrary. In the order selected the dry and then the wet drawing materials are discussed successively in separate sections.

In describing the drawing materials Van Gogh's own praises and other comments on the relevant material will be dealt with first.[4] In every case this is followed by a description of one or more drawings made with this material – or, in the case of mixed techniques, these materials. Next, the drawing materials are placed in their historical perspective by giving a brief history of the origin of each one and its use in Van Gogh's time. In some cases the history is continued up to the present day and supplemented by information about the composition of the material.

PENCIL

One of the first materials with which Van Gogh attempted to develop his artistic talent was pencil.[5] After starting with 'fine and expensive Fabers' (a make already on sale in the eighteenth century) he replaced these during his Hague period by a carpenter's pencil. This attracted him because of the fairly thick lead with which he could work more expressively. During the time he spent in Drenthe, too, Van Gogh would set out, armed with his favourite carpenter's pencil. His clear preference for this coarse instrument was based on his admiration for the art of the old masters. He asked himself what they would have drawn with and concluded: 'Certainly not with Faber B, BB, BBB etc., but with a piece of raw graphite. The tool used by Michelangelo and Dürer was probably very much like a carpenter's pencil'. In the summer of 1883, however, Van Gogh discovered 'a kind of Faber pencil' which was softer and of better quality than the carpenter's pencils. They produced 'a wonderful black' and worked 'very nicely for large studies'. Pencil, particularly the soft types which invite you to use them for black and dark effects, has a metallic gleam on paper, besides which it smudges readily. This 'shiny' effect, especially, was not particularly appreciated by Van Gogh (and his contemporaries), but was in fact regarded as 'unattractive' and hence undesirable.

One fascinating aspect of Van Gogh's drawing technique is his experiments with fixing agents aimed at remedying the troublesome gloss and smudging of pencil, but also of other materials, as we shall see. After some experimentation he hit upon the idea of fixing pencil drawings with milk, which made the pencilled lines look 'singular and intensely black'. Sometimes the milk – undoubtedly full-cream in those days – was diluted with water. In a letter, he gave his brother Theo the following advice: 'If I have not fixed your drawing, or if after I have fixed it I have worked on it again here and there, so that

there are places which are unpleasantly shiny, then don't hesitate to throw a big glass of milk, or water and milk, over it'.

Pencil Drawings In the 'Almshouse Man with Long Overcoat and Stick' (F 962) only (soft) pencil has been used. The paper is a thick quality of watercolour paper. What makes this picture especially interesting is the ring or 'halo' around the figure of the almshouse man. On the basis of remarks made by Van Gogh in his letters, and the greasy layer of white 'powder' which is clearly visible under the microscope, we may safely assume that what we have here is one of his drawings fixed with milk. To judge by the shape of te ring, the milk was applied with a brush. That the film is thin points to the fact that in this case the milk was diluted with water. *cat. 47*

Another drawing predominantly in pencil is 'Male Nude, Standing' (F 1364c). The dark accents on the hands, head, genitals and feet were obtained with pencil alone. The dark tone of the background has been created by stumped charcoal. The line of the nude's back was accentuated with a charcoal line which was probably intended to create an extra-dark effect. *cat. 139*

History In the second half of the sixteenth century a graphite quarry was discovered in England (Borrowdale). The highly expensive material – only high-ranking personages wrote with a Borrowdale pencil – very rapidly came into use as a writing medium everywhere in Europe. For this purpose graphite was sawn into rods and wrapped in paper or thread. Since the nature of the material was initially unknown and it looked like a kind of lead, the name for graphite writing instruments in various languages was derived from lead: lead pencil in English, *potlood* in Dutch, *Bleistift* in German, *mine de plomb* in French. To overcome the objections to the irregular transfer of graphite to the paper, experiments aimed at binding powdered graphite into a solid mass were made at a very early date. Until the end of the eighteenth century these experiments were not very successful. The most important discovery in this field was made by the French engineer and inventor Nicolas Jacques Conté (1755-1803) of Paris. He mixed very finely ground graphite with clay powder, made it into a paste, pressed the paste into rods and after drying, baked them in a furnace. Depending on the baking time, temperature and the ratio of clay to graphite, pencils of varying hardness were obtained. Broadly speaking, this is the way in which pencils are still made today.

The Conté firm's invention was patented in 1795. From that time onwards the pencil slowly but surely gained in popularity and its effect was also greatly valued by artists. For his pencils – confusingly enough, like chalk, they were called crayons – Conté introduced a hardness scale ranging from 1 to 5 (1 is soft). Conté's scale practically coincided with that of the Englishman Brookmann, who at the start of the nineteenth century introduced a hardness scale expressed in letters: B, BB, F, HB, H and HH. Here B stands for Black, a soft and dark pencil resulting from a relatively high graphite content, F for Firm and H for Hard, which meant a higher clay content. In our times the number of available hardnesses has been increased to more than 15. Although pure graphite pencils were initially referred to as lead pencils, from the time of Conté's discovery this name has become a general term for the graphite-clay pencils now considered commonplace. References to graphite as lead pencil in describing pre-nineteenth century drawings must therefore be regarded as anachronisms.

CHARCOAL

Van Gogh did not only use charcoal for the background.[6] From as early as 1881 onwards he made attempts to use charcoal as a sketching material. Self-taught as he was, he consulted books about this such as *Le Fusain* (Charcoal) by Karl Robert and *Exercices au Fusain pour Préparer à l'Etude de l'Académie d'après Nature* by Ch. Bargue. With plans in mind for canvases to be painted in a somewhat larger format later on, he particularly wanted to practise on large charcoal sketches. Van Gogh was encouraged in the use of charcoal by his cousin Anton Mauve (1838-1888), one of the great masters of The Hague school. And although in a letter to Van Rappard he said that he understood the enthusiasm of the writer of *Le Fusain*, Van Gogh had to admit that he himself did not know how to handle the material properly. Since he made only slow progress Van Gogh sometimes became so impatient that he 'trampled on his charcoal and became totally disheartened'. In spite of that he persevered. His greatest objection to the material was the fact that charcoal 'rubs out so easily, you lose things you have found because of this erasure if you do not work very carefully'. Handling drawing materials cautiously was not Van Gogh's style. As he himself said, he felt 'the need not to be over-cautious'.

Drawing details was also a stumbling block with charcoal. Fine accents are not easy to apply with the brittle material and make great demands on the artist's drawing skill. The objections decreased to some extent when Van Gogh had found a fixing agent (not described in further detail) for charcoal which made it possible to work with other materials in the charcoal sketch. Nevertheless, charcoal never became one of Van Gogh's favourite materials. In 1882 he wrote to Van Rappard, saying that – after repeated practice following the books of examples and reading the instructions – he was not making much progress with charcoal. 'I prefer to work with a carpenter's pencil'. Accordingly, Van Gogh worked on most of his charcoal sketches with other drawing materials such as Italian chalk and printing ink.

Van Gogh knew of the existence of oil-impregnated charcoal, which might have gone some way towards meeting his objections to the vulnerable lines and other difficult aspects of the technique. But one of his principles was that an artist, at the start of his career, must not have recourse to material that quickly created an attractive effect. As an example of this Van Gogh mentioned 'charcoal which has lain in oil' and which produced a smooth, velvety-black line. He wanted to gain an absolute mastery of drawing technique, without any tricks, so that 'the beauty should [not] come through my material, but through me'.

Charcoal Drawings After the foregoing it will not surprise the reader to learn that we know of only a few sketches which Van Gogh executed entirely in charcoal. One of them is 'Female Nude, Seated' (F 1368). In this case the shadow effects, *cat. 13* produced in many drawings with other materials, are obtained with hatching in charcoal and polishing with the stump. As already mentioned, Van Gogh had difficulty with drawing details in charcoal. In this drawing we see that from the clumsy execution of the hands and feet which show a somewhat undifferentiated shape. When comparing Van Gogh's charcoal sketches such as 'Female Nude, Seated' with, for instance, the pencil drawing 'Almshouse Man with Long Overcoat and Stick' *cat. 47* described above, one is struck by the fact that Van Gogh developed a great skill in pencil drawing which did not emerge to full effect with charcoal.

History The use of charcoal as a drawing material is probably as old as mankind itself. The method of preparing it has not changed radically throughout the centuries. In this process wooden sticks are tied together in bundles and carefully charred in a vacuum. Excessive and prolonged heating results in charcoal that does not adhere well to paper. In the course of time various kinds of (soft) wood have been used for charcoal as a drawing material, including walnut, myrtle and vine stocks, willow, fruit trees, palm trees and birch. In the nineteenth century it was mainly branches of birch, lime, spindle tree and hazelnut that were charred for this purpose. Artists made certain demands on charcoal. In particular, it had to be uniform in structure and not too soft or crumbly. In every case it kept making smudges on the drawing and a fixing agent was actually essential to keep it in place. From about the middle of the sixteenth century, as a variation on the technique, charcoal began to be impregnated with drying oil (linseed oil) which made it unnecessary to fix the drawing. The sticks of charcoal obtained in this way could be used for half a year, after which they became too hard to draw with. Nowadays charcoal powder is in fact compressed into sticks with a binder (Siberian charcoal) to eliminate adverse properties such as pulverisation and scratching.

DRAWING MATERIALS

BLACK CHALK

Van Gogh repeatedly wrote that he used black chalk or Conté.[7] Sometimes in the form of sticks and sometimes set in wood like a pencil. Although he frequently worked with this out of doors in Etten and The Hague, among other places, he found black Conté less appropriate for working in the open countryside, for 'because of the glaring light you do not see properly what you are doing, and notice that it has become too black'. For outdoor use Van Gogh therefore preferred the greyer 'graphite' (pencil) which could always be made 'a few octaves' darker by shading in later with pen and ink.

Van Gogh was not entirely happy with Conté for other reasons as well. Briefly, he thought it was (too) hard and made scratches, and also that the sticks without wood offered too little to hold on to and were prone to break. In addition, because of the intense, unrelieved blackness the effect of black chalk could, in Van Gogh's view, have something 'dead or iron-like' about it. For him the disadvantage of its size was not solved by using a holder, because he did not feel comfortable working with it.

To intensify the effect of black chalk Van Gogh occasionally wetted the drawing, after which he worked on the shadowy parts as in a painting (made them 'flow') and then 'took the lights out again', as he called scraping the chalk off the light parts. The main subjects of Van Gogh's purely black chalk drawings are figure studies and studies of limbs such as arms, legs, hands and feet. The landscapes with black chalk are frequently worked up with other materials.

Black Chalk Drawings An example of a drawing with black chalk is 'Peasant Woman, Gleaning, Seen from Behind' (F 1269). To obtain nuances the drawing was stumped at various places. Like the 'Almshouse Man with Long Overcoat and Stick' (pencil) already mentioned, this drawing is fixed with milk. Under the microscope the veil of milk over the 'Peasant Woman, Gleaning, Seen from Behind' shows up as a powdery, white film. The layer is relatively thick, so we may assume that in this case the milk would only have been diluted slightly, if at all. The white patches visible here and there, as on the mouth, the right arm and below the left foot, are not white body colour as has hitherto often been assumed. They are dried drops of milk which display craquelures under the microscope. The 'milk fixer' has been applied with a brush. The contour of the fatty ring largely follows the outer line of the figure and can be seen particularly clearly with the naked eye as a vertical line between the head and hand. Van Gogh missed some places with his somewhat primitive fixing agent: the leftmost fold, the figures at the top of the sheets and a patch under the armpit. As a result, these appear to be of a slightly deeper black than the rest of the drawing.

In the sketch 'Kasteel het Steen' (F 1350 r) the black chalk is brightened up with fine accents in coloured pencil. The 'Double-Bass Player' (F 1244c v) and the 'Violinist' (F 1244a r) are both executed unerringly with a greasy kind of coloured chalk, without any preliminary sketch.

History The term 'chalk' often causes confusion. In the case of the black types, chalk has nothing to do with limestone, while in the case of the white types chalk is generally used – mostly incorrectly – as a synonym for limestone. (Blackboard chalks in 1990, incidentally, have long since ceased to consist of limestone and are made of gypsum). At the start of the nineteenth century the best kinds of artificially made black chalk came from Paris, and were therefore sometimes also called Paris chalk.

One of the first manufacturers in Paris was the firm of Conté, already mentioned, which exported chalk to every country in Europe, in addition to pencils. Through time, Conté's black chalks became so widely known that the brand name became a generic term. Regardless of the make, Conté meant (and still means) a moderately soft, slightly greasy kind of chalk. This in spite of Conté's wide range of other drawing materials. In the second half of the nineteenth century black chalk was prepared in various ways – frequently with soot – depending on the application. In the last quarter of that century black synthetic chalk had become so commonplace that the name 'black chalk' no longer meant a natural type but the artificial product. Both then and now Conté made black chalk in three degrees of hardness. Of these, the soft type is often described – wrongly – nowadays as greasy.

LITHOGRAPHIC CHALK

For a long time Van Gogh hoped to find work as an illustrator. With that in mind he regularly made drawings which he hoped Theo would bring to the attention of publishers. Obtaining work as an illustrator was also the underlying idea in acquiring a mastery of a printing technique. During his period in The Hague, Van Gogh made acquaintance with lithography, a technique which – as he himself remarked – was not very popular in his times.[8]

The special chalk used in the process for drawing on the stone intrigued him: 'an excellent material'. It need not surprise us, therefore, that he hit upon the idea of experimenting with it as a material for making drawings on paper. Very soon he was 'toiling with heart and soul [...] to make it good and usable'. The fatty consistency of lithographic chalk makes it virtually impossible to remove lines once they have been made on paper, so that it is hard to make corrections. To overcome this problem, Van Gogh first worked the drawing out as far as possible with a (carpenter's) pencil. This was next fixed with milk, after which he worked on it with chalk. The greasy lithographic chalk adhered much better to the pencil lines than

cat. 115

cat. 47

cat. 122

cat. 127 – 12...

ordinary (Conté) chalk. In addition, the places with 'the greatest strengths' – Van Gogh's usual expression for the darkest parts – were further reinforced with pen or brush or ink. The lighter parts were heightened with white body colour.

The device of working in a wet black chalk drawing was also employed by Van Gogh when using lithographic chalk. Writing from The Hague he described the method to Theo in graphic detail: 'Today a [man's head] which I drew with lithographic chalk. Then I slapped a bucket of water over the drawing and began to model with the brush in the soaking wet. As a result you get very fine tones if it is successful, for it is a risky method that can sometimes also end up wrongly. But if it succeeds you have a very *non ébarbé* result, fine tones of black'. Van Gogh regularly used the term *non ébarbé* in his letters to mean a less polished, not so clean effect.

Lithographic Chalk Drawings There are various drawings in the exhibition which, according to the literature, have been made with lithographic chalk. For example, 'Girl with Shawl, Half *cat. 52 - 53* Figure' (F 1008), 'Fisherman's Head with Sou'wester' (F 1014) *cat. 45* and 'Almshouse Man with Top Hat, Head' (F 985). On the basis of Van Gogh's own descriptions it is highly probable that these three drawings were indeed made with this material. We cannot be certain of this, however. As already mentioned in the introduction, even a microscope study cannot provide an answer in the case of lithographic chalk. The point is that under the microscope a 'fresh' line drawn with lithographic chalk looks completely different from the lines in the now century-old drawing by Van Gogh. The former shows characteristic, semi-upright 'scales'. In Van Gogh's drawings, on the other hand, the chalk has dried in to form a fairly uniform, solid mass. Here science must provide the answer. We will only know for certain that Van Gogh worked on these drawings with lithographic chalk when the composition has been clarified by a chemical analysis of a (minuscule) sample.

cat. 53 'Girl with Shawl, Half Figure' is executed as a rough pencil sketch on a thick quality watercolour paper which has been worked on further in broad lines with a greasy type of chalk. The pencil sketch has been fixed with milk applied with separate brushstrokes. This can clearly be seen to the left of the figure. On some parts of the drawing the pencil lines have not been reinforced with chalk, such as the hand, the blouse and the contour of the face. Most parts, however, are covered with a thick layer of chalk. Next, scratches have been made in this with a sharp instrument to obtain lighter tones. This is the case, for example, in the shawl and the hair, but Vincent's signature has also been applied in depth (*intaglio*). At the hair the thin paper has hardly been able to withstand the crude scratching method and it is crinkled and damaged. The signature, too, was not entirely satisfactory. At the first letter 'V' Vincent scratched too deeply. As can still be seen this ruined a piece of the paper, so that he started again beside it.

As with 'Girl with Shawl, Half Figure', thick watercolour paper was used for 'Fisherman's Head with Sou'wester'. In the *cat. 52* face drawn with pencil, the eyes and nose are reinforced with ink. The hat, face and coat are heightened with white. The coat is further deepened with black paint.[9] The dull white layer on the chalk – visible under the microscope as a grey veil, particularly on the hat – shows that the whole drawing has been coated with milk.

Van Gogh used the same method in the 'Almshouse Man *cat. 45* with Top Hat, Head'. The use of pencil can be clearly distinguished as the silver-grey lines in the face and on the brim of the hat. On the hat itself the chalk has been partially scraped away to create a shimmering effect. In addition to the treatment with a rubber or stump, the drawing was worked up with (brown) ink in the eyebrows, eyes and hair (right), among other places. The dirty white patches above the right ear and on the right shoulder are dried drops of milk, as we saw in the case of the black chalk drawing 'Peasant Woman, Gleaning, Seen *cat. 115* from Behind'. And as in the 'Girl with Shawl, Half Figure', here again the name *Vincent* has been scratched out with a sharp instrument.

History Lithography, or printing from stone, was invented around 1792 by a native of Prague, Alois Senefelder (1771-1834), who obtained a patent on it in 1799. In this planographic technique – initially used only for printing music – the drawing was frequently made directly on to the stone with a type of chalk specially developed for this purpose, or with ink. Senefelder made his lithographic chalk with lampblack, soap, wax, tallow, resin and a fatty fluid obtained from the heads of sperm whales (spermaceti). More resin – particularly copal – made the chalk drier and more brittle.

Cooking lithographic chalk, as it was called, was a very laborious process and required a great deal of experience. Although much doctoring went on in the nineteenth century in order to keep the price down, the actual recipe underwent little change. Lithographic chalk was made in four degrees of hardness, copal chalk being the hardest. In spite of that, this type was no harder than a soft pencil.

ITALIAN CHALK[10]

While Van Gogh was happy with lithographic chalk as a drawing material he was positively lyrical about his 'discovery' of Italian chalk.[11] 'In Italian chalk there is a lot of sound or tone. I would almost say that Italian chalk understands what you want, listens intelligently and obeys, and the Conté is indifferent and uncooperative', Van Gogh wrote to Theo. 'If you want to do me a very great favour, then send me some pieces of Italian chalk by post', he added. Van Gogh's enthusiasm for Italian chalk is also evident from a letter to Anton van Rappard: 'And now something else – do you know about *Italian chalk* [...] it is as though there is soul and life in that commodity...' In the same letter Van Gogh compared the 'soul' of Italian chalk to the soul of a gipsy, for which reason he proposed to call it 'gipsy chalk' from then on.

Van Gogh saw Italian chalk as having various advantages over Conté. This mainly related to its colour, which he described as a 'warm, singular black' and 'the colour of plough-ed-up land on a summer evening'. In addition, it did not make scratches and 'half tones' could be applied with it. By this he meant that lines (and planes) could be rubbed out to a lighter hue. For this purpose Van Gogh used bread crumbs, which was a fairly widely used medium at that time. This method could not be employed with the jet black Conté without making the whole drawing look smudged and blotchy. For that matter, his remark about 'non-scratching' Italian chalk is astonishing. In Van Gogh's times this material was of poor quality (many small stones, uneven in colour) which was partly why it had become obsolete. He probably found some good pieces by chance. In spite of the magnificent colour the 'very deepest shadows' could not be obtained with Italian chalk, so Van Gogh combined it with lithographic chalk. Besides using this material, Van Gogh also worked on Italian chalk drawings with charcoal, autographic ink, sepia, printing ink, etc. All in all, he liked the 'new' material so much that he remarked in a letter to Theo: 'From now on I shall perhaps use little else for the ordinary work any more'.

Very soon after his discovery of Italian chalk Van Gogh came to the conclusion that, after all, this was 'not so unusual' and so unknown as he had thought. He therefore expected that it would be on sale everywhere. Nevertheless, it was hard to come by. This is apparent from the following remark in a letter to Theo: 'When I asked Leurs [a dealer in artists' materials in The Hague] about it once again, he told me that Jaap Maris had asked him for it so frequently'. Van Gogh eventually found some 'very small remnants' of the coveted drawing material at a druggist's in The Hague.

The fact that Italian chalk, as a natural product, was not constant in quality and dimensions emerges from a reply to Theo when the latter had sent him a quantity of this material for the second time: 'it is softer than what I first received and the pieces are a half shorter'. We know exactly how big the first pieces were. In a letter to Van Rappard, Van Gogh made a sketch of a piece of Italian chalk to show him what it looked like. Below it, he wrote: 'this is the actual size', which meant about 13 cm. Van Gogh described the remnants he had managed to lay hands on at a druggist's in The Hague as 'everything in little pieces'.

Italian Chalk Drawings On the envelope of a letter to Theo, Van Gogh drew some small figures, adding that this was Italian chalk.[12] This is, of course, the most ideal way to find out what Italian chalk looked like at that time and how we can recognise it. The Italian chalk Van Gogh used was generally brownish-black in colour. Under the microscope it looks fairly dull and dry. The line sometimes shows a deep indentation and the material contains very small white to colourless crystals in various forms. The fact that Van Gogh described some of his Italian chalk drawings to Theo and Van Rappard can also assist us in identifying this material. For example, Van Gogh mentioned 'Peat Diggers', 'Infant in Various Attitudes', 'Girl Beside a Cradle' and 'Women and Children at a Window in the Soup Kitchen' in this connection.

The latter could be the drawing 'Public Soup Kitchen (Distributing the Soup)' (F 1020a) dating from Van Gogh's cat. 58 period in The Hague. The warm tone of Italian chalk emerges clearly in it. Under the microscope we see a characteristic picture: the chalk has left scratches of varying depth in the paper and contains crystals of various colours. In this drawing Van Gogh tried to get the darkest possible effect at some places by applying the chalk thickly and forcefully. This can be seen, for example, in the opening of the serving hatch. Here he has worked with such force that the scratches of the tiny stones in the chalk are even visible to the naked eye. In the hem of the skirt of the woman on the left the chalk is intensified with paint. At some places the drawing is heightened with white, as in the case of the cap of the girl opposite, the contour of the woman behind the serving hatch, the baby on the left and the cuff of the woman on the right.

A drawing which is only partly outlined with Italian chalk is 'The Head of a Man, Profile' (F 1244d r). It is a sketch with only cat. 129 broad-lined drawing materials, namely blue, red, orange-red and white chalk. In addition to the coloured materials Van Gogh used brownish-black chalk, which proved to be Italian chalk. The 'gipsy chalk' was worked over with a stump, particularly in the hair and face.

History Black chalk of natural origin – sometimes also called black 'stone' or Italian chalk – is a mineral consisting of a type of slate (clay shale), the dark colour coming partly from carbon and partly from bituminous slate. This colour can vary from grey and bluish-grey to brownish-black and deep black. The colour and hardness depend on the place where it is found. The mineral was sawn into rods for use as a drawing material. Although Italian chalk was probably first used as a drawing material in the fifteenth century, it was most generally in use in the eighteenth century, when it was able to hold its own side by side with synthetically manufactured soot chalk and graphite. Towards the end of the eighteenth century Italian chalk was used less and less, among other things because its quality was poor, while synthetic chalk (made of soot) was good and inexpensive. In Van Gogh's time Italian chalk was almost completely out of fashion and only available in limited quantities.

DRAWING MATERIALS

Particularly in Van Gogh's first years as an artist, the pen drawing was almost always preceded by a pencil sketch which was often even developed into a complete drawing. He next worked the drawing up with ink[13], possibly supplemented with other materials. Examples of the drawing materials with which he enlivened ink drawings were chalk (black or coloured) and printing ink or watercolour (sepia), for washing them. It is striking to note that the use of pencil in his 'Dutch' pen drawings is functional: it contributes to the *chiaroscuro* effect. In his 'French' pen drawings, on the other hand, pencil was only an aid with which a rough preliminary sketch was made.

As will be clear from the preceding descriptions of Conté, Italian chalk and lithographic chalk, Van Gogh preferred drawing materials with a thick lead with which he could draw a broad line. It is therefore not so surprising that he dwelt at length on the possibilities of a fine drawing pen combined with (thick flowing) autographic ink, such as that used by an acquaintance of Van Rappard. Van Gogh himself thought that the thick ink was unsuitable for (the fine line of) a drawing pen; a nib at least the size of that in a drawing pen must be used for this purpose.

The fact that Van Gogh had absolutely no use for fine (metal) pens can be guessed from an incisive typed comment in a letter to Van Rappard: 'Very fine pens, like very elegant *people*, are sometimes surprisingly useless'. He therefore described the expensive, special penholders and pens he had purchased in the course of 1883 as 'all rubbish'. The 'milder, cheekier stroke of e.g. an ordinary quill pen' was more to Van Gogh's liking. As early as his Etten period he came to know and appreciate the reed pen, with its broad action, from which he later became virtually inseparable in France.

Initially, Van Gogh mainly regarded his pen drawings as a good preparation for etchings he might make later on. He had various sources of inspiration for these drawing exercises such as the work of his favourite painter J.F. Millet, books of examples and subjects from nature. As a book of examples Van Gogh mentioned: John, *Esquisses Anatomiques des Artistes*. Pen sketches by old masters such as Van Ostade and 'Boeren Breughel' served as a shining example to him. Through time, the aim of the pen drawings changed: drawing exercises became preliminary studies. During his time in Drenthe they mainly served as preliminary studies for his paintings. Van Gogh found that a more detailed study of the object to be painted could be made with the pen than with paint. After that, he made a second preliminary study with paint for the colour impression. While pen drawings were mainly drawing exercises and/or preliminary studies during his Dutch period, that changed during his time in France. Now he often made ink sketches – preferably with a broad reed pen – based on (sometimes almost) completed paintings. He enclosed such sketches in his letters to give an impression of the painting on which he was working. A reed pen, sharpened slantwise like a goose quill pen, was used to draw the thick lines, while the fine lines were drawn with a goose quill.

In Van Gogh's pen drawings we find both black and brown ink. The black inks are mainly Indian ink, autographic ink or printing ink. It may be assumed that the brown ink was generally an originally black, non-light-fast iron-gall (or gallnut) ink. This was a cheap kind of ink which was commonly used for writing. However, to dismiss all brown ink as 'faded' is to take too simple a view of things. Particularly in some nature studies Van Gogh tried to reproduce 'the effect of light and brown – the momentary mood of nature'. It is very probable that he used brown materials such as sepia or brown ink for this purpose. As examples of such nature studies he mentioned 'Ditch', 'Pine Trees in the Fen' and 'Thatched Roofs'.

Various pen drawings from Van Gogh's Dutch and French periods show a whole range of brown hues; both shape and shadow effects are obtained with dark and lighter coloured lines. Very probably non-light-fast iron-gall ink is involved here too. A plausible explanation for the variety of hues is provided by the action of the reed pen which Van Gogh frequently used. Generally speaking, when drawing with a pen the ink is applied increasingly sparingly. The lines become thinner and thinner, until the ink finally runs out. With the reed pen, the process is somewhat different. Since a reed pen, unlike a metal or quill pen, more or less absorbs the ink, the last lines drawn with it are not only somewhat thinner, but also increasingly light in colour.

Another possible way to obtain this effect is to dilute the ink with water until the required colour is obtained. This was (and still is) a favourite method of artists for creating a lively effect in lines and planes. Van Gogh did not mention the latter method in his letters. It is therefore not very likely that he used diluted ink.

Ink Drawings No purely pen and ink drawings were found among those investigated. In every case, there was a combination of ink with one or more drawing materials, varying from a rough preliminary sketch in pencil to a complex mixed technique. For example, the pen drawing 'A Sower (after Millet)' *cat. 1* (F 830) was first sketched in pencil, then washed and worked up with colour. In particular, green paint was used for this, as can be seen below the peasant with oxen ploughing on the horizon to the right. In addition, the shirt of the peasant who is sowing is heightened with grey paint on the collar and cuff. The grey of the sky, on the other hand, was not obtained with drawing material: instead of this, Van Gogh allowed the grey tone of the paper to come into its own.

The drawing 'The Paddemoes' (F 918) was first worked out *cat. 19* extensively in pencil, after which it was finished in ink. The roofs of the houses and the dark areas behind the hedge are washed with ink, as are the man and woman (centre left and in the foreground, respectively). The areas 'with the greatest strengths' are given extra depth with soft pencil, such as the edge of the pavement, the edge of the little wall on the right and the gap between the wall and the pavement. The street paving and the house on the left were shaded in grey with pencil. The brown ink is generally applied with a very fine pen; at some points a coarser pen (a reed pen?) has been used, as in the street paving and the skirt of the woman in the foreground.

cat. 69   In the drawing 'Country Road in Loosduinen near The Hague' (F 1089), after a preliminary sketch, the contrasts have been introduced with brown ink. Here predominant use has been made of a pen: at some places, such as the bottom, very dark edge of the reed mat along the gardens, the ink has been applied with a brush; at this part the ink has soaked right through the paper. Van Gogh next worked up the ink parts with soft pencil, which still has a metallic gleam in spite of being fixed. White paint is used to accentuate the cloudy sky.

cat. 157   The Parisian street scene 'Boulevard de Clichy' (F 1393) was drawn with a fairly hard pencil: its lines are light grey in tone and have left a deep dent in the paper. These pencil lines can be seen in the trees, persons and hatching on the right. They were next drawn over with a fine pen and ink and coloured in with (mainly) orange-red and blue chalk. Even the building on the left, which is only roughly indicated, was first drawn in pencil. On the far right, on the roof and beside the women in the foreground, traces of vigorously rubbed out white chalk or paint can be seen. The light stains on the rest of the buildings are not drawing materials, but patches which for some unknown reason have yellowed less than the rest of the paper – containing, incidentally, a high proportion of wood pulp.

cat. 177   The preliminary sketch for the drawing 'Bank of the Rhône' from Arles (F 1472a) was made in pencil and stumped, after which the drawing was executed with purple ink and pen in various thicknesses, a reed pen and a goose quill (?). The ink has become intensely discoloured, fading from purple to brown; in fact, a patch of the original colour can be seen only at the bottom left. This has probably always been concealed under a passe-partout. We may assume that here Van Gogh made the drawing with purple aniline ink (aniline violet), at that time a fairly modern ink derived from coal-tar. Like almost all dyes prepared from coal-tar, aniline violet cannot withstand daylight. In addition, in this drawing the ink has been applied very strongly at some places, as in the boats; the drawing has not been washed. The sky and the sun's rays are indicated by short ink strokes.

cat. 186   In Arles Van Gogh also drew the 'Rocks with Trees: Montmajour' (F 1447). After a rough preliminary sketch in pencil, he went on to draw the landscape in Indian ink alone, using both a broad reed pen and a finer type. A noteworthy feature here is that he used scarcely any uninterrupted lines, but mainly worked with short pen strokes. Van Gogh's intention in doing

this was to emphasise the shape of what was portrayed in an expressive manner with the 'direction of the pen scratches'. In the lumps of rock, for example, the shape is accentuated by pen strokes which have 'followed the shape expressively'. At some places dark accents have been applied with a brush, as in the grass and the rocks on the left. We see a similar effect in the sun's rays in 'Wheat Field with Sun and Cloud' (SD 1728) from   cat. 225
Saint-Rémy-de-Provence. Here the rays are drawn with small strokes around the sun, so that the shape and radiation are emphasised.[14]

History Various drawing and writing inks were available in the second half of the nineteenth century, including gallnut or iron-gall ink, aniline ink and Indian ink.[15] The most commonly used and also cheapest kind was iron-gall ink. The oldest known recipes for this date from the seventeenth century. Iron-gall ink was made from extracts of gallnuts (oak apples) or other vegetable materials containing tannic acid, such as acorn cups, chestnuts and sumac. The method of preparation was, in fact, very simple. The tannic acid in the extract (tannin) was mixed with an iron salt (ferrous sulphate), after which a black-coloured fluid formed on exposure to air. To enable the ink to flow smoothly from the pen and prevent deterioration, gum arabic and phenol, respectively, were added to the black fluid. Dilute hydrochloric acid or sulphuric acid was sometimes added to obtain a deep black colour. In many cases, the use of iron-gall ink had disastrous consequences for the paper. Through time, the ink ate into it to such an extent that holes formed. This effect was further intensified by the added acids. Iron-gall ink proved to have another adverse property: it is frequently not light-fast. The fact that it can fade to light brown and even become colourless is sufficiently well-known from the many old documents in archives which have become unreadable as a result.
The inks, which were originally brown in colour, were mostly made with bistre (soot from deciduous wood) or sepia. These were not very light-fast either. Of the coloured types of ink developed from coal tar dyes in the second half of the nineteenth century, purple aniline ink is the best known. This type was made on an aniline violet base – both toxic and carcinogenic – and was mainly used as a copying ink; among other things, in pencil form until well into the twentieth century. These were the pencils which generations of unsuspecting grocers licked in blind faith, before jotting down the amounts spent by their customers on the slate. The inks prepared from tar dyes are generally not very light-fast.
Indian ink was made from lampblack (soot) and fish glue perfumed with musk or camphor. The latter is also a preservative. The mixture was pressed into sticks and dried. Prior to use they then had to be dissolved in water; nowadays Indian ink is mainly available in liquid form. Artists have valued Indian ink from as long

ago as the seventeenth century for its good fluidity, transparency and light-fastness. In spite of its steep price it found general application.

Autographic ink was used in lithography to transfer a picture or text from the paper to the stone. It was prepared from a mixture of soap, resin, wax, tallow and soot. The ink could be diluted with water.

The ingredients of which printing ink was composed included paraffin oil, colophony and soot and it could not be diluted with water but only with an organic solvent such as turpentine.

WATERCOLOUR

First, a few remarks about the (rapidly vanishing) distinction between drawing and painting. Van Gogh himself regarded his works in watercolour as drawings.[16] For example, in a letter to Theo he said: 'The two drawings I have made in the last few days are both watercolours'. In various other letters, too, he used the term drawing as a synonym for watercolour. To Van Gogh, painting and paintings were associated with oil paint.

Assuming that paper is the carrier, this distinction is obvious, but it is a definition which is no longer used in some circles. Depending on the way in which the modern artist handles his materials, in 1990 we speak of the art of drawing or painting.[17]

In our times, the terms aquarelle for transparent watercolour and gouache for opaque watercolour are so general that confusion might arise on this point with regard to the work of Van Gogh. In fact, most of his watercolour paintings cannot really be covered by one of these two terms. Particularly in his Dutch period, watercolour – as we shall see, partly through inexperience – was often used in one work both opaquely and transparently. As far as Van Gogh is concerned, it is therefore preferable to keep to the more general term 'watercolour'.

After first having practised drawing with dry materials and ink, Van Gogh was already experimenting in Etten with the use of sepia and watercolour in order to introduce colour into his drawings. As we have also seen in relation to other techniques, Van Gogh tried to learn the tricks of the trade from a book. In this case he used Cassagne's *Traité d'Aquarelle*. He also learned a great deal from his cousin, Anton Mauve. During a stay of almost a month in The Hague, Van Gogh received many hints and practical tips: 'In this way, I have acquired through Mauve some insight with regard to the mysteries of the palette and painting watercolours', Van Gogh wrote enthusiastically to Theo. But more despairing letters also reached Theo which showed that the learning process was a laborious one. It was not so much working with colour that presented a problem – Van–Gogh found that 'no more difficult' than 'with black and white' – but keeping the paint fresh and transparent. Particularly when he wanted to apply the colours in a somewhat

darker tone, Van Gogh initially did not succeed in preventing the paint from becoming opaque: 'It is sometimes desperate enough when one wants to heighten it a bit and it becomes thick'. When his drawings became 'heavy, thick, muddy, black, dead', Mauve consoled him with the remark that it would bear witness to 'a certain chic' if he would work in 'thin' (transparent) paint directly.

Van Gogh was not against using opaque paint in itself. On the contrary. In his eyes Mauve 'and all the others' used it with good results. Van Gogh could not yet handle it, however, and would therefore have liked Mauve to give him some guidelines for this, in addition to the hints about the transparent watercolour paint. Later, things increasingly improved and Van Gogh found more pleasure in the use of watercolour. He wrote to Theo saying that the aquarelles were becoming 'somewhat stronger and fresher in colour and without body colour'. He sent him composition sketches of the watercolour paintings on which he was working.

Besides producing watercolours, Van Gogh also experimented with the technique of (watercolour) sketching in shades of brown – known as sepias – which he had seen Van Rappard making on the moorland near Etten. Just as with watercolour painting, Van Gogh did not find this easy either. 'That can't be done in one go', he wrote to Theo from Etten. Prior to that he had already tried to make a sepia in Brussels after 'Oven on the Moor' by Theodore Rousseau.

When Van Gogh had settled in The Hague, he considered he had made so much progress that a major purchase was justifiable. He bought a box of watercolours with a lid which could be used as a palette. As regards the colours, he confined himself to buying 'simple colours', which in fact meant fairly common basic colours: three shades of ochre, sepia, sienna, Naples yellow, gamboge, cobalt blue, Prussian blue, ultramarine, carmine, vermilion, white and black. Van Gogh never used black unmixed in his watercolour paintings because he thought that in nature nothing is 'absolutely black', but always consists of 'an endless variation of greys'.

In 'real' watercolourist circles it was a fairly generally held view that white was undesirable and even impermissible. The reason for this was that in 'real', transparent watercolours white areas had to be left untouched. Lighter hues were obtained by diluting the paint with water. White paint is always more or less opaque, so that transparency was lost. This is evident in many of Van Gogh's watercolour paintings. As we shall see later, lighter, colourful hues, in particular, are in many cases not very transparent. This is because Van Gogh tried to make the colours lighter with white paint instead of diluting them.

Watercolour Sketches In the watercolour sketch 'The Poor and the Money (A Flock of People in Front of the Lottery Office)' (F 970) Van Gogh made a preliminary drawing with black

cat. 60

chalk and a (fairly hard) pencil. The chalk is still visible on the cap of the man on the left, seen from behind; the pencil line betrays itself by the deep dent in the sleeve of the woman in the centre. The painting, in general, is executed with body colour. The purple, blue and grey tints, in particular, are opaque, partly as a result of mixing with white. The other dark colours such as black, greenish-black and also red, have been kept fairly transparent. As against this, a black body colour has been used for the background of the entrance. The inscription 'Today ... State Lottery' is written in ink.

The 'Weaver, Interior with Three Small Windows' (F 1115) is outlined fairly roughly. After a hasty pencil sketch, some lines of which can still be seen below the weaver's right hand, the drawing was further developed with watercolour. In the case of the weaver (clothing, face, hand) and the loom the paint is opaque; in the woven cloth and foreground it has been kept transparent. Some details in the windows and small trees are accentuated with pen and ink. In the 'Weaver, Facing Left' (F 1107) the paint used is likewise predominantly opaque, again after a preliminary sketch in pencil. In the background the paint is fairly transparent. A third sketch with a weaver as its subject is 'Weaver, Facing Left' (F 1114). In contrast to the other two, the watercolour this time has been applied thinly almost everywhere. It is not really transparent, however, so that here again there is no question of a watercolour in the traditional sense of the term. On the warp beam at the front left various preliminary sketch lines in pencil can still be seen, as can some accents with pen and ink.

The colourful garden scene from Saint-Rémy-de-Provence, called 'Flowering Bushes in the Asylum Garden' (F 1527), was drawn with rough brushstrokes without a preliminary sketch. Blue predominates in the picture. The blue and green touches of watercolour are frequently opaque. In the vista in the background at the left the (red) paint is noticeably much more transparent than on the rest of the paper. It is not clear what Van Gogh intended this difference to convey.

The drawing 'Cottages with Thatched Roofs' (F 1640 r), also from Van Gogh's French period (Auvers-sur-Oise), is sketched with short brushstrokes in blue watercolour. The paint is used in many dilutions, varying from transparent to opaque. The preliminary sketch has been made with a (soft) pencil. A landscape from the same place and with the same 'atmosphere' as 'Cottages with Thatched Roofs' is 'Old Vineyard with Peasant Woman' (F 1624). After a preliminary outline made with soft pencil once again, the picture has been sketched with predominantly blue watercolour, both opaque and transparent. By mixing it with white, the light blue has also become opaque. The roofs and trees form brown accents in the overall blue, while the woman provides a white accent. The paint has been kept transparent for the sky.

History Water paint is a collective name for watercolour and gouache, among other things.[18] Watercolour consists (and consisted) of very finely ground pigments, mixed with a binding agent. The paint is marketed both as a paste (in tubes) and in dried form (in cubes). To make the paint which has been pressed into cubes soluble again, glycerine or sugar is added. Watercolour paper has an important function. It must be absorbent so that the paper fibres, as it were, are coloured, resulting in the transparent, characteristic effect of a watercolour painting. If too many layers are applied one on top of the other, or if the paint is not diluted sufficiently, this effect is lost. The use of white paint produces the same result; here, too, the transparent or glazing effect is lost. It is for this reason that, particularly in watercolourists' associations in nineteenth century Britain, white paint (for lighter hues) was forbidden. White was not applied in a watercolour but left blank on the paper.

The same binding agents are used for gouache as for watercolour. Apart from (not very finely ground) pigments, however, gouache also contains white fillers such as barytes, pipeclay or opaque pigments. This results in an opaque watercolour which enables gouache to be used either on white or coloured paper. This paint can be applied both diluted and in a fairly paste-like consistency. On the other hand, if gouache is too highly diluted a patchy effect is rapidly created as a result of the less fine particles of pigment.

Sepia is named after the cuttlefish *Sepia officinalis* and is obtained from this or other species of Cephalopods. The pigment from the ink sac is used by the cuttlefish as a means of defence. Like other watercolours, the ink sac extract is mixed with gum arabic as a binding agent. Because of the fine particles and the transparent effect, the pigment is eminently suitable for use as watercolour. In addition to sepia drawings with pen or brush, there are also drawings and prints which are washed with sepia. The history of sepia as a writing ink probably dates back to the classical period.

MIXED TECHNIQUES

As has already become clear from the foregoing, Van Gogh liked to work with several materials in one drawing. By using this mixed technique he was able to compensate for any missing or adverse properties of one material by introducing others. This procedure was more the rule than the exception with Van Gogh, so that 'mixed techniques' is not a remaining group, but rather a group which must be regarded as one which includes the vast majority of his drawings.

One of the materials with which Van Gogh liked to 'work up' his drawings was printing ink. As with lithographic chalk, this was, in fact, an unconventional way of using the material. As early as his Hague period he wrote about this extensively in his letters.[19] He even wrote: 'At present, there is now no longer

cat. 77

cat. 81

cat. 78

cat. 217

cat. 241

cat. 242

any drawing which I do not work on with the brush with the printing ink'. Van Gogh mixed the pasty printing ink with turpentine, highly diluted for washing and slightly less diluted for being mixed with paint to make what was frequently a grey body colour. The kinds of paint used by him in this respect were Kassel earth, Chinese white and zinc white (in powder form). In these experiments, Van Gogh preferred printing ink to Indian ink because it had a 'much intenser' (read: blacker) effect. He combined printing ink with almost every drawing material, but particularly with charcoal, Italian chalk, lithographic chalk and, in addition, also with autographic ink which he used for his lithographs.

For his drawings, Van Gogh preferred to use tinted paper 'which has something of the colour of unbleached cotton or linen'. In that case, it was not necessary to temper the bright white of the paper in advance with drawing material, or, as he himself put it: 'If one draws on white, one must necessarily apply a flat tone over the whole paper before one begins'.

Besides his preference for particular materials, Van Gogh also showed a special liking for unusual methods. After applying body colour and dry black and coloured drawing materials, Van Gogh 'scratched' with pen and ink wherever he thought necessary. In addition, lights were scratched out just as he thought fit and were sometimes worked over again with light body colour. Van Gogh had apparently been criticised for this somewhat rigorous method and he admitted that there was something 'harsh' about it. But, he said: 'there are also people who, just as it is sometimes pleasant and invigorating for a sound constitution to go for a walk when the wind is blowing hard [...], are not afraid of that harshness'.

Drawings and Watercolour Sketches with Mixed Techniques 'Barn with Moss-Covered Roof' (F 842) from Van Gogh's Etten period is a complex and interesting drawing as regards the use of materials. For this, Van Gogh first employed pencil, pen and ink; both the former over the latter and vice versa. The grey sky was depicted with stumped (soft) pencil and hatching with pen and ink. The sky was then washed, resulting in the virtual disappearance of the ink lines and leaving only the pen scratches in the paper. This constitutes an indication that iron-gall ink was used here and not Indian ink, which, of course, is water-resistant. From the fine, deep scratches it can be deduced that Van Gogh used a drawing pen here. This an also clearly be seen from the deep strokes scratched into the roof of the barn. The foreground is very dark in treatment, with a great deal of pencil, pen and brown ink and splashes of black ink. As a result, details such as, for example, the wheelbarrow (centre, right) are almost no longer perceptible. We see the same method and materials in the trees: pencil, pen and brown ink and black splashes. The smock of the peasant (centre) and patches to his right and left, as well as the patch to the right of the faggots, form extra dark accents in the whole scene and

cat. 10

have been applied with a brush and black ink. The black ink in this drawing is printing ink or autographic ink, both of which are matter in appearance than Indian ink after drying. The vegetables in the kitchen garden on the left beside the barn and some clumps of reeds in the foreground have been painted with grey body colour. The fact that iron-gall ink was used in 'Barn with Moss-Covered Roof' can not only be deduced from the ink lines which have been washed away. Its effect on the paper also points to this. The destructive action of the acid ink, applied to excess, can be seen particularly clearly on the back of the paper. The light 'patches' in the sky have not been inserted with drawing material. It is possible that residues of glue, with which this drawing was stuck to another carrier, have prevented the paper from yellowing evenly.[20]

'A Boy Cutting Grass with a Sickle' (F 851) has been drawn with black chalk. Both the foreground and background have been stumped with charcoal, after which they have been washed with transparent watercolour in green, grey and yellow. As a result, the charcoal particles have started 'floating' and have dried in black rings here and there. This can be seen, for example, in the foreground under the boy's feet. The light blue of his stockings and shirt, as well as the brown of his hair and the bushes on the horizon, are painted transparently; the clouds are opaque grey in colour. The horizon is drawn as a white line, which has then been worked over again with black chalk.

cat. 12

The third example of sketches with mixed techniques which we are discussing here is 'Windmills at Dordrecht' (F 850). The landscape has first been drawn with pencil, which can clearly be seen in the windmills and the fence. In addition, the hedge has been heightened with white body colour. The large windmills on the right and in the centre have been deepened with ink. In addition, the windmills have been washed and accentuated with chalk. The groups of trees on the horizon have also been washed. Van Gogh gave the houses red roofs with a brush and watercolour. The blue in the clothing of the man on the white-heightened path is also watercolour. Black chalk can be recognised on the horizon and in the grass (right). In the foreground the green mainly consists of washed coloured pencil.[21] The heavy, cloudy sky has been painted with white and grey body colour. The clouds lit up by the (setting?) sun may possibly have turned out more opaque than was intended.

cat. 15

Another black chalk drawing which has been coloured is 'Woman Sewing' (F 1221). At some places – for example, around the head and clog – the chalk is heavily accentuated. The drawing has been washed transparently in restrained colours such as red (the jacket, the roof behind the window), beige-green (the table-top), reddish-brown (the foreground) and beige (the face and hand). The cuff of the shirt on which the woman is working has been heightened in greyish-white with body colour.

cat. 8

In 'Sien with Cigar, Sitting on the Ground by the Stove' (F 898), Van Gogh has kept everything completely in grey tones. The drawing has been sketched and elaborated with a soft pencil, without the 'strength' of black chalk. Sien's jacket has been washed with water after first being sketched in pencil and has then been deepened again with pencil; the colour of the jacket is the colour of the paper. A similar procedure of pencil/wash/pencil has been followed in the back wall. The white between the stovepipe and Sien's hands has been applied with white chalk, in which Van Gogh has again worked with pencil. The brown colour of her hair, the stovepipe and the background has been applied with a brush and possibly consists of diluted printing ink. As at various other places, here too the hair has again been touched up with pencil afterwards.

'Landscape in Drenthe' (not included in De la Faille) has been painted with predominantly opaque paint, mainly in greenish-grey, blackish-grey and yellow ochre. The trees are drawn with black chalk and the foliage has been washed with (more or less diluted) ink. Apart from chalk, black body colour has also been used in the tree trunks and has been applied so thickly on the right that craquelures have occurred in it after drying. The fairly 'solidly' painted group of bushes on the left have been further worked on with chalk. The sky has been washed in pink and white, which is possibly intended to represent the sunset glow. The black material in this picture is almost certainly printing ink, possibly mixed with paint to achieve broken colours.

For 'Town Wall with Horse-Drawn Tram and Walkers' (F 1400) Van Gogh used a range of drawing materials such as pencil, ink, pastel chalk and watercolour. Details such as grass at the roadside (on right, sloping upwards), houses and persons are drawn with pencil, while the horse and tram and a house in the centre were drawn with pen and ink. The touches of white body colour on the road show yellow accents in pastel chalk. For that matter, coloured accents in pastel chalk are distributed over the whole drawing: blue and green in the group of trees on the left (where watercolour has also been used), blue in the wall on the right, orange in the parasols and the roofs on the horizon, two colours of green in the grass at the roadside (partly applied over green watercolour), and yellow in the wheat field on the right.

CONCLUSION

Clearly, Van Gogh used his drawing materials in an original way. Initially, he drew with traditional instruments such as a pencil, black chalk, charcoal, ink and watercolour, attempting to penetrate the secrets of their specific action and properties. It is obvious that he did not succeed in doing this with all his materials. Depending on the result which confronted him – he was particularly interested in the chiaroscuro effect – he frequently looked at several materials which he used in a

drawing side by side with each other. In this way, he was largely able to overcome the limitations of every material.

Through time, Van Gogh did not hesitate to use a more rigorous drawing technique. Forceful scratching and a painterly treatment of, for example, wetted chalk were the result of his own single-minded view of drawing. Here, he sometimes found himself compelled to replace the normal, relatively thin drawing paper by a thick quality of watercolour paper. In addition, his experiments led to surprising combinations and sometimes to a peculiar and unconventional use of materials such as, for example, milk as a fixing agent and lithographic chalk and printing ink as drawing materials. Van Gogh also took the trouble to lay hands on materials which, in his times, were already out of fashion. This was particularly the case with Italian chalk which intrigued him so much that it led him to use lyrical descriptions such as 'gipsy chalk with a gipsy soul' with a colour like 'ploughed-up land on a summer evening'.

Van Gogh's drawing techniques and materials constitute a fascinating aspect of his work – an aspect which until now has unjustly been left in comparative obscurity. Obviously, with this study the last word about this side of Van Gogh as a draughtsman has not yet been written. The research described here is intended to initiate a discussion about Van Gogh's use of materials. A similar study relating to other artists from his period could constitute an interesting addition to this.

[1] This article is a continuation of the research which I carried out at the Centraal Laboratorium voor Onderzoek van Voorwerpen van Kunst en Wetenschap in Amsterdam (further referred to as CL). It was prompted by the problem of the (un)recognisability of drawing materials which Johannes van der Wolk pointed out and submitted to the CL. The author of the present article next carried out a source study and an opinion survey at the CL relating to this subject. The results are incorporated in two internal reports (Ineke Pey, *De tekenmaterialen van Vincent van Gogh en de samenstelling van droge tekenmaterialen in de 19e eeuw*, Amsterdam 1987; ditto, *Onderzoek naar de herkenbaarheid van zwarte, droge tekenmaterialen*, Amsterdam 1987). The information for the history of the dry drawing materials in this article is derived from the source study mentioned above. For literature on the wet drawing materials, see the relevant note. I am very grateful to the director, Mrs A. Gräfin Ballestrem, for her permission to publish the information and results from the study. I also wish to express my sincere thanks to Professor E. van de Wetering for his advice and support during the research. The title of this article has been taken from Van Gogh's description of Italian chalk [R 30].

[2] The study of Van Gogh's sketchbooks by Johannes van der Wolk is an exception to this. In his research he attempted to reconstruct the sketchbooks by devoting attention not only to the iconography but also to the kinds of paper and drawing materials used. As far as the latter is concerned, the problem of recognisability quickly emerged. Johannes van der Wolk *The Seven Sketchbooks of Vincent van Gogh*, New York/London 1987. See, in particular, Chapter 1 and Conclusion.

[3] This conclusion can be drawn from the research performed in 1987 into the recognisability of dry, black drawing materials (see note 1). In this connection a test was devised consisting of various drawing materials applied to different kinds of drawing paper. This was presented in the form of an opinion survey to a group of Dutch experts.

[4] The following were consulted for the letters of Van Gogh: J. van Gogh-Bonger (ed.), *Verzamelde Brieven van Vincent van Gogh*, I-III, Amsterdam/Antwerp 1952, 1953; V.W. van Gogh (ed.), *Verzamelde Brieven van Vincent van Gogh*, IV, Amsterdam/Antwerp 1954. Use was also made of the card index system built up by Brigitte Blauwhoff (CL) relating to the techniques mentioned in the letters.

[5] *Letters* 187, 195 and R 37.

[6] *Letters* 135, 169, 195, 287, 288, 296, R 1, R 13 and R 36.

[7] *Letters* 150, 153, 195, 263, 270, 273, 277 and R 1.

[8] *Letters* 241, 242, 243, 256, 259, 284, R 18 and R 35.

[9] Here, De la Faille and Hulsker speak about 'heightened with black and white', which is a contradiction in terms as regards black. Black has a receding effect, so that the terms 'to deepen' (deepened) or possibly 'to strengthen' are preferable. J.B. de la Faille, *The Works of Vincent van Gogh. His Paintings and Drawings*, Amsterdam 1970; Jan Hulsker, *The Complete Van Gogh. Paintings. Drawings. Sketches*, New York/Oxford 1980, p. 76. See also drawings F 1003 and F 1011.

[10] Dutch *bergkrijt* or *steenkrijt*, German *Bergkreide* or *Steinkreide*, is known in English as *Italian chalk, natural black chalk* or *black stone*. See J. Watrous, *The Craft of Old-Master Drawings*, Madison 1957, pp. 100-106 and J. Meder, *Die Handzeichnung. Ihre Technik und Entwicklung*, Vienna 1923, pp. 109-115.

[11] *Letters* 270, 272, 273, 274, 276, 277, 287, R 30, R 31 and R 36.

[12] Not in the exhibition. The envelope is in the Rijksmuseum Vincent van Gogh in Amsterdam, under number B 5631.

[13] *Letters* 137, 138, 146, 150, 221, 280, 326, 478, 498a, R 30 and R 45.

[14] In various paintings, too, we see that Van Gogh emphasises the shape of the sun by his use of paint. For example, in 'Mountain Landscape Seen across Walls with Rising Sun and Green Field', Otterlo (F 720), 'Sower with Setting Sun', Otterlo (F 422) and 'Enclosed Field with Young Wheat and Rising Sun', Princeton, New Jersey (F 737), the brushstroke contributes strongly to the expressive effect of the sun and its rays.

[15] For the history and composition of inks see: C. Ainsworth Mitchell, *Inks. Their Composition and Manufacture*, London 1916 (2nd Edition); G.A. Buchheister, *Handbuch der Drogisten-Praxis*, Berlin 1893 (3rd Edition); M. Schürer-Waldheim, *Chemisches-Technisches Recept Taschenbuch*, Vienna/Leipzig 1921 (3rd Edition); G. Banik, et al., 'Untersuchung der destructiven Wirkung von Tinten auf Schriftträger-materialien', *Restauro* 94 (1988), pp. 302-310; W. Schwahn, 'Braune Tinten – Lavierungstechniken', *Maltechnik-Restauro* 93 (1987), pp. 24-31.

[16] *Letters* 146, 151, 152, 163, 171, 173, 176, 177, 214, 215, 219, 222 and R 1.

[17] Nowadays the difference between drawing and painting is becoming increasingly blurred. In my view, the fact that in museums both drawings and paintings on paper are looked after by the same curator is based more on a practical reason – such as the similarity in the carrier – than on the technique. However, no consensus exists about the distinction between drawings and paintings-on-paper. This distinction is not always immediately clear in Van Gogh either. This, however, is not the place for a detailed discussion of the difference between drawing and painting for the purpose of dividing Van Gogh's drawings and watercolour sketches into these two categories. As regards Van Gogh's watercolours, it has been decided to adopt the more general terms 'watercolour sketches' or 'watercolour paintings' in the present article.

[18] M. Doerner, *Malmaterial und seine Verwendung im Bilde*, Stuttgart 1954.

[19] *Letters* 205, 278, 280, 284, 287, 288, 294, 296, R 29, R 30, R 33, R 35 and R 37.

[20] The paper restorer Louis Damen (Museum Boymans-van Beuningen, Rotterdam) was kind enough to draw my attention to the fact that the drawing had been stuck onto a backing and to the possible effect of glue on the paper.

[21] A good quality coloured pencil is very suitable for use as (cubes) of watercolour.

Catalogue

Brussels

A HARD AND DIFFICULT BATTLE

'What a tremendous amount of work and study must be done, that is the condition' [141], Van Gogh wrote to his parents from Brussels. At the start of October 1880 he had moved from Cuesmes in the Borinage district of Belgium to Brussels. One of the reasons for this was the lack of space in which to work in Cuesmes. In his little room there, and also in the garden, he had been hard at work copying the albums *Exercices au Fusain* and *Cours de Dessin* produced for that purpose by Charles Bargue. He also frequently copied the work of Jean-François Millet, doing his 'Sower' at least five times. He had cherished his memories of art as he had come to know it when working for the art and reproduction business of Goupil & Co in The Hague, London and Paris. But he had also begun to realise that 'in the Borinage there are no paintings, that [there] people in general even absolutely do not know what a painting is' [127]. He had become homesick for *le pays des tableaux*, for the imaginary country of paintings. In Brussels, Van Gogh hoped to come into contact with an older artist who could give him hints about how to acquire proficiency as a draughtsman.

Van Gogh wanted to see 'good things' and artists at work. He was in search of 'a more artistic environment [...] for how will one learn to draw unless someone shows you how to do it. With the best will in the world one will not succeed without also being and remaining in contact with artists who are already further on' [138]. Only shortly before that he had travelled to Courrières (in vain, incidentally) in order to meet there in the person of Jules Breton a living being belonging to the species 'artist', an *être vivant de l'espèce Artiste* [136]. Arriving in Brussels he asked advice from V. Schmidt, the local representative of Goupil & Co., and, by letter, also from his brother Theo in Paris. Schmidt lent him photographs Braun had made of 'The Diggers' and 'The Evening Prayer' by Millet. Van Gogh drew copies based on both photographs and sent them to his father in Etten 'so that he would see that I am doing something' [138].

On Theo's advice, Van Gogh visited Anton van Rappard, his junior by five years, in Brussels. And he also visited Roelofs who, like Schmidt, advised him to start taking lessons at the drawing academy. Van Gogh threw himself into the study of the anatomy of man and animals. He 'aims to try this winter to acquire some capital in terms of anatomy here; waiting longer to do this is impermissible, and when all is said and done would work out even more expensively, for it would be losing time' [138]. Full of devotion and dedication, Van Gogh invests in his future. But he does sigh that 'drawing is a hard and difficult battle' [138].

Van Gogh very quickly felt that drawing was coming to him somewhat more easily. Besides his anatomical studies and copies after Millet, he now flung himself into what he calls *études de moeurs* [140], into studies of manners and customs, of human behaviour. In this, he was inspired by the French illustrator Auguste Lançon and British wood engravers. By practising thoroughly on these worker types *ces types d'ouvriers* he hoped to become proficient enough to find work as a book or magazine illustrator in due course.

He reports to his parents as follows: 'Things continue to go fairly successfully with my work, although it is still imperfect, and must become much better' [141]. He says that he is planning to start a collection of costumes and to use these as attributes for his models. 'This is the only true way to get there, to draw from a model, with the necessary costumes' [141]. He also writes that he has again begun 'collecting wood engravings, in the manner of these scrapbooks, such as Theo and Willemien also had in the past. For when I have that fairly complete, then I can benefit by it, for it could still very well turn out that with time I will indeed start working for wood engraving' [141]. To Theo he writes: 'This winter I have collected many woodcuts [...] But drawing by myself is the main thing, and everything must work towards that' [142].

It cannot be established with certainty whether all three of the drawings presented here – 'A Sower (after Millet)' (F 830), 'The Evening Prayer (after Millet)' (F 834) and 'The Bearers of the Burden' (F 832) – actually did originate in Brussels. In *letter* 143 Van Gogh writes to tell Theo that, among other things, he is bringing the drawing 'The Bearers of the Burden', made at Van Rappard's, to Etten where he hopes to meet Theo on a visit to their parents in order 'to confer [with him] about what to do further. To complete them, I will have to have the necessary models in one way or another, and then I am confident that something good will come of it, namely a few compositions which I can show to Smeeton Tilly, or the people at the *Illustra-*

tion or the like'. It is not possible to determine whether 'The Bearers of the Burden' shown here originated in Brussels or, shortly afterwards, in Etten. That is not of essential importance, of course. The same applies to the two copies made after Millet which were perhaps not produced in Brussels, but already in Cuesmes, or perhaps were only made during Van Gogh's stay in Etten or The Hague. What is beyond all doubt – and it is therefore justifiable to open the exhibition with these three drawings – is that their themes occupy a central position at the start of the artistic development of Van Gogh the draughtsman.

fig. 12
P.E. LeRat after J.F. Millet
The Sower
Amsterdam, Rijksmuseum Vincent van Gogh
(Vincent van Gogh Stichting)

fig. 13
Martinez after J.F. Millet
The Evening Prayer
Amsterdam, Rijksmuseum Vincent van Gogh
(Vincent van Gogh Stichting)

I

A Sower (after Millet)
Early 1881
Pencil, ink and paint on wove paper, 480 x 368 mm
F 830 JH 1
Amsterdam, Rijksmuseum Vincent van Gogh
(Vincent van Gogh Stichting)

2

The Evening Prayer (after Millet)
Early 1881
Pencil, ink and watercolour, 470 x 620 mm
Annotated l.l.: d'après J.F. Millet L'Angélus du Soir
F 834 JH 0
Otterlo, Rijksmuseum Kröller-Müller

3

The Bearers of the Burden
Early 1881
Pencil and ink on laid paper, 430 x 600 mm
Watermark: ED&CIE PL BAS
Annotated l.r.: The Bearers of the burden
F 832 JH 0
Otterlo, Rijksmuseum Kröller-Müller

Etten

FAITHFULNESS TO NATURE

Coming from Brussels, Van Gogh did not only have the drawings he had made there with him, but he also brought along a stock of Ingres paper. He liked that paper because he could draw on it well with a pen and reed pen. He disliked pure white paper and cold hues. His preference was for paper the colour of unbleached linen. He used paper both in its original size and reduced to the size of the sketchbooks he made himself.

Among the first subjects he tackled, just as in Brussels, were the examples of Millet: 'The Sower' and 'Les Travaux des Champs'. He continued to be fascinated by the latter's simplicity and faithfulness to nature. When Van Gogh speaks about 'nature' – particularly at this period – he means both the landscape and the figure. The combination of both in Millet's work probably led Van Gogh to take this view, or at least reinforced it. When he is practising drawing figures, he says that at the same time he is practising concentration and that, in turn, has an influence on his landscape drawing. Van Gogh: 'When one draws a pollard willow as if it were a living being, and after all that is actually the case, then the surroundings themselves follow relatively if one has but concentrated one's attention on the tree in question, and has not rested before something of life has entered it' [152].

He compares his struggle with reluctant nature with what Shakespeare called 'taming the shrew', with 'overcoming the opposition by perseverance, *bon gré et mal gré*' [152]. Van Gogh: 'And now that I am drawing figures I shall continue to do that until I am a bit further ahead, and when I work out of doors, then it is to make tree studies, but actually looking at the trees as if they were figures. I mean mainly looking at them with my eye on the contour, the proportion and how they hang together. That is the first thing one has to deal with. Next comes the modelling and the colour and the surroundings' [165].

In an – also otherwise – amorous mood (which is further irrelevant here) Van Gogh in a letter to Van Rappard [R 4] advises him to abandon his studies at the Academy in Brussels and instead of that to devote himself entirely to 'your actual beloved *Dame Nature* or Reality'. Van Gogh: 'I have also fallen in love like this, and head over heels at that, with a *Dame Nature* or

Reality and since then have felt so happy although she still resists me strongly and she will not have me yet and often raps me over the knuckles if I should already dare prematurely to regard her as mine. I am therefore far from saying that I have already won her, but certainly that I am wooing her and seek the key to her heart in spite of painful raps on the knuckles' [R 4].

Van Gogh also familiarised himself in various publications with the practical aspects of the artist's trade: in books and albums by Bargue and Robert about drawing with charcoal, in those of Cassagne about watercolour and perspective. On Theo's advice he also used photographs to practise portraiture. In the method of Bargue, Van Gogh mainly felt himself attracted to the latter's sheets of examples, using large lines, masses and simple, finely felt contours. He describes Bargue's method indirectly in a letter to Theo when he mentions the style of one written previously: 'It would not surprise me, Theo, if my last letter made a more or less strange impression on you. But I hope, however, that as a result you will have obtained an impression which will give you an overview of the lie of the land to some extent. With straight and large strokes of charcoal I tried to indicate the proportions and planes. Once the indispensable basic lines have been found, then we knock the charcoal off again with a handkerchief or a wing, and then start looking more intimately at the contours' [154].

Van Gogh made his first drawings in Etten with pencil and pen: pencil for the main lines of the composition and pen for the further detailing and filling in. But when he was given a box of Paillard paints as a present by his Uncle Cent, he also set to work with watercolour. First, he used this almost exclusively for colouring-in pictures. After a lesson in watercolour painting from his famous cousin Anton Mauve, Van Gogh wrote with great satisfaction: 'What a wonderful thing watercolour is for expressing space and sky, so that the figure is in the atmosphere and it comes to life' [163]. Van Gogh never became a watercolourist in the traditional sense, however. Apart from a few exceptions, he preferred to use watercolour in opaque form.

Van Gogh quickly made the transition from copying examples from books to drawing living models, albeit never entirely definitively. When Van Rappard once commented on a particular sower, saying that Van Gogh had not drawn a man who was sowing but a man who was posing as a sower, Van Gogh readily admitted that, but he added: 'However, I also regard my present studies as studies after the model, they do not pretend to be anything else. In a year or a few years from now, only then will I succeed in doing a sower who is sowing, I agree with you there' [R 2].

BRABANT TYPES

The borderline between the model purely as a 'model' and the model engaged in doing something, or endowed with an attribute as a 'type', is seldom a rigid one in Van Gogh's work, however. On the basis of what Van Gogh writes on this subject in his letters, it would seem that his common sense told him that with his drawings after a model he must, above all, not pretend to make them more than what they actually were, but that his enthusiasm quickly led him to place his models in a setting and thus also to make them depict a subject or a theme. This enthusiasm was probably also born partly of necessity. The point was that in Etten it was not easy for Van Gogh to find models who realised that modelling is something different from sitting for a portrait. The choice was limited and the models would have felt the understandable desire to look their best rather than serve the study requirements of an artist in the making. Van Gogh therefore had to put them to work: 'I also hope to succeed in finding a good model, e.g. Piet Kaufman the labourer, but I think that it will be better to let him pose with a spade or a plough or something else, not here at home, but either in the yard, or in his own home or in the field. But what a hard job it is to make people understand what posing means. Both peasants and townspeople are hopelessly adamant about a point which they refuse to abandon, namely that they do not want to pose otherwise than in their Sunday suit, with impossible folds in which neither knees, elbows, shoulder blades nor any other part of the body have made their characteristic dents or bumps. Truly, that is one of the small adversities in a draughtsman's life' [148].

Very soon he starts depicting 'Brabant Types' engaged in their daily tasks: a peasant with a spade, a sower, a girl with a broom, a woman with a white cap peeling potatoes, a shepherd *cat. 6* leaning on his crook, an old sick peasant sitting on a chair by the open fire with his head in his hands and his elbows on his *cat. 12* knees (F 863), a boy cutting grass with a sickle (F 851), a man and a woman sitting by the fire, a labourer drinking coffee and cutting a slice of bread at dinner time, the spade with which he has come into the field on the ground beside him, a peasant boy lighting the fire in the hearth in the morning with the kettle *cat. 7* hanging above it, an old man putting dry rice on the hearth (F 868), and so on and so forth.

In the group of drawings from Etten in the present exhibition, two are linked in a special way and one is separate to some extent. The two which are connected with each other are 'A Man with a Broom' (F 890) and 'Road with Pollarded Willows *cat. 9* and a Man with a Broom' (SD 1678). In the latter drawing, *cat. 11* Van Gogh placed a reduced version of the man with the broom who is the subject of the first drawing. Van Gogh took a certain pleasure in being able to benefit from preparatory work. Most of all he wanted to build up a stock of figures in all kinds of attitudes which he could introduce at will in larger compositions. In The Hague this would even become an activity on which he was constantly engaged. The separate drawing is 'Windmills at *cat. 15* Dordrecht' (F 850), in other words not windmills at Etten but at Dordrecht and, in fact, on the Weeskinderen Dyke. Van Gogh probably made this drawing (or the preliminary study for it which has not been preserved) during a break in one of his excursions to The Hague.

Van Gogh seems almost constantly to have had the idea of qualifying as a magazine illustrator at the back of his mind. He had already mentioned such a career to his family when in Brussels. In Etten, and for a long time afterwards, he would continue to toy with this idea. More than that, he would seriously consider this option over and over again. He asks Theo to keep a good lookout to see whether there might be a position for a draughtsman here or there and in that case to think particularly of him. With his 'draughtsman's fist' [160] surely there must be something to be earned?! Although at the end of 1881 Van Gogh still saw his field of activity as lying in Brabant, and although he regarded the 'Brabant Types' as his actual work, he nevertheless preferred to move temporarily to The Hague in order to 'come among people a bit more' there. He wanted to have contact with painters again. The incidental visits from and to Mauve and Van Rappard were not enough for him.

4

A Marsh
Summer 1881
Pencil and ink, 425 x 565 mm
F 846 JH 8
Ottawa, National Galleries of Canada /
Musée des Beaux-Arts du Canada

5

The Garden of the Parsonage with Arbor
Summer 1881
Pencil, ink and watercolour on laid paper, 445 x 565 mm
Watermark: HVI
F 902 JH 9
Otterlo, Rijksmuseum Kröller-Müller

6

Worn Out
Summer 1881
Pencil, ink and watercolour on laid paper, 234 x 312 mm
Annotated and signed l.l.: Worn out Vincent
F 863 JH 34
Amsterdam, Stichting P. en N. de Boer

7

An Old Man Putting Dry Rice on the Hearth
Late 1881
Pencil, chalk and paint on laid paper, 560 x 450 mm
F 868 JH 80
Otterlo, Rijksmuseum Kröller-Müller

8

Woman Sewing
Late 1881
Black chalk and watercolour on laid paper, 625 x 475 mm
Signed l.l.: Vincent
F 1221 JH 70
Otterlo, Rijksmuseum Kröller-Müller

9

A Man with a Broom
Autumn 1881
Black chalk and watercolour on laid paper, 550 x 275 mm
F 890 JH 45
Otterlo, Rijksmuseum Kröller-Müller

10

Barn with Moss-Covered Roof
Spring 1881
Pencil, ink and paint on laid paper, 473 x 620 mm
Watermark: ED&CIE PL BAS
F 842 JH 5
Rotterdam, Museum Boymans-van Beuningen

II

Road with Pollarded Willows and a Man with a Broom
Autumn 1881
Black chalk, ink and watercolour on laid paper, 395 x 605 mm
SD 1678 JH 46
New York, The Metropolitan Museum of Art
(Robert Lehman Collection, 1975)

12

A Boy Cutting Grass with a Sickle
Autumn 1881
Black chalk, charcoal and watercolour on laid paper,
470 x 610 mm
Watermark: ED&CIE PL BAS
Signed l.l.: Vincent
F 851 JH 61
Otterlo, Rijksmuseum Kröller-Müller

13

A Girl Raking
Autumn 1881
Black chalk and watercolour on laid paper, 580 x 460 mm
F 884 JH 57
Utrecht, Centraal Museum
(on loan from Stichting Van Baaren Museum)

14

A Digger
Autumn 1881
Pencil, chalk and watercolour on laid paper, 621 x 471 mm
Watermark: ED&CIE PL BAS
Signed l.l.: Vincent
F 866 JH 54
Amsterdam, Rijksmuseum Vincent van Gogh
(Vincent van Gogh Stichting)

15

Windmills at Dordrecht
1881
Pencil, chalk, ink and paint on laid paper, 260 x 600 mm
Watermark: ED&CIE PL BAS
Signed l.r.: Vincent
F 850 JH 15
Otterlo, Rijksmuseum Kröller-Müller

JOHANNES VAN DER WOLK

The Hague

SEARCHING AND TOILING

When Van Gogh moved from Etten to The Hague at the end of 1881 he had mixed feelings about the correctness of his decision. On the one hand, he was far from having finished his studies of the 'Brabant Peasant Types' [169]. He felt that his work in Brabant was just beginning to go smoothly. He was busy moving to a studio of his own. But on the other hand, he did not feel at ease in his parents' home. 'Quarrelling and nagging' induced in him 'a mood of weariness and coolness' [R 7].

One of the advantages of a town such as The Hague for Van Gogh was its artistic life, filled as it was with the activities of artists, art societies, art dealers and all that goes along with these. Van Gogh was already familiar with it in terms of the art trade from the time when he had worked there as an assistant with Goupil & Co at the Plaats. Now he was back again as an artist, filled with positive expectations which, as he would soon find out, were pitched too high. After a year in The Hague he confessed to Theo: 'I sometimes think back to a year ago when I came to the town here, I had imagined that the painters here formed a kind of circle or club, where warmth and sincerity and a certain unity prevailed. To me, that was in the nature of things and I did not know it could be otherwise. Nor would I wish to lose the ideas I had about this when I came here, even if I have to change them and make a distinction between what is and what might be. I could not believe that it is a natural situation for so much coolness and disunity to exist' [256].

In his letters to Anton van Rappard, too, Van Gogh regularly mentions 'the cooperation of the painters' [R 32]. In answer to the rhetorical question: 'Is it a good time for the painters???' Van Gogh replied: 'When I came here to the town I went to all the studios I could possibly visit precisely to seek contact and make friends. Now I have cooled down a lot in that respect and think there is a regrettable shadowy side to it because the painters do appear to be sincere but only too often trip you up as well. That's the fatal thing. People should help and trust each other, for in society there are by nature enmities enough'. Van Gogh had no choice other than to accept his disappointment in this respect. He was even able to give it a positive turn. Van Gogh: 'Contact with artists has, so to speak, ceased for me entirely, without my being able to explain to myself precisely how and why. I pass for everything that is eccentric and bad. As a result, I sometimes have a certain feeling of abandonment, but on the other hand it concentrates my attention more on those things which are unchanging, namely the eternally beautiful in nature. I often think of the old story of Robinson Crusoe who did not lose courage because of his loneliness but set about things in such a way that he created employment for himself so that he developed a very active and very stimulating life as a result of his own searching and toiling' [R 13].

cat. 17

TOWNSCAPES

Van Gogh had two uncles who were art dealers: Uncle Cent and Uncle Cor (C.M.). Much to Van Gogh's delight, the latter twice commissioned him to draw a series of townscapes of The Hague. The first commission was prompted by some pen drawings of townscapes which Van Gogh had been able to show him, including that of 'The Paddemoes'. Van Gogh had cat. 19 roughed out this drawing in pencil after a walk with Breitner at midnight and filled in the further details with ink the next morning. The wall and the railings on the right enclose the site of the Nieuwe Kerk (New Church). Strikingly enough, Van Gogh did not choose the massive church as his subject, but the street scene, a choice which was probably a natural one for him.

Van Gogh reports to Theo on the visit of their mutual Uncle Cor: 'Could you do more of these townscapes for me, said C.M. Yes of course, for I amuse myself doing that when I have sometimes tired of working with the model. Here is the Vleersteeg – the Geest – the Vischmarkt. Do 12 like that for me. Certainly, I said, but then we do a little business and immediately talk about the price. My price for a small drawing of this size, made either in pencil or with the pen, I have fixed for myself at two and a half guilders. Does that seem unreasonable to you. No, but, he says if they turn out well I will ask for another 12 of Amsterdam, provided you then let me fix the price, then you will earn a bit more with them' [181]. Van Gogh did not look for the subjects for this series of 12 among the traditional monuments and monumental townscapes of The Hague, but much closer to home, among the things in which he was really inter-

fig. 14 (JH 132)
Vincent van Gogh
Diggers in a Torn-Up Street, 1882
Amsterdam, Rijksmuseum Vincent van Gogh
(Vincent van Gogh Stichting)

fig. 15 (F 1078)
Vincent van Gogh
Two Men and a Cart, 1882
Otterlo, Rijksmuseum Kröller-Müller

ested: the Rijnspoor Railway Station and surrounding area, the Geest and the Gasworks.

Van Gogh writes to Van Rappard 'I like the new studio I have and I find my subject matter close by me here' [R 11]. 'Close by' means the neighbourhood of the Rijnspoor Station, the predecessor of the present Central Station. Van Gogh lived in a side street off the Schenkweg. From the window at the back he looked out over a carpenter's workshop and a laundry to the coal shed, the engine shed and the workshops of the Rijnspoor. There, Van Gogh was living on the outskirts of the town. In that way, he could go walking in the meadows towards Delft or Voorschoten, but the town itself was also readily accessible. We find the immediate surroundings of the Rijnspoor station in numerous drawings. The trains, with their impressive locomotives, are only depicted sporadically, however, and not as the main subject but more as additions to the landscape. Van Gogh was very much taken with the subjects he found to draw in The Hague. He writes to Van Rappard and Theo respectively: 'Only, should it happen that you [Van Rappard] do not know the 'Geest', the 'Slijkeinde', etc., namely the Whitechapel of The Hague with all its alleyways and courtyards, I suggest that when you come to The Hague again sometime I will go there with you' [R 8]. 'The Hague is beautiful – and there is tremendous diversity' [R 30]. 'I think it is wonderful being in The Hague and I find such an infinity of beautiful things, and I must try to reproduce something of that' [166].

Van Gogh felt most at ease in his working gear: 'Rooting about in dockyards, and in alleyways and streets, and in the hospitals, waiting rooms, even the taverns, that is not a nice occupation, unless you are an artist. As such, you would rather be in the dirtiest neighbourhood, provided there is something to draw, than at a tea party with pretty ladies. Unless you are drawing ladies, then a tea party is nice even for an artist. All I mean is that looking for subjects, moving about among the workers, bargaining and struggling with models, drawing after nature and on the spot itself is rough work, sometimes even dirty work, and really the shapes and clothing of a shop assistant are not exactly the most suitable things for me or for anyone who does not have to speak to beautiful ladies and rich gentlemen and sell them expensive things and make money (i.e. earn) but, for example, draw diggers in a hole on the Geest' [190].   fig. 14 - 15

The second commission Van Gogh received from his Uncle Cor was not to draw Amsterdam townscapes but instead of that a series of locations in The Hague once again. Uncle Cor ordered six of them, but Van Gogh sent him seven drawings. Uncle Cor never mentioned ordering sketches of Amsterdam again. Van Gogh, for his part, did make an attempt to interest his uncle in a series of 50 x 100 cm compositions of 'Works on the Dunes', but as far as is known he never even reacted to that very serious proposal of Van Gogh's.

THE HAGUE

Around the time of Theo's birthday on 1 May 1882, and more or
less to mark this occasion, Van Gogh sent him two drawings
which he most emphatically regarded as companion pieces:
'Sorrow' and 'Tree Roots in Sandy Soil'. Referring to two
almost identical drawings, Van Gogh wrote to Theo: 'Now
I have tried to infuse the landscape with the same sentiment as
the figure. Rooting oneself, as it were, convulsively and pas-
sionately in the earth, and yet being half torn out by the storms.
Both in that white, slender female figure and in these black
gnarled roots with their knots, I wanted to express something
of the battle of life. Or rather, since I tried to be faithful to
nature, which I had before me, without philosophising about
it, something of that great battle has come into it almost involuntarily in both cases. At least it occurred to me that there was
some sentiment in it, but I may be mistaken, anyhow you will
just have to see' [195].

Van Gogh saw in the whole of nature, as it were, a soul, not
only in human beings but also in the trees, the young corn, the
grass, and so on. Van Gogh: 'A row of pollarded willows sometimes resembles a procession of men from an almshouse.
Young corn can have something inexpressibly pure and tender
about it, which arouses the same kind of emotion as the expression of a sleeping child. The flattened grass by the roadside has
something of the weariness and dustiness of the population of
a slum. The other day, when it had been snowing, I saw a group
of savoy cabbages growing numb with cold, which reminded
me of a group of women I had seen standing early in the morning in a hot water and coal shop in their thin petticoats and old
shawls' [242].

Against the advice of many friends, Van Gogh devoted a great
deal of time and energy to drawing from the model. Van Gogh:
'I do not believe I am deceiving myself in thinking that being
and remaining productive is connected with the studies one
makes and goes on making. The more variety there is in them,
the more one toils on them, the more easily one works later
when it comes to making actual paintings or drawings.
Anyhow, I regard the studies as the seed, and the more one
sows the more one may hope to reap' [232]. If there had been a
place in The Hague for artists 'where models met daily as at the
Graphic in the past' [R 32], then Van Gogh would have gone
there frequently. In the absence of such a meeting place he had
to look for his models himself and he certainly did that
successfully. 'My ideal is gradually to work with more and
more models, a whole herd of poor people to whom the studio
could be a kind of harbour or refuge on cold days, or when they
are out of work or in need. Where they know that there is
warmth, food and drink for them and a few cents to be earned.

fig. 16 (F 1662)
Vincent van Gogh
At Eternity's Gate, lithograph
Amsterdam, Rijksmuseum Vincent van Gogh
(Vincent van Gogh Stichting)

fig. 17 (F 1658)
Vincent van Gogh
Almshouse Man with Long Coat and Stick, lithograph
Amsterdam, Rijksmuseum Vincent van Gogh
(Vincent van Gogh Stichting)

At the moment that is still on a very small scale which, I hope, will increase. For the time being I am confining myself to just a few, without giving up any of them – I cannot do without a single one, but can use even more' [278]. 'It is maddeningly difficult to forge the figure. And indeed it is the same as with iron – you work on a model and keep working on it, at first unsuccessfully, but at the very end it becomes compliant and you find the figure, just as iron becomes malleable when it is white-hot, and then you have to go on with it' [288].

Van Gogh preferred to take his models to his studio with him to supply them with the garments and attributes he thought desirable. 'A model is not always wearing a nice, picturesque smock; you change that and it becomes more true to life and expressive' [288]. The special garments available to him included, among other things, various smocks and jackets, trousers, a sou'wester, a Scheveningen hat, a lady's hat, a cape and a fisherman's jacket with an upturned collar. From the rubbish dump he took broken street-lighting lanterns. Van Gogh describes this refuse dump: 'It was something for one of Andersen's fairy tales that collection of discarded buckets, baskets, kettles, soldiers' mess kettles, oil cans, iron wire, street lanterns, stovepipes' [R 28].

The almshouse men and Sien with her children and mother were Van Gogh's favourite models. One of the almshouse men inspired Van Gogh to repeat with his new model the drawing
cat. 6 'An Old and Sick Peasant Sitting by the Fire (Worn Out)' (F 863), which he had made in Etten. 'How very beautiful such an old workman is in his patched bombazine suit, with his bald head' [247]. In Etten the title was 'Worn out'; in The Hague it
cat. 41 became 'At Eternity's Gate' (F 997; the title is taken from F 1662,
fig. 16 the lithograph of the same subject). Over seven years later, when he was in Saint-Rémy-de-Provence, Van Gogh would tackle the Hague composition once again, but then in colour and not as a drawing but as a painting (F 702). For another
cat. 47 drawing, 'Almshouse Man with Long Coat and Stick' (F 962) Van Gogh put a large, old overcoat on his model 'as a result of which he acquired a curious, wide figure. I believe you would perhaps be pleased with this collection of almshouse men in their Sunday best and working suits. Then I also caught him once again sitting with a pipe. He has a nice bald head – large, nota bene, deaf ears and white side whiskers' [235].

Van Gogh had an intimate relationship with Sien during his period in The Hague. She posed patiently for him. Sien's daughter and mother can also regularly be recognised on the surviving drawings, as can Sien's baby with whom Van Gogh was particularly charmed. 'The younger woman does not have a beautiful face because she has had smallpox, but her figure is very graceful and has a certain charm for me. They also have good clothes. Black merino woollens and a nice style of hats, and a beautiful shawl, etc.' [178]. To Van Rappard Van Gogh writes: 'I am pleased with that model I have; I mean that woman who was in my studio when you came, for she is learn-

ing every day and understands me. For example, if I sometimes get angry because something is not going well and I fly into a rage and stand up and say 'It's not worth a damn' or even much worse things, she does not take it as an insult as most people would naturally do, but lets me calm down and start all over again. And as regards the tedious searching for this or that position or pose, she has the patience for that. And so I think she is a darling. If I need to find the size of a figure outside or have to search for the position of a figure in a drawing which I am making outside, for instance seeing how a figure shows up against a fishing smack on the beach and where the light strikes, I only have to say: be there at such and such a time and she is there' [R 8].

COMBINED COMPOSITIONS AND LITHOGRAPHS

Van Gogh had a slightly ambivalent attitude to models: 'I see no other way than working with models – one must most certainly not extinguish one's powers of imagination, but it is precisely the fact of having nature constantly before one's eyes and wrestling with it that sharpens the imagination and makes it more accurate' [238]. 'Two things which remain eternally true and complement each other are in my view: do not extinguish your inspiration and imagination, do not become a slave to the model, and the other: take the model and study it, for otherwise your inspiration will not acquire a plastic body' [241]. At least that is how he formulated it in letters to Theo.

At the same time, Van Gogh had a whole series of secondary intentions in drawing his figure studies. First and foremost, he wanted to build up a collection of separate figures on which he could later draw at will for larger compositions. Some examples of this can be seen in the exhibition. For instance, the figure in 'Old Woman with Walking Stick and Shawl' (F 913)
cat. 16 can be found in two other drawings, namely 'Bakery in the
cat. 17 Geest' (F 914) and 'Broken up Street with Diggers' (F 930a). From
cat. 20 these two drawings it can clearly be seen that when Van Gogh made them he still had difficulty in fitting such figures, which had first been designed separately, into a larger whole. The mutual proportions and the perspective, including those of the surroundings, were difficult factors which would continue to be a problem for Van Gogh for a long time to come.

In the summer of 1883 Van Gogh devoted himself entirely to making large, drawn compositions about 50 cm high and 100 cm wide. It is impossible to find out how this came about, but the sad fact is that none of these large drawings has survived. They are known only from Van Gogh's descriptions of them in his letters, from small sketches which he sent to Theo and his Uncle Cor and from some photographs he had had made of
fig. 18 - 19 them. These photographs were intended to convince Theo, and through him magazine publishers, of Van Gogh's budding talent as an illustrator. He also planned to visit publishers in London personally and offer his services as an illustrator,

although he never put this plan into effect. Van Gogh: 'Now that things are going well, I want to carry on with some larger compositions suitable for illustrations [...] I would, I think, venture to undertake to supply about one large drawing for a double page engraving every month, and will also apply myself to the other formats sometime, the whole page and the half page. I am well aware that one can make large and small reproductions, but the double page lends itself better to what is done in breadth, while the smaller ones can be drawn in a different way, for instance, with pen and pencil' [288].

There was another reason for a second way in which Van Gogh used his model studies. Theo had drawn his attention to the existence of a particular kind of paper from which a drawing could easily be transferred to a stone. From this stone, in turn, a lithograph could be produced. Van Gogh succeeded in buying this kind of paper in The Hague and immediately started to experiment. By making several copies of a picture, Van Gogh was suddenly in the attractive position of being able to bring the same work to the attention of various people simultaneously: Theo, Van Rappard, publishers, etc. 'I have always regarded printing as a miracle – the same kind of miracle as a grain of wheat becoming an ear. An everyday miracle, precisely because the everyday is all the greater, you sow one drawing on the stone or in the etching plate and you harvest a whole host of them' [277]. But Van Gogh became most enthusiastic about the idea of making an initial series of some thirty lithographs of 'figures from the people for the people'.

Employees of the stationery business and printing works where Van Gogh had his lithographs printed had asked their employer if they could have a copy of the lithograph

fig. 17
cat. 47

'Almshouse Man with Long Coat and Stick' (F 1658, after F 962) to hang up on the wall. Van Gogh: 'No result of my work would please me more than ordinary working people hanging such prints up in their room or workshop. For you – the public – it is really done: I regard these words of Herkomer's as true. Naturally, a drawing must have artistic value, but in my view this must not exclude the ordinary passers-by from being able to find something in it. Anyhow, I still count this very first print as being nothing, but I hope with all my heart that it may become something more serious' [245]. In his enthusiasm, Van Gogh foresaw a market growing up, especially in the Netherlands, for a 'people's edition' which was to consist of a series of some thirty 'types of workmen' such as a sower, digger, woodcutter, ploughman, washerwoman and, in addition, at some point also a child's cradle or a man from an almshouse. Van Gogh: 'Anyhow, the whole vast field is open, there is attractive material in abundance – may one undertake such an enterprise or must one not – It goes even deeper than that – is it a duty and a right or is it wrong? That is the question. If I were a man of means I would not hesitate to decide, I would say: *en avant et plus vite que ça* [go ahead and do it faster than that ...] I would think that the following would have to be

decided upon: since it is useful and necessary for Dutch drawings to be made, printed and distributed, intended for workers' dwellings, farmhouses, in one word for every working man, some persons therefore undertake to do their very utmost and to devote their best efforts to this end' [249].

In this connection, it was important to Van Gogh that the persons depicted by him were doing something, were actively engaged on something: 'All these fellows are doing something, and that in particular must generally be maintained in the choice of the subjects, I think. You know yourself how beautiful are the numerous figures at rest which are drawn so very, very frequently. More drawings are made of them than of figures at work. It is always very tempting to draw a figure at rest; expressing action is very difficult, and in the eyes of many people the effect is 'more pleasant' than anything else. But this pleasantness must not lose sight of truth, and the truth is that there is more toiling than resting in life' [251].

Van Gogh hoped that from all his studies after the model he would succeed in creating types. He was then no longer concerned with the reproduction of a particular model, but with the characteristics of a particular action or activity. Van Gogh: 'You will understand my intention: in real studies there is something of life itself and the person who makes it will not respect himself but the nature in it, and will thus prefer the study to what he may possibly make of it later. Unless something entirely different emerges from it as the final result of many studies, namely the type concentrated out of many individuals. That is the pinnacle of art, and there art is sometimes above nature... just as, for instance, in Millet's Sower there is more soul than in an ordinary sower in the field' [257].

But above all, to Van Gogh the drawings of models were 'ammunition' for obtaining the greatly coveted appointment as an illustrator. 'I think it is possible that within a relatively short time there will perhaps be a demand for employees for making illustrations, more so than at present. If I fill my portfolios for myself with studies after these models which I can lay hands on or capture, then I will have something to offer, as a result of which I hope that I can be considered for employment. To keep on making illustrations as, for instance, Morin, Lançon, Renouard, Jules Farat and Worms did in the past, you must have a whole lot of ammunition in the form of various studies in all kinds of fields. I am attempting to collect these as you know and will see sometime' [241]. Van Gogh did, however, worry to some extent about the kind of subjects he would have to illustrate when employed by a magazine. 'Topical events – they would ask for these, if by that they meant such things as, for example, illuminations on the occasion of the King's birthday I would have very little pleasure in that – but, if it pleased the gentlemen to include among topical events scenes from the everyday life of the people, then I would have nothing against doing my very best for that' [272]. 'And a few more tugs and I believe they will be willing and able to use me for one

THE HAGUE

fig. 18 (F 1031)
Vincent van Gogh
Peat Diggers, photograph only

fig. 19 (F 1028)
Vincent van Gogh
Sand Diggers, 1883
Amsterdam, Rijksmuseum Vincent van Gogh
(Vincent van Gogh Stichting)

fig. 20 (F 41)
Vincent van Gogh
Potato Harvest, 1883 (?)
Otterlo, Rijksmuseum Kröller-Müller

illustration job and another. For humble as this may seem, I am made for a job such as this, I have the zest and the energy for it' [290].

As already mentioned, Van Gogh also made an attempt to interest his Uncle Cor in giving him a third commission. He sent him a few small sketches of the large (50 x 100 cm) compositions he had put together from separate drawings of models. 'I wanted the result of this to be that he would perhaps be willing to help to carry out the whole of my plan, namely to make a series of drawings about work in the dunes' [289]. It appears that Uncle Cor never reacted to this suggestion, much to Van Gogh's sorrow and annoyance, of course. One letter later, Van Gogh writes about something else again, namely that he is considering converting the large drawn compositions into painted versions. He also did that, among other things, with the composition of five potato diggers.

One year later, according to current opinion – Van Gogh was then in Nuenen – he painted another large 'Potato Harvest' (F 41). He did that in the manner of the large compositions from his Hague period: a collection of individual figures which appear to have little more in common than the canvas on which they are painted. The painting is so strongly reminiscent of the description of the theme in the Hague period and it is so out of keeping with the other paintings from the Nuenen series of paintings for a dining room that it raises the question of whether it should not be redated to the Hague period.

Van Gogh described to Van Rappard the plan which was never carried out and, in retrospect, was the most astonishing of them all. Again it relates to large, combined compositions – now no longer topical, however, but historicising. Van Gogh: 'Both you and I learned something about history at school, but if you are like me that is not enough and it is too dry and too conventional. Now, for my part, I would particularly like to have a clear overview of the period from 1770, for instance, up to the present. The French Revolution is the very greatest modern event around which everything turns, even at the present time. When I read something like the London and Paris of Dickens (*Tale of Two Cities*) and think about it I find that one can take such splendid motifs for drawings from that period of the revolution. Not directly relating to the actual history as much as to incidents from ordinary life and the aspect of things as they used to be [...] Now, starting in those days and allowing one's thoughts to continue until today one has an overview of a period in which everything has changed. And various moments are exceptionally interesting. And one finds them so grippingly and thoroughly described in various French and English books that it becomes possible to picture to oneself clearly the things of the past. Dickens, who mostly described his own times, could not refrain from writing the *Tale of Two Cities* and over and over again one sees that he inserts descriptions of former days, for instance, a description of the London streets before there were lanterns. The question is

fig. 19

fig. 20

THE HAGUE

could one find Dutch subjects, for instance, from the times when the first lanterns were put up or before they were there. Just imagine a church pew or something about a burial from the time of 1815, or thereabouts. A removal, a place where people go walking, a street on a winter's day from that period or slightly later. In *Les Misérables*, although it deals with a later age, I find what I am looking for: aspects of former times which inspire me to imagine how things looked in my great-grandfather's time, or back to no later than my grandfather even [...] When I was at your place I saw a few fragments of the town which I imagined to be animated by figures from olden times. Well, we will probably have a talk sometime about drawings from an earlier period' [R 36]. It is not known whether Van Gogh and Van Rappard ever discussed this plan with each other. No traces of it can be found either in later letters or in the surviving work. What is clear, however, for instance also from the letters from Drenthe and Nuenen, is that Van Gogh was disturbed by the all-too-thorough disappearance of traces from the past. But here again there was the same kind of ambivalence as with regard to his models: in The Hague, Van Gogh drew the traditional life of the people in the Geest with just as much dedication as he portrayed modern phenomena such as the gasometers and the station.

BLACK & WHITE VERSUS COLOUR

An entirely different ambivalence in Van Gogh's period in The Hague was his attitude towards the media 'black and white' (line drawings), 'aquarelle' (watercolour drawing) and 'painting' (oils). A few brief quotations from letters to Van Rappard clearly show his feelings about the three techniques: 'Painting is so congenial to me that it will cause me a lot of difficulty not to keep on painting always. It is somewhat more manly than doing watercolours and there is more poetry in it' [R 11]. 'I mean it Rappard. I would just as soon be, for example, a waiter in a hotel as some kind of manufacturer of watercolours as some Italians are' [R 13]. His real preference was for 'black and white'. He regarded that as a powerful, manly technique. The outlines, the contours, could not be strong enough for him. Van Gogh: 'Take Millet's etching *Les Bêcheurs*, take an engraving by Albert Dürer, take above all the large woodcut *La Bergère* by Millet himself and then you see to the full what can be expressed by such a contour [...] I for my part declare frankly to you that with all the love and respect I have for these masters, I find it particularly regrettable that when Mauve and Maris speak to others they no longer point to what can be done by the contour and advise them to draw cautiously and softly. And so it is that nowadays doing watercolours is the order of the day and is regarded as the most expressive medium and, in my view, too little work is made of Black & White, even to such an extent that there is a certain antipathy towards it. In watercolour there is, so to speak, no black and on that basis people

refer disparagingly to 'these black things'. It is, however, unnecessary to fill this letter with comments on this subject now' [R 37].

Van Gogh looked disapprovingly at those artists who did not take enough time to develop their skills as draughtsmen first before starting to do watercolours or paint. Van Gogh: 'When I see how various painters whom I know here muddle along with their watercolours and paintings, in such a way that they can make nothing of them, then I sometimes think – my friend, the trouble is your drawing. I have not for one moment regretted the fact that I did not carry on immediately with doing watercolours and painting. I know for certain that I will catch up if I soldier on, so that my hand does not hesitate in drawing and perspective, but when I see young painters composing and drawing out of their own heads – then daubing all kinds of things onto the canvas at random also out of their heads – then holding it away from them and putting on a very pensive, sombre look in order to find out what in God's name it may possibly resemble, and finally, and always simply going on, making something or other of it out of their heads, then it sometimes makes me feel sick and faint and I think it is nevertheless tremendously boring and pretentious [...] And I hope you will understand that if I simply go on drawing and drawing I do this for two reasons. Because at all costs I want to acquire a firm hand for drawing above all and secondly because painters' materials and watercolour entail a great deal of expense, nothing of which is regained at first, and these expenses double and increase tenfold when one is working on a drawing which is not yet correct enough. And if I got into debt or surrounded myself with canvases and papers covered completely in paint, without being sure of my drawing, then my studio would soon become a kind of hell, as I have sometimes seen a studio which appeared to me to resemble that. Now I always come to it with pleasure and enjoy working in it' [221].

Some fifty letters later, the tone is already much more moderate, although Van Gogh certainly still does not give up 'black and white' as his first love: 'I will still have to go through even more failures, however – for I believe that with watercolour much depends on great dexterity and speed of working. You have to work in the semi-wet to create harmony and then you do not have much time for thought. It is therefore not a question of completing things one by one, no, you have to put these twenty or thirty heads on in succession almost simultaneously. Here are a few nice sayings about doing watercolours: 'The watercolour is something diabolical', and the other words come from Whistler who said: 'Yes, I did that in two hours, but I worked for years to be able to do something like that in two hours'. But enough about that. I love watercolour painting enough never to abandon it completely, I keep on dabbling in it repeatedly. But the basis of everything is to have a knowledge of the figure, so that one can readily draw men and women and

fig. 21 (F 952 r)
Vincent van Gogh
Bench with Four People, 1882
Otterlo, Rijksmuseum Kröller–Müller

fig. 22 (F 980)
Vincent van Gogh
On the Beach at Scheveningen, 1882
Otterlo, Rijksmuseum Kröller–Müller

children engaged in all kinds of actions. So I work most on this, for I do not think one can achieve what I want in any other way' [270].

WATERCOLOUR DRAWINGS

In fact, Van Gogh never entirely gave up painting in watercolour. He never became a watercolourist in the traditional sense of the term, however, for apart from a few exceptions he preferred to use watercolour as body colour rather than transparently. It seems that as a rule he liked to use watercolour as a means to colour in a composition rather to build up a picture with it. Entirely in line with this somewhat aloof attitude towards the medium of watercolour, when making watercolour drawings, he was not only concerned with the technique itself, but particularly also with compositional problems, for instance, with the phenomenon of *moutonneries*.

Van Gogh: 'But how difficult it is to get life and movement into them, and to get the figures correctly in place and separate from each other. It is that great problem *moutonner* – groups of *fig. 22* figures which, although constituting a single whole, look over each others' heads or shoulders from above, while in the foreground the legs of the first figures stand out strongly, and higher up the skirts and trouser legs again form a kind of confused muddle, in which there is nevertheless a pattern. Then to the right and left, depending on the location of the angle of view, the greater extension or shortening of the sides. As regards composition, every possible scene with figures – whether it be a market, the arrival of a barge, a flock of people at the soup kitchen, in the waiting room, at the hospital, the lending bank, the groups chatting or walking on the street – is based on the same principle of the flock of sheep, which is certainly where the word *moutonner* comes from, and it all boils down to the same questions of light and shade and perspective' [231]. Good examples of *moutonneries* include the watercolour *cat. 57 - 62* drawings 'On the Beach at Scheveningen' (F 982 and F 1038), 'The Poor and the Money (A Flock of People in Front of the Lottery Office)' (F 970) and 'People's Soup Kitchen (Distributing the Soup)' (F 1020a and F 1020b).

Here is Van Gogh on 'The Poor and the Money (a Flock of People in Front of the Lottery Office)': 'In the last few days I have done almost nothing else but watercolours [...] Perhaps you remember Moorman's State Lottery office at the beginning of the Spuistraat? I passed it on a rainy morning, when a crowd of people were standing waiting there to buy lottery tickets. For the most part they were old women and of that type of person of whom one cannot say what they do or how they live, but who nevertheless apparently scrape along and struggle hard and somehow make their way in the world. Of course, viewed superficially such a crowd of people, who seem to attach so much importance to the phrase 'drawing today', is something that almost makes you and me laugh, in this respect that you and I are not in the least concerned about the lottery. But the group of people – and their expectant expressions – struck me – and while I was doing it, it took on a greater and deeper significance for me than in the first moment. Then, I think, it becomes more meaningful when one sees in it – the poor and the money. For that matter, it is the same with almost every group of figures – you have to think deeply about it before you realise what you are faced with. The curiosity and illusion about the lottery appear more or less childish to us – but it becomes serious when you think of the opposite picture of wretchedness and those kinds of desperate efforts of the poor fellows to possibly be, as they imagine, rescued by buying a lottery ticket, paid for with cents saved from the food they have taken out of their own mouths. However that may be, I have a large watercolour of this in hand [...] Needless to say in this group of figures, of which I am sending a rough sketch in black, there were magnificent touches of colour, blue smocks and brown jackets, white, black, yellowish workers' trousers, faded shawls, an overcoat gone greenish, white bonnets and black top hats, soaking wet paving stones and boots, contrasting with pale or wind- and weather-beaten faces. And that is where oil painting or watercolour comes into its own. Anyhow, I am hard at work on it' [235].

There are two drawings of the subject 'People's Soup Kitchen (Distributing the Soup)' in the exhibition. Van Gogh did them both on the same day: one in the morning with watercolour and the other in the afternoon with Italian chalk. It seems as if he did both of them on location. But that is not the case: it is a composition staged with Sien and her family as models in his studio. Van Gogh had just been able to make a number of improvements in his studio, the most important of which was certainly that he could regulate the light incidence better than before by opening or closing window shutters. He had, however, first observed the subject in reality, probably in the company of G.H. Breitner with whom he quite frequently went 'subject hunting' in the Geest. Van Gogh sent the 'rough sketch' he had made (F 1020) to Theo along with *letter* 271. In the letter itself he outlined the scenario he had devised in his studio (JH 328). 'I have tried to recreate this situation in the studio. I put a white screen in the background and drew the window on it in the proportion and dimensions it has in reality, with the back window closed and the centre window closed from below [...] You will understand that if I now make the figures pose there I get them back again precisely as they were in the actual people's soup kitchen [...] Of course I can now look for the poses of the figures for as long and as often and as exactly as I like. Yet always staying faithful in size to what I have seen' [271].

cat. 57 - 58

fig. 23

fig. 24

fig. 23 (F 1020)
Vincent van Gogh
Sketch with letter 271
Amsterdam, Rijksmuseum Vincent van Gogh
(Vincent van Gogh Stichting)

fig. 24 (JH 328)
Vincent van Gogh
Sketch in letter 271
Amsterdam, Rijksmuseum Vincent van Gogh
(Vincent van Gogh Stichting)

THE HAGUE

In The Hague, Van Gogh kept on regularly recalling his stay in the Borinage in Belgium. He even asked Van Rappard whether he would perhaps like to go there with him. From a coal porter in the station yard he finally learned how to carry bags of coal. First, the mouth of the bag is tied up. Next, the bag is set bottom upwards. Then the corners of the bottom are stuck into each other, thus creating a kind of monk's cowl which can be carried on the head. Happy with his new knowledge, he drew a whole series of studies of 'Miners' Wives Carrying Bags' and the watercolour 'Women Carrying Bags of Coal in the Snow' (F 994). Van Gogh: 'In the watercolour I have, I believe, the effect, but it is still not great enough in character for me. The reality is something like *Les Glaneuses* by Millet, stern, so you will understand that one mustn't turn it into an *effet de neige* [snow scene], which would only be an impression and would only have a *raison d'être* if it were a question of the landscape' [241].

cat. 64

Van Gogh always loved to travel. He was constantly making plans to go and work somewhere else. Prompted by a travel description of the Netherlands by Boughton, with illustrations by Abbey, he thought it would be interesting to settle on the island of Marken. Van Gogh: 'Who knows, if one ever got round to settling down somewhere where everything was very beautiful, how good one would feel in that situation. But in such a case one must have at least one point of contact with the art world, for of course the fisherfolk understand nothing about it and you have to be able to live' [297]. Van Gogh also sees reasons precisely for remaining in the town: 'As regards living entirely in the country – I find nature beautiful and yet there are many things which tie me to the town, also particularly the magazines and the possibility of making reproductions. It would greatly please me not to see any locomotives [Van Gogh lived beside the station], but it would be much more difficult for me never to see a printing press again' [297]. Scheveningen would be a nice compromise: outside the town, yet close to it. But there the prices are again too high; so what about the Hook of Holland or Katwijk or, after all, Marken? Van Gogh: 'One of the things I have sometimes thought about, namely moving, could be solved in a different way. Yesterday and the day before I walked around in the neighbourhood of Loosduinen. Among other things I went from the village to the sea and found numerous cornfields, certainly not as beautiful as those in Brabant, but nevertheless there one must have reapers, sowers, ear gatherers, and one of those things I have missed this year and why I occasionally needed something else' [307].

Finally, Van Gogh decided to follow Van Rappard to Drenthe: 'He [Van Rappard] is going back there again sometime soon and he is going even further, namely to the fishing villages on Terschelling. For my part, particularly now after Rappard's visit, I would very much like to go to Drenthe. So much so, in fact, that I have been finding out whether it would be easier or more awkward to move the whole show. Through the intermediary of Gend and Loos the furniture, even the stove and bed, can be taken along by taking half of a goods wagon, even if few or no packing cases were needed. Naturally I am thinking about it, for although the things I have are not worth much, it is nevertheless a great expenditure if you have to settle in again right from the start. My plan then, however, would be to go with my wife and children. We would be confronted with the expenses of this move and travelling costs. Once there, I think, I would remain permanently in this moorland and peat-cutting region to which more and more painters are coming and through time a kind of colony of painters might probably grow up [...] I would imagine that if I were to settle down somewhere there, Rappard would come even more to that same region than he does now and we would have some companionship from each other. As I am telling you, particularly since his visit and what we discussed together with regard to work, I have set my mind on Drenthe. For that matter, if necessary I can also look for cheaper accommodation here, and I think it is also beautiful here, but nevertheless – I would like to be alone with nature sometime – without the town' [316]. And in fact, Van Gogh did go to Drenthe. Sien and her children did not accompany him, however. Van Gogh went alone.

But even before he was due to set off for Drenthe he already had plans for a following destination: England. Van Gogh: 'My plan is to make great strides with painting in Drenthe so that I will be eligible for membership of the Drawing Society when I come back. That, in turn, is connected with a second plan about going to England. I believe it is permissible to speculate, provided one does not do it aimlessly or on shifting sands. So, concerning England. I most certainly think I can sell something there more easily than here – that is so – therefore I sometimes think about England. But I do not know how the point at which I have arrived will appeal to the English art lovers and because I do not know I first want to make a small positive start here with selling before I consider it advisable to take steps over there. When I start selling a few things here then I won't hesitate a moment longer but will start to send things over there or go over there. But as long as I sell absolutely nothing here, then I would be making a very slight mistake about the timing if I did not have the wisdom to wait until I see even a beginning here [...] I was very pleased with your letter for I observe that you see something in the plan about Drenthe, and that is enough for me, it will emerge automatically later how it can be turned to advantage. But I have already made my mind up, directly in connection with ensuring I become a member of the Drawing Society, and furthermore with England – because I know for certain that the subjects to be found over there, if I succeed in infusing them with some sentiment, will find favour in England. Anyhow, let's just go ahead with Drenthe, whether we can spend a lot or only a little for the time being' [319].

16

Old Woman with Walking Stick and Shawl
Early 1882
Pencil, ink and watercolour on wove paper, 575 x 319 mm
Signed l.l.: Vincent
F 913 JH 109
Amsterdam, Rijksmuseum Vincent van Gogh
(Vincent van Gogh Stichting)

17

Bakery in the Geest
Early 1882
Pencil and ink on wove paper, 204 x 336 mm
Signed l.l.: Vincent
F 914 JH 112
The Hague, Haags Gemeentemuseum

18

Blacksmith Shop
Early 1882
Pencil, ink and paint on wove paper, 370 x 260 mm
F 1084 JH 137
Otterlo, Rijksmuseum Kröller-Müller

19

The Paddemoes
Early 1882
Pencil and ink on wove paper, 250 x 310 mm
Signed l.l.: Vincent
F 918 JH 111
Otterlo, Rijksmuseum Kröller-Müller

20

Broken up Street with Diggers
1882
Pencil, ink and watercolour, 430 x 630 mm
Signed l.l.: Vincent
F 930a JH 131
Berlin, DDR, Nationalgalerie der Staatlichen Museen
zu Berlin

21

Corner of Herengracht and Princessegracht
Early 1882
Pencil, ink and paint on laid paper, 240 x 335 mm
Signed l.l.: Vincent
SD 1679 JH 121
Amsterdam, Rijksmuseum Vincent van Gogh
(Vincent van Gogh Stichting)

22

The Entrance of the Pawnshop
Early 1882
Pencil, ink and paint on laid paper, 240 x 340 mm
Signed l.l.: Vincent
F o JH 126
Amsterdam, Rijksmuseum Vincent van Gogh
(Vincent van Gogh Stichting)

23

The Gas-Works
Early 1882
Pencil, ink and paint on laid paper, 240 x 335 mm
Signed l.l.: Vincent
F 924 JH 118
Amsterdam, Rijksmuseum Vincent van Gogh
(acquired with aid from the Vereniging Rembrandt)

24

De Prins van Oranje (Iron-Foundry)
Early 1882
Pencil and ink on laid paper, 240 x 330 mm
Signed l.l.: Vincent
F 925 JH 117
Karlsruhe, Staatliche Kunsthalle (Kupferstichkabinett)

25

Rijnspoor Station
Early 1882
Pencil and ink on laid paper, 237 x 333 mm
Signed l.l.: Vincent
F 919 JH 123
The Hague, Haags Gemeentemuseum

26

Ditch along the Schenkweg
Early 1882
Pencil, ink and paint on laid paper, 185 x 340 mm
Watermark: VDL
Signed l.l.: Vincent
F 921 JH 116
Otterlo, Rijksmuseum Kröller-Müller

21
22

23
24

25
26

28

Nursery-Garden
Early 1882
Pencil, ink and paint on laid paper, 295 x 585 mm
Signed l.l.: Vincent
F 930 JH 138
New York, The Metropolitan Museum of Art
(Bequest of Walter C. Baker, 1971)

27

Nursery-Garden and Houses near the Schenkweg
Early 1882
Pencil and ink, 400 x 690 mm
F 915 JH 122
The Hague, Mrs. W. Nieuwenhuizen Segaar

29

Nursery-Garden
Early 1882
Pencil, ink and paint on laid paper, 235 x 330 mm
Signed l.l.: Vincent
F 923 JH 125
Amsterdam, Rijksprentenkabinet (Rijksmuseum)

THE HAGUE

30

Fish-Drying Barn at Scheveningen
Summer 1882
Pencil, ink and paint on laid paper, 280 x 440 mm
Watermark: ED&CIE
Signed and annotated l.l.: Vincent del. Scharrendroogerij
te Scheveningen
F 938 JH 152
Otterlo, Rijksmuseum Kröller-Müller

31

Carpenter's Yard and Laundry
Summer 1882
Pencil, ink and paint on laid paper, 285 x 470 mm
Watermark: PL BAS
Signed l.l.: Vincent del.
F 939 JH 150
Otterlo, Rijksmuseum Kröller-Müller

32

Barns and Houses at Scheveningen
Summer 1882
Pencil, chalk and watercolour on wove paper,
435 x 597 mm
F 1041 JH 167
Amsterdam, Rijksmuseum Vincent van Gogh
(Vincent van Gogh Stichting)

33

View of the Schenkweg and the Railway-Yard
1882
Watercolour and ink, 380 x 560 mm
F 910 JH 99
Geneva, Private Collection

34

Tree Roots in Sandy Soil
April 1882
Pencil, chalk, ink and watercolour on wove paper,
500 x 690 mm
F 933 r = F 1076 r JH 142
Otterlo, Rijksmuseum Kröller-Müller

35

Sorrow
April 1882
Pencil and black chalk on laid paper, 445 x 270 mm
Signed and annotated: Vincent del. Sorrow Comment se fait-il
qu'il y ait sur la terre une femme seule – délaissé Michelet
F 929a JH 130
Walsall, West Midlands, Walsall Museum & Art Gallery
(Garman-Ryan Collection)

36

Bent Figure of a Woman
Spring 1882
Pencil and ink on double laid paper, 580 x 420 mm
Watermark: ED&CIE PL BAS (double)
F 935 JH 143
Otterlo, Rijksmuseum Kröller-Müller

37

Sien Sewing, Half-Figure
Early 1883
Pencil and chalk on laid paper, 530 x 375 mm
Signed l.l.: Vincent
F 1025 JH 346
Rotterdam, Museum Boymans-van Beuningen

38

Woman Praying
Spring 1883
Pencil, chalk and paint on wove paper, 630 x 395 mm
F 1053 JH 357
Otterlo, Rijksmuseum Kröller-Müller

39

Sien with Cigar, Sitting on the Ground by the Stove
1882
Pencil, white chalk and ink on double laid paper,
455 x 560 mm
Watermark: ED&CIE PL BAS (double)
F 898 JH 141
Otterlo, Rijksmuseum Kröller-Müller

40

Woman Sitting on a Basket, with Head in Hands
Early 1883
Pencil, black chalk and paint on watercolour paper,
490 x 305 mm
F 1069 JH 325
Chicago, The Art Institute
(Gift of Mrs. G.T. Langhorne and the Mary Kirk Waller Fund
in memory of Tiffany Blake)

41

At Eternity's Gate
Autumn 1882
Pencil on watercolour paper, 503 x 308 mm
Watermark: DAMBRICOURT FRERES
Signed l.l.: Vincent
F 997 JH 267
Amsterdam, Rijksmuseum Vincent van Gogh
(Vincent van Gogh Stichting)

THE HAGUE

42

Sien with Girl on her Lap
Spring 1883
Charcoal, pencil, ink and paint on wove paper,
539 x 355 mm
Signed l.l.: Vincent
F 1067 JH 356
Amsterdam, Rijksmuseum Vincent van Gogh
(Vincent van Gogh Stichting)

43

Sien Sewing and Girl
Early 1883
Charcoal, ink and watercolour on wove paper,
555 x 299 mm
Signed l.l.: Vincent
F 1072 JH 341
Amsterdam, Rijksmuseum Vincent van Gogh
(Vincent van Gogh Stichting)

44

Almshouse Man with Top Hat, Head
Late 1882
Pencil and chalk, 400 x 245 mm
F 954 JH 287
Worcester, Massachusetts, Worcester Art Museum
(Gift of Chapin and Mary Alexander Riley,
in memory of Francis Henry Taylor)

45

Almshouse Man with Top Hat, Head
Late 1882
Pencil, lithographic chalk and ink on watercolour paper,
601 x 360 mm
Signed l.l.: Vincent
F 985 JH 286
Amsterdam, Rijksmuseum Vincent van Gogh
(Vincent van Gogh Stichting)

46

Almshouse Man with Cap, Seen from Behind
Winter 1882-83
Pencil and black chalk on laid paper, 500 x 280 mm
Signed l.r.: Vincent
F 965   JH 298
Private Collection

47

Almshouse Man with Long Coat and Stick
Autumn 1882
Pencil on watercolour paper, 504 x 302 mm
Watermark: DAMBRICOURT FRERES
F 962 JH 212
Amsterdam, Rijksmuseum Vincent van Gogh
(Vincent van Gogh Stichting)

48

A Digger
Autumn 1882
Pencil on watercolour paper, 313 x 505 mm
Watermark: DAMBRICOURT FRERES
F 906 JH 260
Amsterdam, Rijksmuseum Vincent van Gogh
(Vincent van Gogh Stichting)

49

A Digger
Autumn 1882
Pencil on wove paper, 505 x 283 mm
Watermark: HALLINES 1877
F 907 JH 261
Amsterdam, Rijksmuseum Vincent van Gogh
(Vincent van Gogh Stichting)

50

A Digger
Autumn 1882
Pencil and ink on watercolour paper, 485 x 292 mm
Watermark: DAMBRICOURT FRERES
F 908 JH 258
Amsterdam, Rijksmuseum Vincent van Gogh
(Vincent van Gogh Stichting)

51

Man and Woman, Arm in Arm
Autumn 1882
Pencil on watercolour paper, 497 x 310 mm
Watermark: DAMBRICOURT FRERES
F 991 JH 233
Amsterdam, Rijksmuseum Vincent van Gogh
(Vincent van Gogh Stichting)

52

Fisherman's Head with Sou'wester
Winter 1882-83
Pencil, lithographic chalk, ink and paint on watercolour paper,
505 x 315 mm
F 1014 JH 310
Amsterdam, Rijksmuseum Vincent van Gogh
(Vincent van Gogh Stichting)

53

Girl with Shawl, Half Figure
Winter 1882-83
Pencil and lithographic chalk on watercolour paper,
508 x 313 mm
Watermark: HALLINES 1877
Signed l.l.: Vincent
F 1008 JH 301
Amsterdam, Rijksmuseum Vincent van Gogh
(Vincent van Gogh Stichting)

54

Woman with Baby on her Lap
Autumn 1882
Pencil, chalk, ink and paint on watercolour paper,
405 x 240 mm
Watermark: [DAMBRICOURT] FRERES
F 1061 JH 220
Otterlo, Rijksmuseum Kröller-Müller

55

A Baby
Early 1883
Chalk and brown ink on watercolour paper,
339 x 265 mm
F 912 JH 318
Amsterdam, Rijksmuseum Vincent van Gogh

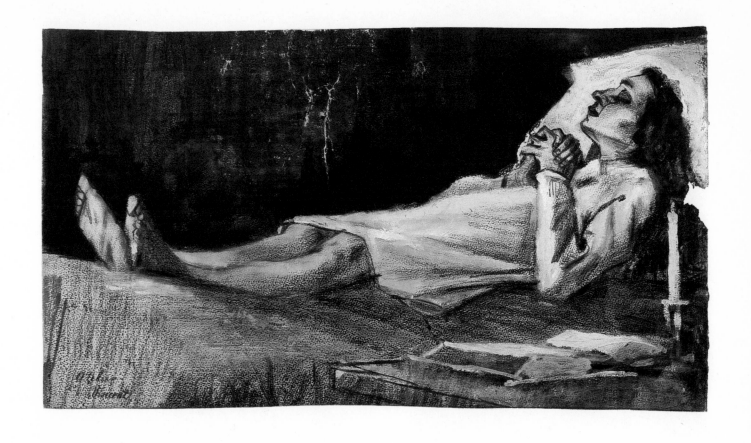

56

Woman on her Deathbed (?)
Spring 1883
Pencil, chalk and watercolour, 350 x 620 mm
F 841 JH 359
Otterlo, Rijksmuseum Kröller-Müller

57

Public Soup Kitchen (Distributing the Soup)
Early 1883
Pencil, Italian chalk and watercolour, 340 x 490 mm
F 1020b JH 331
Private Collection

58

Public Soup Kitchen (Distributing the Soup)
Early 1883
Italian chalk and paint on watercolour paper,
570 x 445 mm
Signed l.l.: Vincent
F 1020a JH 330
Amsterdam, Rijksmuseum Vincent van Gogh
(Vincent van Gogh Stichting)

59

Church Pew with Almshouse Men and Women
Autumn 1882
Watercolour, ink and pencil on wove paper, 280 x 380 mm
F 967 JH 225
Otterlo, Rijksmuseum Kröller-Müller

60

The Poor and the Money (A Flock of People
in Front of the Lottery Office)
Autumn 1882
Black chalk, pencil, watercolour and ink on wove paper,
380 x 570 mm
F 970 JH 222
Amsterdam, Rijksmuseum Vincent van Gogh
(Vincent van Gogh Stichting)

61

On the Beach at Scheveningen
Autumn 1882
Watercolour, 270 x 450 mm
F 982 JH 247
Private Collection

62

On the Beach at Scheveningen
Autumn 1882
Watercolour, 340 x 495 mm
F 1038 JH 228
Baltimore, The Baltimore Museum of Art
(The Cone Collection, formed by Dr. Claribel Cone
and Miss Etta Cone of Baltimore, Maryland BMA 1950.301)

63

Town View of The Hague with the Nieuwe Kerk
1882-83
Watercolour and ink, 245 x 355 mm
Watermark: [J WHATMAN] TURKE[Y MILL]
Signed l.l.: Vincent
SD 1680 JH 97
Private Collection

64

Women Carrying Sacks of Coal
Late 1882
Watercolour on watercolour paper, 321 x 502 mm
F 994 JH 253
Otterlo, Rijksmuseum Kröller-Müller

65

A Sower
Late 1882
Pencil and ink on watercolour paper, 613 x 398 mm
F 852 JH 275
Amsterdam, Stichting P. en N. de Boer

66

Scheveningen Woman with Wheelbarrow
Spring 1883
Pencil, black chalk and watercolour, 670 x 450 mm
F 1021 JH 362
Private Collection

68

A Potato Field in the Dunes near Loosduinen
Summer 1883
Ink and watercolour on laid paper, 275 x 420 mm
Watermark: JV
Signed l.r.: Vincent
F 1037 JH 390
Otterlo, Rijksmuseum Kröller-Müller

67

Weed Burning
Summer 1883
Watercolour on wove paper, 194 x 360 mm
Signed l.l.: Vincent
F 1035a JH 375
Private Collection

69

Country Road in Loosduinen near The Hague
Early 1882
Pencil and brown ink on laid paper, 247 x 342 mm
Signed l.r.: Vincent
F 1089 JH 124
Amsterdam, Rijksmuseum Vincent van Gogh
(Vincent van Gogh Stichting)

THE HAGUE

Drenthe

INDESCRIBABLY BEAUTIFUL

Van Gogh did not stay in Drenthe for as long as he had originally intended. With Hoogeveen as his home base he moved, in accordance with Van Rappard's advice, to the south-eastern part of Drenthe, to Nieuw Amsterdam and to Zweeloo. And eventually he did not return to The Hague, let alone go via The Hague to England, but to his parents' home which was then no longer in Etten but now in Nuenen. Loneliness, financial worries and bitter cold forced him to give up his stay in Drenthe.

In spite of the problems, Van Gogh was exceptionally enthusiastic about the unspoilt landscape of Drenthe: 'Drenthe is so very beautiful, it fascinates me completely and satisfies me absolutely, so much so that if I could not be here forever I would prefer not to have seen it. It is indescribably beautiful' [338]. Van Gogh wanted to see as much of Drenthe as possible so that in the second place, and only then, he could develop a plan for his work: 'As you see I simply go into action, I tackle everything head on, it will fall into place and sink in automatically later on. But I do not want to start here with a pre-arranged plan, on the contrary I want my plan to take shape from my studies. I do not yet know the actual character of the land at present, I am drawing everything I come across now, and then later when I have experience I will try to render it in what are basically its most characteristic aspects. Things are so closely interrelated that one has to seize upon everything, however much one may wish to concentrate, one cannot miss a thing' [332].

One day, Van Gogh got a lift in the early morning to Zweeloo, a small place where, among others, Max Liebermann also painted. Van Gogh almost went out of his mind, so magnificent did he find the landscape with the winter corn coming up: 'It was really so beautiful driving into the village. Enormous moss-covered roofs of houses, stables, sheepfolds, barns. Here the dwellings are very broad-fronted, standing between oak trees of a superb bronze. Tones of golden-green in the moss; of reddish or bluish or yellowish dark lilac greys in the ground; tones of indescribable purity in the green of the cornfields; tones of black in the wet tree trunks, contrasting with golden showers of swirling, swarming autumn leaves, which hang in loose clusters as if blown onto them, loose and with the sky still shimmering through them, from poplars, birches, lime trees and apple trees. The sky smooth and clear, luminous, with white, but of an indecipherable lilac, a white shimmering with red, blue and yellow which reflects everything and which one feels above oneself everywhere, which is hazy and merges into the thin mist below. Which brings everything together in a gamut of delicate greys. At Zweeloo, however, I did not find a single painter, nor did any ever come in the winter, said the people. I hope I will be there this winter. Since there were no painters I decided, instead of waiting for my landlord to return, to walk back and draw something on the way. In this way I began to make a sketch of the particular apple orchard of which Liebermann made his large painting. And then back along the road we had driven in the early hours. This region around Zweeloo is at present entirely covered in young corn – sometimes endlessly, that very, very first green that I know. With a sky of a delicate lilac white above it that creates an effect – which I believe cannot be painted, but for me it is the basic tone with which one must be familiar in order to know what the basis of other effects is. A black stretch of earth – immense – a clear sky of delicate lilac white. This earth sprouts young corn, it is as though mildewed with that corn. At bottom, that is what the good fertile lands of Drenthe are; all that in a hazy atmosphere [...] What do you bring back from such a day? Only a number of rough sketches. But you do bring something else back too – a calm delight in work' [340].

Van Gogh in Nieuw Amsterdam: 'This time I am writing to you from the very remotest part of Drenthe where I have come after an interminably long journey by canal boat through the moorland. I see no possibility of describing the land to you as it ought to be described for words fail me, but imagine the banks of the canal as miles and miles of Michels or Th. Rousseaus, van Goyens or Ph. de Konincks. Flat plains or strips differing in colour, which become narrower and narrower as they approach the horizon, accentuated here and there by a turf hut or small farmhouse, or a few gaunt birch trees, poplars, oaks. Stacks of peat everywhere, and one repeatedly sails past barges carrying peat or bulrushes from the marshes. Here and there delicately coloured scrawny cows, often sheep and pigs' [330].

A subject characteristic of the peat moors of Drenthe is the at. 75 'Peat Stumps' (F 1095). Van Gogh: 'Yesterday I drew rotted oak roots, so-called peat stumps, which are oak trees that have been buried under the peat for perhaps a century, from which new peat has formed; when it is being dug out, the peat stumps then come to light. The roots were lying in a pool, in black mud. Some black ones were lying in the water in which they were reflected, some lay bleached white on the black surface. A white pathway ran alongside, behind it more peat, as black as soot. Then a stormy sky above it. This pool in the mud with these rotted roots was absolutely melancholy and dramatic, just like Ruijsdaal, just like Jules Dupré' [331].

JV PAPER

cat. 71 The drawing 'A Digger' (F 1307) has hitherto always been dated as belonging to the Nuenen period in the literature. From the stylistic viewpoint, however, this drawing is out of place among the Nuenen peasants. A quotation from a letter and the kind of paper used justify a dating in the Drenthe period. The quotation is: 'Fortunately the men here wear short trousers, which brings out the shape of the leg and makes the movements more expressive' [324]. The digger in F 1307 is indeed wearing short trousers, at least as compared with the trousers of other diggers portrayed by Van Gogh. The watermark in the paper is JV, which makes it identical to the watermark of the watercolour cat. 72 drawing 'Landscape in Drenthe', now published for the first time. The assumption that this landscape is situated in Drenthe (although it cannot be localised exactly) is based on the close cat. 73 stylistic relationship with the watercolour F 1099 which can certainly be dated in the Drenthe period. The fact that drawing cat. 68 F 1037 of a potato field in the dunes near Loosduinen was also done on JV paper leads to the assumption that when Van Gogh left The Hague he took a batch of that paper to Drenthe with him.

Van Gogh also firmly intended to do a lot of painting in Drenthe: 'I am also drawing, but you know very well that painting must be the main thing as far as possible' [325]. 'I have a few studies of the moors, which I will send you when they are thoroughly dry, and have also started doing watercolours. And I have also begun doing pen drawings again, precisely with painting in mind, because with the pen one can enter into such details as painted studies cannot do, and one does well to make two studies, one completely drawn for putting the things together and one painted for the colour. If it is, in fact, possible and the opportunity permits, this is a way to heighten the cat. 74 painted study later' [326]. It is probable that 'Landscape with Canal' (F 1104) is one of these pen drawings which Van Gogh made in preparation for a painting. No painting depicting this subject has survived, however.

70

Drawbridge in Nieuw-Amsterdam
Autumn 1883
Watercolour, 385 x 810 mm
F 1098 JH 425
Groningen, Groninger Museum

71

A Digger
Autumn 1883
Black chalk, ink and watercolour on laid paper,
437 x 302 mm
Watermark: JV
F 1307 JH 853
Amsterdam, Rijksmuseum Vincent van Gogh
(Vincent van Gogh Stichting)

72

Landscape in Drenthe
Autumn 1883
Black chalk, ink and watercolour on laid paper,
275 x 420 mm
Watermark: JV
F o JH o
Private Collection

73

Landscape at Nightfall
Autumn 1883
Watercolour, 416 x 541 mm
F 1099 JH 399
Amsterdam, Rijksmuseum Vincent van Gogh

74

Landscape with Canal
Autumn 1883
Pencil, ink and paint on laid paper, 280 x 400 mm
Watermark: VDL PRO PATRIA EENDRAGT MAAKT MAGT
F 1104 JH 424
Amsterdam, Rijksmuseum Vincent van Gogh
(Acquired with aid from the Vereniging Rembrandt)

75

Landscape with Bog-Oak Trunks
Autumn 1883
Ink and pencil, 310 x 375 mm
F 1095 JH 406
Boston, Museum of Fine Arts
(Gift of John Goelet)

Nuenen

A BIG ROUGH DOG WITH WET PAWS

Van Gogh felt it as a great victory over himself that, although actually compelled to do so by circumstances, he had nevertheless returned from Drenthe to his parents' home in Nuenen of his own accord, 'having been the first to swallow his own pride' [345]. He had far from forgotten his annoyance about his parents' lack of understanding which had forced him in the past to move from Etten to The Hague. He reports to Theo on the reception he now received from his parents in Nuenen: 'I feel what Father and Mother instinctively (I do not say reasoningly) think of me. There is the same reluctance towards taking me into their home as there would be about having a big rough dog. He would come into the room with wet paws – and besides that he is so rough. He would get into everyone's way. And he barks so loudly. He is a filthy creature [...] The dog is only sorry he has not stayed away, for he was not so lonely on the moors as in this house, in spite of all the friendliness. The visit by the beast was a weakness which I hope will be forgotten and which he will avoid repeating' [346].

Van Gogh wanted to leave again as soon as possible. He thought about going to Van Rappard in Utrecht and then, perhaps, back to The Hague, to Mauve. But he has second thoughts: 'Since I wrote the enclosed letter, I have thought about your remarks again and I have also spoken with Father again. My decision definitely not to stay here was as good as certain, regardless of how that would be taken or what would come of it. Then, however, the conversation took a different turn because I said: I have now been here for a fortnight and feel I have come no further than in the first half hour. If only we had understood each other better, we would now have had this and that in order and put to rights. I can lose no time and I must decide. A door must either be open or closed – I do not understand anything in between and it is actually impossible. It has now ended up with the decision that the room in the house where the mangle now stands will be available for me as a storage place for everything, and also as a studio whenever this may be desirable because of circumstances. And with a start being made with emptying the room, which was not the case at first and the matter was still undecided' [347].

Van Gogh collected his things which he had left in

The Hague, visited Van Rappard in Utrecht and was now firmly intending to stay with his parents in Nuenen for some length of time. The financial advantages settled the matter. Van Gogh to Theo: 'Business is business, and to you and to me it is clear enough that this is a good move. For much too long I have not had this refuge and I think that it must go through if we want to succeed in our plan' [348].

BRABANT ARTISANS

As a logical follow-up to the 'Brabant Peasant Types' from Etten and the 'Workmen's Figures' from The Hague, Van Gogh started work on a series of 'Brabant Artisans' in Nuenen. He found the subjects in his immediate vicinity. For the time being, he concentrated on the artisans who worked indoors, the home workers. It was winter and he felt at home among the weavers and the men and women who wound the yarn, more so, in fact, than with his parents in the parsonage. Van Gogh: 'Isolation is miserable enough and a kind of prison [...] For my part I often find it more pleasant among the people who do not even know the word in question – for example, the peasants, the weavers etc. – than in the more cultured world. That is certainly fortunate for me. Thus, for example, while I am here I have become engrossed in the weavers. Do you know of many drawings of weavers? I know of only a few. For the time being I have made three watercolours of them. These people are awkward to draw, because in the small rooms one cannot stand back far enough to draw the loom. I believe that is the reason why attempts to draw them must often fail. Here, however, I have found a room in which there are two looms and where it can be done. Rappard painted a study of them in Drenthe which I found beautiful. Very sombre – for these weavers are very impoverished people' [351].

Clearly, the weavers had all his sympathy. Van Gogh drew them in watercolour and in ink and also painted them. For the *cat. 76* first time, too, Van Gogh made drawings based on his own paintings, something of which he was later to make a fixed practice during his stay in Arles and Saint-Rémy-de-Provence in order to keep his brother and his artist friends up to date with the progress in his work. Van Gogh: 'In a few words I wanted to tell you that, also in response to your letter in which you said something about pen drawings, I have five weavers for you which I have done after my painted studies and are somewhat different – and I think more incisive – in execution than the pen drawings which you have seen from me up to now. I am working on them from morning to night for, apart from the painted studies and the pen drawings, I have also roughed out new watercolours of them' [357]. Van Gogh intended 'to collect a number of pen drawings of Brabant artisans. That is something I would gladly undertake and, assuming that I will now be quite frequently in Brabant, about which I would be very enthusiastic. On condition that we make a series of them which will remain together, I will gladly keep the price low, so that even if there are many drawings of that kind they can remain together as a whole' [359].

Van Gogh himself was quite pleased with the watercolour drawings he made in Nuenen. In any event he found them suitable for sale. Van Gogh to Theo: 'Towards March I will send you some watercolours from here. If you do not want them, I will take them to someone else, but I prefer to do business with you. There will be faults in these watercolours, but nevertheless I do not think that it is silly of me to make a start with having my work looked at in order to send it into the world' [360]. He seems to have made the watercolour drawings of the weavers on the spot, directly from the example. That was probably also the case with the watercolour drawings 'A Wood Sale' (F 1113), 'Interior of a House with a Woman Sewing' and 'A Gardener'. Although I cannot prove it, I suspect that the watercolour 'Four Woodcutters at Work' (F 950) also dates from this period. From the stylistic viewpoint it seems to me to be a work done in Nuenen rather than one from Van Gogh's Hague period as, incidentally, has so far been assumed on relatively vague grounds.

cat. 84

cat. 83

Van Gogh got on increasingly well with his models: 'I have recently been on friendlier terms with the people here than I was at the start, which is worth a great deal to me, for one definitely has such a need to be able to have some diversion and work always suffers where one feels too lonely. One must, however, perhaps prepare oneself for these things not always remaining as they are, but nevertheless I am optimistic about it. It seems to me that the people in Nu[e]nen are generally better than those in Etten or Helvoirt. There is more sincerity here, at least that is my impression now that I have been here for some time. The people admittedly base all their doings on a parson's viewpoint – that is true – but in such a way that I, for my part, have no hesitation about accepting that to some extent. And as regards the Brabant one dreamed about, reality sometimes comes very close to that there. I must admit that my original plan of settling in Brabant, which fell through, again attracts me strongly' [368].

However enthusiastic Van Gogh was about the inhabitants of Nuenen at that time, he was equally full of praise for the local scenery. Van Gogh to an acquaintance in The Hague: 'I am still getting along well here in Brabant, at least I find the scenery here very inspiring' [351a]. And to Theo: 'Today, I went for a splendid walk of several hours with an acquaintance of mine [...] I do not say that, for instance, in Brittany, in Katwijk, in the Borinage, there is not more gripping and more dramatic scenery – yes – but nevertheless, the moors and the villages here are also very beautiful and once I am there I see in them an inexhaustible source of subjects from peasant life, and the question is only to set to and work' [400].

'Peasant life' is, of course, strongly bound up with the changes in the seasons. After concentrating on the weavers and other home workers, Van Gogh first turned his attention to the landscape in and around Nuenen and, following the seasons, only gradually to peasant life, in other words, the peasants of both sexes working on the land. He parted temporarily with his pen and ink drawings of the Nuenen landscape, giving them to Rappard 'for he knows quite a lot of people' [363]. Van Gogh hoped that Van Rappard would be more successful than his own brother Theo in selling one of these drawings. When things turned out otherwise, he still sent them to Theo: 'Garden in Winter' (F 1128 and F 1130), 'Pollarded Birches' (F 1240), 'Lane with Poplar Trees' (F 1239), 'The Kingfisher' (F 1135) and 'Behind the Hedges' (F 1129).

cat. 89 - 94

To prepare for his portrayals of 'peasant life' Van Gogh decided to look for a studio elsewhere in the village. The studio in his parents' home was inadequate. It was much too small and he could not allow his models to pose there. Van Gogh asked Theo whether he could give him a fixed monthly sum of money in return for supplying him with his work. Van Gogh: 'Why I have to know this is because if I can count on it I would again be able to take a more spacious studio somewhere which I need in order to be able to work with models. What I have at present has the following geographical location: [in the letter this is followed by a map showing the studio situated between the coal shed, the dung pit and the sewer]. And my powers of imagination are not strong enough to find that this is any advance on the situation as it was last year' [363]. Fortunately, Theo was able to give his brother the reassurance he requested so that very soon Van Gogh could give him the news which was so important to him: 'And next I will tell you that today I have more or less finished putting a roomy new studio I have rented into order. Two rooms, a large one and a small one, *en suite*. That has kept me fairly busy during the last fourteen days. I believe that I will be able to work much more pleasantly there than in the room at home' [368].

In order to acquire further proficiency in the technical aspects of drawing and painting, Van Gogh purchased some books on human anatomy. He considered the possibility of drawing from nude models in 's Hertogenbosch at the studio of the sculptor Stracké. In Nuenen, and also as a son of the parson, he would probably have found no one who was prepared to pose for him in the nude. Van Gogh writes about his plan as follows: 'Probably, however, one must pay for the model oneself, but that is not so very expensive and in addition one has a good room for which one does not pay. I am going to look into this further, and then it might well be that one day I will go to Stracké in the same way as, for instance, Breitner went to Cormon [in Paris]. This would be in the vicinity, and it would also be the cheapest way [...] The key to many things is a thorough knowledge of the human body [...] And in addition I think that colour, that chiaroscuro, that perspective, that tone, that drawing, in a word everything, also certainly has particular laws which one must and can study just like chemistry or algebra. This is far from being the easiest conception of things and someone who says – Oh, it must be absolutely true to nature – is making light of it. If only that were sufficient, but it is not sufficient, for however much one knows instinctively, one must precisely then do one's best three times more in my view in order to move from instinct to reason' [381]. As far as is known, Van Gogh never worked at Stracké's studio and it would not be until he spent some time at the Academy in Antwerp that he would follow in Breitner's footsteps and go to the Atelier Cormon in Paris.

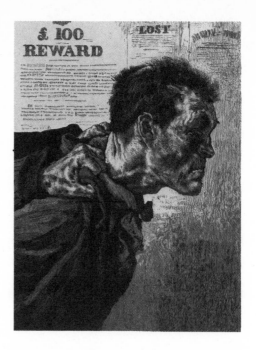

HEADS OF THE PEOPLE

fig. 26

In Nuenen, he flung himself into making a series of painted and drawn 'Heads of the People'. Van Gogh: 'I must do fifty of these heads – while I am still here and can obtain models of all kinds relatively easily during the winter months. Now, however, the winter months are going past – if I do not keep pressing on – without my doing as much as I want to and must' [389]. 'I do not know in advance what I will do with these heads, but I want to derive the motif from the characters themselves. I do know why I am painting them and for what purpose in general' [391]. 'I am busy painting these heads. I paint during the day and draw in the evening. In this way I have certainly already painted thirty and drawn just as many' [394]. Most of these

cat. 97 - 98

heads must be regarded as studies. Van Gogh developed only a few of them into 'fully fledged' drawings.

When Van Gogh's father died suddenly, he expected that his mother and the children still living at home would move away from Nuenen and he would then be the only member 'of the household' who would remain in Brabant. Van Gogh: 'And for me it is not at all unlikely [that] I will also stay there for the rest of my life. After all, I wish for nothing more than to be deep in the heart of peasant country and to paint peasant life. I feel that I can create a place for myself here and so I will keep my hand calmly on my plough and continue making my furrow.

fig. 25
William Small
Heads of the People I
Amsterdam, Rijksmuseum Vincent van Gogh
(Vincent van Gogh Stichting)

fig. 26 (F 1145)
Vincent van Gogh
Head of a Young Peasant, 1885
Amsterdam, Rijksmuseum Vincent van Gogh
(Vincent van Gogh Stichting)

I believe you had other ideas about this and that you would probably prefer to see me taking a different path as regards my place of residence. But I sometimes think that you have more of an eye for what one can do in the town, yet on the other hand I feel more at home out of doors [...] And so, Theo, what we have now begun again, I hope that we will continue on both sides. In expectation of, or rather while I am struggling on with, more important compositions, I am sending the studies just as they come straight from the cottages. People will naturally say they are unfinished, or ugly, etc., but in my view you should nevertheless let them see them. For my part, I firmly believe that there are some people who, caught up in town life and tied down, retain ineradicable impressions of the outdoor life and who continue to feel homesick for the fields and the peasants their whole lives long. Such lovers of the countryside are sometimes struck by sincerity, and are not put off by what repels others. I myself know how I used to walk around for hours in the town looking at shop windows to see somewhere one view or another of anything at all from the outdoors' [398].

Van Gogh: 'If I say that I am a painter of peasants, that is really so, and that will become clearer to you from now on, I feel at home there. And it is not for nothing that I have sat for so many evenings pondering by the fire among the miners and the peat cutters and the weavers and peasants here – unless I had no time to think – because of my work. Through seeing peasant life continually at all hours of the day I have become so involved in it that I actually almost never think of anything else' [400]. Peasant life therefore becomes the central theme in Van Gogh's entire creative output. He wants not only to paint and draw it, he also wants to distribute it in the form of lithographs in a printing run. Van Gogh: 'I am thinking of making a series of subjects from peasant life, enfin, *les paysans chez eux* [the peasants at home]' [400]. In contrast to the procedure he followed in The Hague and in which he first drew on a special type of paper from which the portrayal was printed in mirror image on the stone and from there again in mirror image, and hence once again 'normally' on paper, Van Gogh now drew directly onto the stone. The result was that 'The Potato Eaters' was now in mirror image (F 1661). Van Gogh: 'When I turn the drawing into a painting I also make a new lithograph of it and in such a way that the figures, which to my regret are now reversed, come right again' [401]. The painting mentioned was indeed produced (F 82, the study is F 78), but he never made the second lithograph.

It was only when Van Gogh had successfully completed the theme of 'The Potato Eaters', and with this the most important work from this series 'The Peasants at Home' in the spring of 1885, that he felt free to tackle new subjects again. Van Gogh: 'I have been working hard on drawings in the last few days. The old tower in the fields is being pulled down. Now there was a sale of woodwork and slates and old iron, including the cross. I have completed a watercolour of this in the manner of that

cat. 84
cat. 104
cat. 100 - 101

wood sale, but I believe better' [408]. In preparation for the 'Demolition Sale' (F 1230) Van Gogh made a series of chalk sketches, notes scribbled down on the spot, for example F 1112 r and F 1336 r. It is not clear whether Van Gogh also made the watercolour drawing on location, or whether he sketched it later in his studio on the basis of his chalk studies.

Van Gogh now flung himself once again into the 'drawing of figures' [408]. He tried to start drawing less literally and more to seize the 'expression': 'I am at present busy putting into practice what Delacroix said about drawing: *ne pas prendre par la ligne mais par le milieu* [do not tackle it by the line but by the environment] in drawing a hand and an arm. There one has opportunity enough to start from ovals. And what I am seeking to achieve with this is not to be able to draw a hand, but the gesture, not a mathematically correct head, but the great expression. Breathing in the wind when a digger looks up for a moment, for instance, or speaking. In a word, life' [408]. 'For the rest, I am busy drawing so that I will be able to send a few complete figures in a little while' [411].

HARVEST TIME cat. 107 - 121

Just as in the past, in The Hague, Van Gogh could not get enough of drawing figures. He wanted to make a hundred before starting to paint them, the argument being that on balance this would save him time and money. As always, Van Gogh was apprehensive about starting to paint too quickly. He clearly preferred to gain further proficiency as a draughtsman first. He also hoped for a change compared with the work he had done previously. Van Gogh: 'I aim to find something different from my old drawings and to find the character of the peasants, particularly those from here' [414]. It is harvest time. And like the peasants going to harvest, Van Gogh wants to do the same. Van Gogh: 'And we go harvesting, and then both during the corn harvesting and the potato digging I must set to work. It is then doubly difficult to get a model and yet that is essential for I am becoming more and more convinced that one cannot be too conscientious, that one must always and eternally concentrate one's efforts on what Daudet (in *l'Histoire de mon livre*, an article I have just read by him about kings in exile) calls *la chasse au modèle* [the hunt for the model]' [414].

Van Gogh feels he will be successful: 'I have been keeping watch on these peasant figures and their actions here for one and a half years now, precisely to get some character into it' [416]. But: 'It is just the same here as everywhere, people are far from happy to pose, and if it were not for the money no one would be willing. Since the people are mostly very poor, however, and in particular many weavers are without work, I can still manage to get them to do it' [417].

Van Gogh did not only want to look at the peasants and draw them, he also wanted to experience all their activities to the full. He wanted 'to live in these cottages, day in day out, to be in the fields just like the peasants, to endure the summer heat in summer and the snow and frost in winter, not indoors but outside, and not just to go for a walk, but day in day out, like the peasants themselves [...] It might seem that there is nothing simpler than painting peasants or rag pickers and other labourers, but there are no subjects in painting as difficult as these everyday figures! As far as I know, there isn't a single academy where one learns to draw and paint a digger, a sower, a woman hanging a pot over the fire or a seamstress. But in every town of any importance there is an academy with a choice of models for historical, Arabic, Louis XV and in a word every figure if they do not exist in reality' [418].

At Theo's request, Van Gogh also gave the figures an entourage, an environment and background. He hoped they were suitable for framing, but he was not certain about this. Probably also to please Theo, and perhaps even more as an aid to understanding for those to whom Theo would show the drawings in Paris, Van Gogh occasionally gave the figures a title. These titles enable spectators without a specialised knowledge of farming to identify what the peasants are doing on the land.

cat. 119 - 120

BACK TO THE WORLD OF PAINTING

After working in Nuenen for almost two years, Van Gogh decided to move to Antwerp, partly because of the problem of finding good models. First, however, he sounds out Theo for his opinion of this plan. Van Gogh: 'If I could now be there in the next few months, December and January, wouldn't that be best? In Amsterdam I stayed in a public soup kitchen for 50 cents. I would also do that over there, or better still, make an agreement with some painter or other to be able to work in his studio. There is yet another reason, namely that it is not absolutely impossible that I would find an opportunity somewhere to paint nudes. They would not want me at the Academy, nor would I probably want that either, but with a sculptor, for instance – there must certainly be a few living there – one can easily find some sympathy. Obviously, with money one can obtain as many models as one wants, but without that it is a difficult matter. Nevertheless, there must certainly be people over there who hire nude models and with whom one can share the costs. I need it for many things [...] Write and tell me soon what you think about going to Antwerp, I believe there is nothing against it' [433].

Van Gogh was in a hurry to leave: 'At the moment I am making little headway with my work here. It is freezing hard, so that working outdoors is no longer possible. It is better to hire a model, in short, I will do nothing more as long as I am living in this house [...] Then I will save my paint and canvas in order to have ammunition over there [...] So the sooner I can leave the better [...] I will also take at least forty frames along of the size of the study heads in your possession. And drawing materials and paper so that however things go with me I can always do something. Since I have worked absolutely alone for years, I imagine that although I want to and can learn from others and even take over technical things, I will nevertheless always see through my own eyes and set to work originally. I would try to learn new things, however, nothing is more certain. And if I can, particularly the nude figure. I imagine, however, that in order to hire as many models as I want, and good ones, I will not be ready all at once, but will have to find the money for this by doing other things. Either landscapes, or townscapes, or portraits as I said, or even signboards and decorations. Or something I did not mention among the things in my previous letter, which I certainly could do, give painting lessons, letting students begin by painting still lifes, which I believe is a different method from that of the drawing masters. I did experiments with this on my acquaintances in Eindhoven which I would dare to repeat' [434]. Van Gogh was ready to tackle anything simply in order to be able to earn money for models.

Just as when he moved from Etten to The Hague, Van Gogh was again obsessed by the idea of going to an environment where he could have contact with other artists. He now felt stronger and more confident than he had been then about confronting his colleagues who, unfortunately, were not always sympathetic towards him: 'You will be able to understand that I am leaving next Tuesday when you consider that in the first place I am longing to do so, secondly that here I am in danger of getting stuck with my work for lack of models, while working out of doors has stopped because of the cold. As regards the fact that I will certainly feel the lack of a workplace at Antwerp, yes, that is so. But I must choose between a workplace without work here and work without a workplace over there. I have decided on the latter. And with a cheerfulness that is even so great that I feel it is a return from exile. After all, I have been out of the world of painting for a long time. And in this interval my powers have ripened somewhat, so that I feel more independent of the normal intrigues that are used to kick someone out. I mean that in The Hague, with the brush, I don't say with my drawing, I was weaker than the rest and by concentrating on painting and colour I was easier to overawe than will now prove possible' [435].

76

Weaver, Facing Right
Winter 1883-84
Watercolour, 320 x 470 mm
F 1108 JH 451
Paris, Musée du Louvre

77

Weaver, Interior with Three Small Windows
Spring 1884
Pencil, watercolour and ink on laid paper, 355 x 446 mm
Watermark: HFDC
Signed l.l.: Vincent
F 1115 JH 502
Amsterdam, Rijksmuseum Vincent van Gogh
(Vincent van Gogh Stichting)

78

Weaver, Facing Left
Winter 1883-84
Pencil, watercolour and ink on laid paper, 357 x 452 mm
Watermark: HFDC
Signed l.l.: Vincent
F 1114 JH 444
Amsterdam, Rijksmuseum Vincent van Gogh
(Vincent van Gogh Stichting)

79

Weaver, Facing Right
Winter 1883-84
Pencil, watercolour and ink on laid paper, 326 x 452 mm
Watermark: HFDC
Signed l.l.: Vincent
F 1125 JH 448
Amsterdam, Rijksmuseum Vincent van Gogh
(Vincent van Gogh Stichting)

80

Weaver, Facing Right
Winter 1883-84
Pencil, chalk and ink on wove paper, 245 x 335 mm
Signed l.l.: Vincent
F 1109 JH 439
Otterlo, Rijksmuseum Kröller-Müller

81

Weaver, Facing Left
Winter 1883-84
Pencil and watercolour on laid paper, 342 x 452 mm
Watermark: HFDC
Signed l.l.: Vincent
F 1107 JH 445
Amsterdam, Rijksmuseum Vincent van Gogh
(Vincent van Gogh Stichting)

82

Weaver, Facing Left
Winter 1883-84
Pencil, ink and paint on wove paper, 306 x 401 mm
Signed l.l.: Vincent
F 1123 JH 455
Amsterdam, Rijksmuseum Vincent van Gogh
(Vincent van Gogh Stichting)

83

Four Woodcutters at Work
Winter 1883-84
Chalk and watercolour on wove paper, 350 x 450 mm
F 950 JH 170
Otterlo, Rijksmuseum Kröller-Müller

84

A Wood Sale
Winter 1883-84
Black chalk and watercolour on laid paper, 350 x 448 mm
Watermark: HFDC
Signed l.l.: Vincent
F 1113 JH 438
Amsterdam, Rijksmuseum Vincent van Gogh
(Vincent van Gogh Stichting)

85

A man winding yarn
Spring 1884
Watercolour on laid paper, 440 x 340 mm
F 1140 JH 487
Amsterdam, Rijksmuseum Vincent van Gogh
(Vincent van Gogh Stichting)

86

Woman at the Spinning Wheel
Spring 1884
Watercolour on laid paper, 330 x 440 mm
Signed l.l.: Vincent
F 1139 JH 494
New York, Private Collection

87

Ditch
Early 1884
Sepia or brown ink on wove paper, 390 x 330 mm
F 1243 JH 472
Amsterdam, Rijksmuseum Vincent van Gogh
(Vincent van Gogh Stichting)

88

Pine Trees in the Fen
Early 1884
Sepia or brown ink on wove paper, 345 x 440 mm
F 1249 JH 473
Amsterdam, Rijksmuseum Vincent van Gogh
(Vincent van Gogh Stichting)

89

Garden in Winter
Early 1884
Pencil and ink on wove paper, 390 x 530 mm
Signed l.l.: Vincent
F 1128 JH 466
Amsterdam, Rijksmuseum Vincent van Gogh
(Vincent van Gogh Stichting)

90

Garden in Winter
Early 1884
Ink and paint on wove paper, 515 x 380 mm
Signed l.l.: Vincent
F 1130 JH 465
Budapest, Szépmüvészeti Múzeum

91

The Kingfisher
Early 1884
Ink and paint on wove paper, 390 x 530 mm
Signed l.l.: Vincent
F 1135 JH 468
Amsterdam, Rijksmuseum Vincent van Gogh

92

Behind the Hedges
Early 1884
Pencil and ink on wove paper, 400 x 530 mm
Signed l.l.: Vincent
F 1129 JH 461
Amsterdam, Rijksprentenkabinet (Rijksmuseum)

93

Lane with Poplar Trees
Early 1884
Pencil and ink on wove paper, 540 x 390 mm
F 1239 JH 464
Amsterdam, Rijksmuseum Vincent van Gogh
(Vincent van Gogh Stichting)

94

Pollarded Birches
Early 1884
Pencil, ink and paint on wove paper, 395 x 545 mm
Signed l.l.: Vincent
F 1240 JH 469
Amsterdam, Rijksmuseum Vincent van Gogh
(Vincent van Gogh Stichting)

95

The Parsonage, Seen from the Back
Spring 1884
Ink, chalk and paint on wove paper, 240 x 360 mm
F 1343 JH 475
Toronto, The Art Gallery of Ontario
(Purchased with proceeds from the Annual Giving Fund, 1982)

96

Houses with Thatched Roofs
Early 1884
Pencil, ink and paint on wove paper, 309 x 451 mm
F 1242 JH 474
London, The Trustees of the Tate Gallery

97

Head of a Peasant Woman
Early 1885
Black chalk on wove paper, 403 x 333 mm
F 1182 JH 590
Amsterdam, Rijksmuseum Vincent van Gogh
(Vincent van Gogh Stichting)

98

A Young Peasant with Pipe, Seated
Early 1885
Pencil and watercolour on wove paper, 399 x 284 mm
Signed l.r.: Vincent
F 1199 JH 579
Amsterdam, Rijksmuseum Vincent van Gogh
(Vincent van Gogh Stichting)

99

Head of a Young Peasant
Early 1885
Pencil on laid paper, 346 x 215 mm
Watermark: CONCORDIA RES PARVAE CRESCUNT
F 1146 JH 580
Amsterdam, Rijksmuseum Vincent van Gogh
(Vincent van Gogh Stichting)

100

Demolition Sale (Sketches)
May 1885
Black chalk on laid paper, 345 x 207 mm
Watermark: CONCORDIA RES PARVAE CRESCUNT
F 1336 r JH 767
Otterlo, Rijksmuseum Kröller-Müller

101

Demolition Sale (Sketches)
May 1885
Black chalk on laid paper, 345 x 207 mm
Watermark: VDL
F 1112 r JH 768
Otterlo, Rijksmuseum Kröller-Müller

102

Wheat Field with Mower, Stooping Peasant Woman,
and a Windmill
Summer 1885
Black chalk on wove paper, 287 x 412 mm
Watermark: [TS]&Z
F 1321 r JH 915
Amsterdam, Rijksmuseum Vincent van Gogh
(Vincent van Gogh Stichting)

103

Wheat Field with a Mower and a Stooping Peasant Woman
Summer 1885
Black chalk on wove paper, 270 x 385 mm
Watermark: TS[&Z]
Signed l.r.: Vincent
F 1301 r JH 917
Otterlo, Rijksmuseum Kröller-Müller

104

Demolition Sale
May 1885
Watercolour on watercolour paper, 379 x 553 mm
Signed l.l.: Vincent
F 1230 JH 770
Amsterdam, Rijksmuseum Vincent van Gogh
(Vincent van Gogh Stichting)

105

Peasant, Chopping
Summer 1885
Black chalk on wove paper, 440 x 335 mm
Watermark: TS&Z
Signed l.r.: Vincent
F 1325 JH 903
Otterlo, Rijksmuseum Kröller-Müller

106

Woodcutter
Summer 1885
Black chalk on laid paper, 450 x 583 mm
Watermark: HFDC
F 1327 JH 902
Amsterdam, Rijksmuseum Vincent van Gogh
(Vincent van Gogh Stichting)

107

Landscape with Wheatsheaves and a Windmill
Summer 1885
Black chalk on wove paper, 444 x 563 mm
Watermark: TS&Z
F 1319 v JH 911
Amsterdam, Rijksmuseum Vincent van Gogh
(Vincent van Gogh Stichting)

108

A Peasant Digging
Summer 1885
Black chalk, ink and paint on wove paper, 530 x 357 mm
F 1305 JH 849
Amsterdam, Rijksmuseum Vincent van Gogh
(Vincent van Gogh Stichting)

109

Peasant with Sickle
Summer 1885
Black chalk on wove paper, 445 x 563 mm
Watermark: TS&Z
F 1316 JH 858
Amsterdam, Rijksmuseum Vincent van Gogh
(Vincent van Gogh Stichting)

110

Peasant with Sickle, Seen from Behind
Summer 1885
Black chalk on wove paper, 525 x 370 mm
Watermark: TS&Z
Signed l.r.: Vincent
F 1323 JH 862
Otterlo, Rijksmuseum Kröller-Müller

III

Peasant Woman, Binding a Sheaf of Grain
Summer 1885
Black chalk on wove paper, 555 x 430 mm
Watermark: TS&Z
Signed l.l.: Vincent
F 1263 JH 871
Otterlo, Rijksmuseum Kröller-Müller

112

Peasant Woman, Picking Up a Sheaf of Grain
Summer 1885
Black chalk on wove paper, 450 x 530 mm
Watermark: TS&Z
F 1264 JH 869
Otterlo, Rijksmuseum Kröller-Müller

113

Peasant Woman, Carrying a Sheaf of Grain
Summer 1885
Black chalk on laid paper, 570 x 420 mm
F 1267 JH 870
Oslo, Nasjonalgalleriet

114

Peasant Woman, Carrying Wheat in her Apron
Summer 1885
Black chalk on laid paper, 586 x 382 mm
Watermark: HFDC
F 1268 JH 881
Otterlo, Rijksmuseum Kröller-Müller

115

Peasant Woman, Gleaning, Seen from Behind
Summer 1885
Black chalk on wove paper, 525 x 435 mm
Watermark: TS&Z
F 1269 JH 832
Otterlo, Rijksmuseum Kröller-Müller

116

Peasant Woman, Gleaning
Summer 1885
Black chalk on wove paper, 515 x 415 mm
F 1279 JH 836
Essen, Museum Folkwang

117

Peasant Woman, Kneeling, Seen from Behind
Summer 1885
Black chalk on wove paper, 430 x 520 mm
F 1280 JH 839
Oslo, Nasjonalgalleriet

118

Peasant Woman, Working with a Long Stick
Summer 1885
Black chalk on wove paper, 545 x 370 mm
Signed l.r.: Vincent
F 1277 JH 880
Otterlo, Rijksmuseum Kröller-Müller

119

Peasant Woman, Planting Potatoes
Summer 1885
Black chalk on wove paper, 417 x 452 mm
Signed and annotated l.l.: Vincent Planteuse
de pommes de terre
F 1272 JH 910
Frankfurt, Städelsches Kunstinstitut

120

Peasant Woman, Digging Potatoes
Summer 1885
Charcoal and black chalk on wove paper, 405 x 465 mm
Signed and annotated: Vincent Arracheuse de pommes de terre
F 1273 JH 909
Amsterdam, Rijksmuseum Vincent van Gogh
(Vincent van Gogh Stichting)

121

Wheat Field with Trees and a Mower
Summer 1885
Black chalk on wove paper, 415 x 580 mm
Watermark: TS&Z
Signed l.r.: Vincent
F 1322 r JH 916
Otterlo, Rijksmuseum Kröller-Müller

Antwerp

VERY CURIOUS AND BEAUTIFUL

Arriving in Antwerp, Van Gogh went almost immediately to the local museums. In the 'Museum van Oude Schilderijen' he admired, among other works, 'The Fisherboy' by Frans Hals, in the 'Musée Moderne' he saw 'beautiful things' but also 'horrible things' [436]. In the art trade – at least that was Van Gogh's impression – little was happening: 'I fear categorically that the trade is dead. Nevertheless – it is a good old Dutch saying – never despair'. In spite of everything, Van Gogh nevertheless had high hopes of finding a market for his work through the Antwerp art trade. In search of subjects he undertook various 'crusades'. Particularly in the dock areas he found the 'real thing'. Van Gogh: 'The various bonded warehouses and sheds on the quays are very beautiful. I have already walked along these docks and quays several times in all kinds of ways. Particularly when one comes from the sand and the moorland and the silence of a peasant village and has not been in anything other than a silent environment for a long time, it is curious as a contrast' [437]. Van Gogh was back in the town from his self-elected exile in the country. He had escaped from his isolation. He was again among people, which still did not mean that he could immediately find suitable models prepared to pose for him, let alone do what he wanted most: pose in the nude.

In a letter from Nuenen, Van Gogh had already told Theo that in order to obtain money for models he would first have to do 'other things' in Antwerp: landscapes, townscapes, portraits, signboards, shop decorations, etc. But winter first had to be over before he could work out of doors. In anticipation of the financial resources he hoped to acquire in this way he looked for suitable models in the meantime. He stared his eyes out: 'At one time one sees a girl who is in splendid health and at least apparently entirely loyal, innocent and cheerful. Then again a face so sly and false that it makes one afraid, like a hyena's. Not forgetting the faces raddled with smallpox, having the colour of boiled shrimps, with pale grey eyes without eyebrows and sparse sleek thin hair, the colour of pure pig's bristles or slightly yellower [...] I think it is not impossible that by doing portraits I will succeed in getting good models again [...] Perhaps the idea of doing portraits and having them paid for at the sitting is a safer way' [437]. Van Gogh saw a market for painted and drawn portraits. He felt he was capable of doing them and expected little competition in that field in Antwerp. Van Gogh: 'I must work myself in here until I get in touch with good figure painters [...] and then I imagine that doing portraits is the means to earn something for greater things. I feel I have the power in me to do something, I see that my work is holding its own against other work and that gives me a surprising desire to work' [438].

Van Gogh enjoyed the bustle of the town, of the vibrant life in a seaport: 'Yesterday I was in the Scala café concert, something like the Folies Bergères. I found it dull and, of course, stale, but – I amused myself watching the spectators. There were splendid women's heads, really exceptionally beautiful, among the honest citizens on the back seats and in general I think it is really true what people say about Antwerp, namely that the women are beautiful. Ah! I will say it again: if only I could get models of my choice! [...] The colours in Antwerp are beautiful and it is worthwhile for the subjects alone. One evening I saw a sailors' dance hall at the docks – that was most entertaining [...] It does one good to see people really enjoying themselves' [438]. Van Gogh did not regret his move to Antwerp: 'I am very happy to have come here, for it is useful and necessary to me for many things' [439].

Among other things, Van Gogh painted and drew the 'Kasteel het Steen' (F 1350 r). Referring to this painting he wrote *cat. 122* to Theo: 'It is a good thing for strangers who want to have a souvenir of Antwerp and for that reason I will certainly do more townscapes in the same genre. For example, yesterday I drew a few studies for a little piece showing the cathedral. *cat. 125 - 126* And similarly I also have a small one of the Park. However, I prefer to paint the eyes of people rather than cathedrals, for there is something in the eyes that is not in the cathedral – although it is magnificent and imposing – the soul of a human being, even though he is a poor beggar or a girl of the street, is more interesting in my eyes' [441]. And so Van Gogh has come back from townscapes to his fellow human beings again. Van Gogh: 'The question is whether one takes the soul or the clothes as the starting point or not and whether one allows the form to act as a peg for bows and ribbons or whether one regards the form as a means to express an impression, a sentiment, or whether one models for the sake of modelling because it is so infinitely beautiful in itself. The first alone is transitory, and the last two are both high art' [442].

FRICTION BETWEEN IDEAS

For the time being, Van Gogh had little success with the main purpose of his journey to Antwerp, namely to be able to work from the nude model. Van Gogh: 'It seems to be difficult to get nude models here, at least the girl I had was unwilling. Of course, that 'was unwilling' is probably relative, but at least it does not happen automatically. She would be magnificent, however. From a business viewpoint I can only say – we are in what people are already beginning to call the end of a century – that women have a charm as in a period of revolution – and have as much to say in fact – that one would be withdrawn from the world if one worked without including them. It is the same thing everywhere, both outside and in the town – one must take account of women if one wants to be of one's time' [442].

Because of the models, Van Gogh enquired at the Antwerp Academy of Art about the admission regulations and the extent to which one could work from nude models there. Van Gogh: 'I have an astonishing desire to strengthen my knowledge of the nude' [443]. And in his next letter to Theo: 'I would like to go so far in my knowledge of the nude and the structure of the figure that I could work from memory [...] I hope to succeed in being allowed to paint from the model at the Academy all day long, which would make it easier for me since the models are so terribly expensive that I cannot keep it up. And I must find some way to get help in that respect' [444].

Van Gogh was admitted to the Academy. In the evening he could also draw 'from the antique' with one of the teachers, in other words, from plaster casts of classical statues. Van Gogh: 'I believe that I can do no wrong with either of these two things and I can easily acquire some knowledge which can be useful to me either for painting or for drawing [...] I have already drawn for two evenings there and I must say that I believe it is very good to draw classical statues precisely for doing, for instance, peasant figures [...] I who for years have not seen any good casts of classical statues – and the ones they have here are very beautiful – and who in those years have always had the living model before my eyes, I am amazed about the tremendous knowledge and correctness of sentiment of the ancients now that I see it properly again for once' [445]. At the end of the drawing class in the evening he also went to a 'club' to work from nude models. Van Gogh: 'I have even become a member of two of these clubs [...] And that suits me excellently. And so does drawing after classical models' [447]. 'Didn't Delacroix and Corot and Millet also keep on thinking a lot about antiquity later, and keep on studying it? The people who study it in order to rattle it off, are of course absolutely wide of the mark. Antiquity requires a great deal of serenity, requires one to be already familiar with nature, requires gentleness and patience.

Otherwise it is of no use to one' [448]. 'I will also send you the drawings after classical models. That is unusual for me and I will still manage to do it differently. Just as today, incidentally, I finished a female torso which is more distinguished in model and less brusque than the first ones, where the figures involuntarily have something of peasants or woodcutters about them' [456].

In addition, Van Gogh was already thinking of the future again. He was firmly intending to go to Paris. Antwerp was only an intermediate stage. In Paris he expected to be admitted more easily to one of the studios when 'his greenest edges' had already been knocked off, but he had already spent some time at an academy somewhere. Van Gogh: 'I am still very pleased that I have come here [...] Here I find the friction of ideas that I seek, I am getting a fresh view of my own work, can judge better where the weak points are and in this way make progress in order to improve them' [447].

TO CORMON IN PARIS

When Van Gogh saw the end of the 'winter course' approaching he conferred by letter with Theo who had already been working at Goupil's art shop in Paris for some years. The great question was: go back to Nuenen, remain in Antwerp or move to Paris. Van Gogh: 'As regards whether or not I should start living here permanently – given that the prospects do not exactly look bright in the art trade – and there is a certain striving among each of the painters to be his own dealer – which I imagine will increase in the long run – it might be sensible to keep a studio here. If you have any ideas about this or wishes either for or against, tell me about them as fully as possible. But it is immediately obvious to me that – if after many or a few years you should ever start working for yourself independently of the Goupils, Antwerp might possibly be a field where, given the sorry display of today, something can certainly be done by good display that the other firms do not understand. In addition, it is relatively so easy to go to and fro to England from here' [441].

To Van Gogh's great satisfaction, Theo proposes that he should come to Paris in order to work there in Cormon's studio. From English acquaintances who had formerly worked in Paris but now, just like Van Gogh, were staying in Antwerp, he had heard 'that in Paris one is relatively freer and one can even, for instance, choose what one wants to do, more than here, but that the correction is casual. Do you know what I think? This: in Paris I would certainly work more than here, for instance, one drawing a day or every two days. And we know, or rather you know, enough good people who will not refuse to look at them and give hints [...] Precisely because I now have the opportunity to talk to various people about my drawings, I feel my errors myself and much has been won towards overcoming them. Let's gird up our loins in any event.

But you must now write once again and we must see to it that we play our cards right with him. I have heard that Cormon lets you work for four hours in the morning, then in the evening you can go and work in the Louvre or the Ecole des Beaux Arts or another studio where drawing is done' [448].

Van Gogh expected to find a greater opportunity to work from female nudes in Paris than he had had in Antwerp. Van Gogh: 'They make almost no use of nude female models [in the Academy here] at least not at all in the class, apart from great exceptions. Even in the antique class there are ten male figures to one female figure. That is easy, of course. Things are certainly better in Paris, and it occurs to me that one learns so much from constantly comparing the masculine and the feminine, which are so very different in everything and always. It may be a supreme difficulty, but what would art and what would life be without that?' [452].

Apart from a few exceptions it is not easy to be certain about the question of which paintings and drawings Van Gogh made in Antwerp. Of the townscapes he drew, the sketches of 'The Grote Markt' (F 1352), of the 'Onze Lieve Vrouwekerk' (F 1356) and the 'Kasteel het Steen' (F 1350 r) are easily recognisable as such because of their subjects. Some small drawings of people dancing have also survived from the same sketchbook (SB 3) as that in which Van Gogh made the latter drawing. None of these drawings is the completed version. They are clever, but fleeting, notes.

From the stylistic viewpoint, the differences between the Antwerp and the subsequent early Parisian drawings are negligible. In view of the brief time interval between both periods, a recognisable difference would also certainly have been remarkable. Of the large drawn portraits, F 1357, 'Portrait of a Woman' has been regarded as an Antwerp drawing up to now. The paper of F 1357 has the watermark J WHATMAN 1884 and is thus identical to that of the drawings F 1363g, F 1370, SD 696, SD 1698, SD 1699 and SD 1706. It is, of course, very possible and certainly not improbable that the plaster casts which Van Gogh drew in F 1363g were available both at the Academy in Antwerp and at Cormon's studio in Paris. If it were assumed that Van Gogh was using the J WHATMAN 1884 paper either in Antwerp or in Paris, but not in both places, the whole group would have to be attributed either to Antwerp or to Paris. As long as no other arguments for a dating become available, the choice which has been made at present – namely for a dating during the Antwerp period – is relatively arbitrary.

There need, however, be little doubt about the redating of the drawing 'The Discus Thrower (Plaster Cast)' (F 1364e), which has so far been attributed to the Paris period, but is here placed in the Antwerp period. The point is that Van Gogh made the drawing on paper with the watermark TS&Z, the same paper on which he frequently worked in Nuenen. F 1364e is the only drawing on this paper which cannot be dated in the Nuenen period because of the subject. It seems plausible to assume that it is a drawing on the paper which Van Gogh had taken with him from Nuenen to Antwerp for safety's sake 'so that however things go with me I can always do something' [434]. I cannot really imagine that Van Gogh had not used up all the Nuenen paper in Antwerp and had then taken the remainder with him to Paris.

122

Kasteel het Steen
Winter 1885-86
Black chalk and coloured pencil on wove paper,
92 x 166 mm
F 1350 r JH 976 SB 3|5
Amsterdam, Rijksmuseum Vincent van Gogh
(Vincent van Gogh Stichting)

123

Dance-Hall
Winter 1885-86
Black and coloured chalk on wove paper, 92 x 163 mm
F 1350a JH 968 SB 3|7
Amsterdam, Rijksmuseum Vincent van Gogh
(Vincent van Gogh Stichting)

124

Women Dancing
Winter 1885-86
Black and coloured chalk on wove paper, 92 x 164 mm
F 1350b JH 969 SB 3|4
Amsterdam, Rijksmuseum Vincent van Gogh
(Vincent van Gogh Stichting)

125

Onze Lieve Vrouwekerk
Winter 1885-86
Black chalk on pink laid paper, 300 x 225 mm
F 1356 JH 974
Amsterdam, Rijksmuseum Vincent van Gogh
(Vincent van Gogh Stichting)

126

The Grote Markt
Winter 1885-86
Black and coloured chalk on blue laid paper,
225 x 300 mm
F 1352 JH 975
Amsterdam, Rijksmuseum Vincent van Gogh
(Vincent van Gogh Stichting)

ANTWERP

127

Double-Bass Player
1886
Coloured chalk on wove paper, 348 x 258 mm
F 1244c v JH 1153
Amsterdam, Rijksmuseum Vincent van Gogh
(Vincent van Gogh Stichting)

128

Violinist
1886
Coloured chalk on wove paper, 349 x 258 mm
F 1244a r JH 1154
Amsterdam, Rijksmuseum Vincent van Gogh
(Vincent van Gogh Stichting)

129

The Head of a Man, Profile
1886
Italian chalk, coloured and white chalk on wove paper,
348 x 258 mm
F 1244d r JH 1158
Amsterdam, Rijksmuseum Vincent van Gogh
(Vincent van Gogh Stichting)

130

Clarinettist and Flutist
1886
Coloured chalk on wove paper, 258 x 349 mm
F 1244b r JH 1155
Amsterdam, Rijksmuseum Vincent van Gogh
(Vincent van Gogh Stichting)

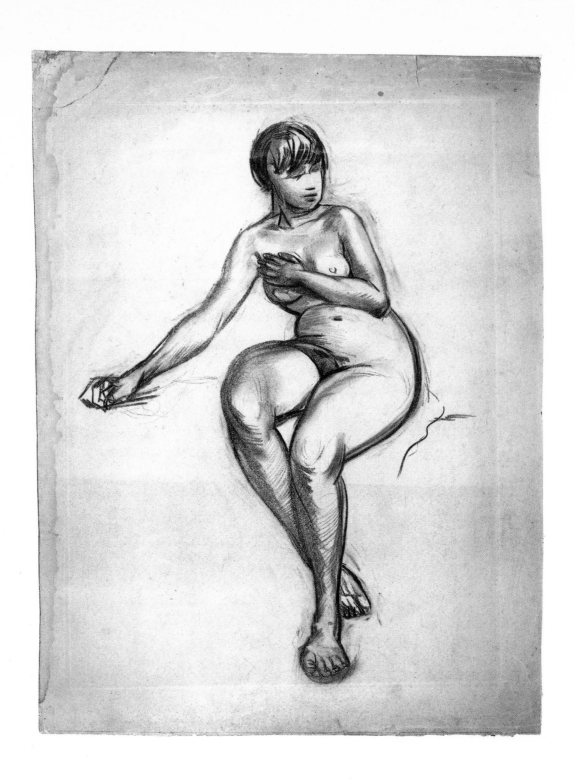

131

Female Nude, Seated
Early 1886
Charcoal on wove paper, 737 x 567 mm
F 1368 JH 1015
Amsterdam, Rijksmuseum Vincent van Gogh
(Vincent van Gogh Stichting)

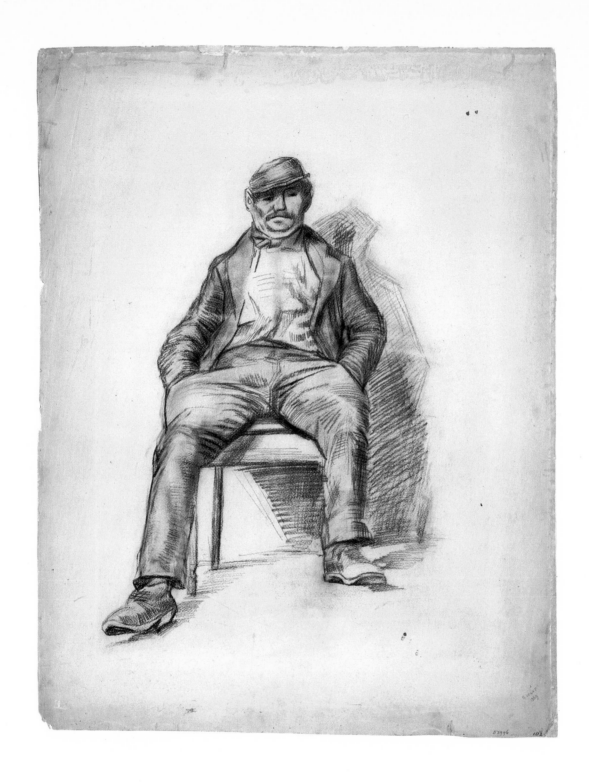

132

Man with Cap, Seated
Early 1886
Charcoal on wove paper, 745 x 582 mm
F 1369 r JH 1017
Amsterdam, Rijksmuseum Vincent van Gogh
(Vincent van Gogh Stichting)

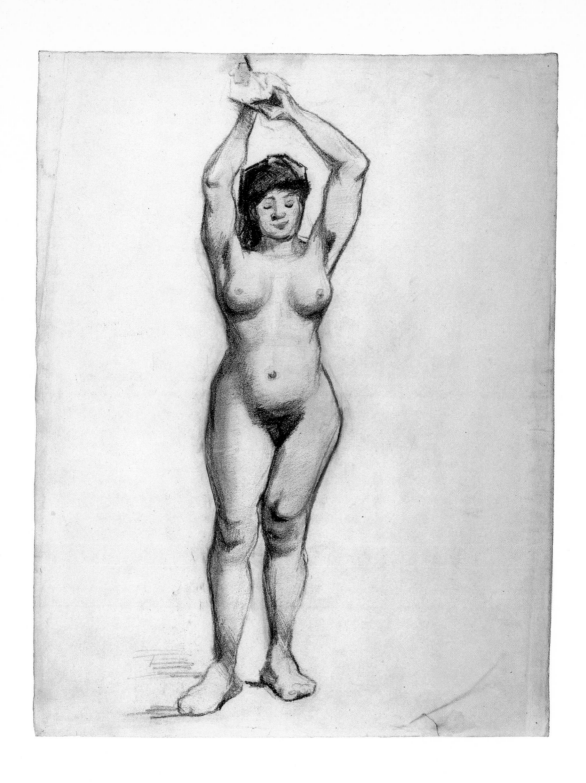

133

Standing Female Nude, with Raised Arms
Early 1886
Black and coloured chalk on wove paper, 504 x 392 mm
Watermark: J WHATMAN 1884
SD 1696 JH 1011
Amsterdam, Rijksmuseum Vincent van Gogh
(Vincent van Gogh Stichting)

134

Study of a Standing Man
Early 1886
Pencil and black chalk on wove paper, 509 x 395 mm
Watermark: J WHATMAN 1884
SD 1706 JH 1088
Amsterdam, Rijksmuseum Vincent van Gogh
(Vincent van Gogh Stichting)

135

A Man, Seated
Early 1886
Black chalk on wove paper, 508 x 396 mm
Watermark: J WHATMAN 1884
F 1370 JH 1087
Amsterdam, Rijksmuseum Vincent van Gogh
(Vincent van Gogh Stichting)

136

Portrait of a Woman
Early 1886
Pencil, black and coloured chalk on wove paper,
507 x 394 mm
Watermark: J WHATMAN 1884
F 1357 JH 981
Amsterdam, Rijksmuseum Vincent van Gogh
(Vincent van Gogh Stichting)

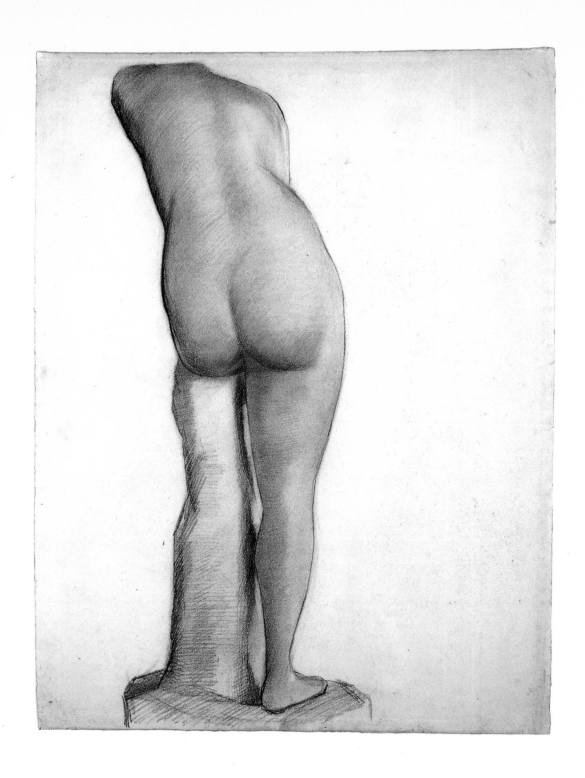

137

A Female Torso (Plaster Cast)
Early 1886
Black chalk on wove paper, 508 x 396 mm
Watermark: J WHATMAN 1884
F 1363g JH 1052
Amsterdam, Rijksmuseum Vincent van Gogh
(Vincent van Gogh Stichting)

138

The Discus Thrower (Plaster Cast)
Early 1886
Black chalk on wove paper, 561 x 445 mm
Watermark: TS&Z
F 1364e JH 1080
Amsterdam, Rijksmuseum Vincent van Gogh
(Vincent van Gogh Stichting)

Paris

THERE IS ONLY ONE PARIS

When Van Gogh arrived in Paris from Antwerp at the begin-ning of March 1886 the city was not entirely unfamiliar to him. In the days when he had worked as an assistant in various branches of Goupil & Co's art business, Paris was one of the cities in which he had lived between 1875 and 1876. At a later date, Theo had also found a job there. Judging by Van Gogh's reactions to letters he had received from Paris, Theo could describe the city in very lively and vivid terms. For example Van Gogh, who was then staying in The Hague, wrote to his brother in Paris as follows: 'Thank you very much for your description of that scene with the work people in Montmartre, which I found very interesting because you also mention the colours, so that I can picture it' [228]. Van Gogh had also regu-larly asked his brother to write and tell him the latest news about what was going on in the art world in Paris. But he liked nothing better when Theo came home on a visit than to be told about what was happening in Paris. Van Gogh: 'If you, for your part, say you sometimes wish we could talk to each other a bit more about various things in art, for my part I have a constant and sometimes very strong desire to do that. I would so often like to know your opinion about this or that [...] I would often like to have even more information about things of which you certainly know more than I do, and I would so much like to hear more about what is going on, namely everything that is being done there [that is: in Paris]. All of which can certainly be partly discussed by letter, but writing takes time and one does not get down to it so readily, nor can it be done in the necessary detail' [274].

When Van Gogh moved from The Hague to the quiet moor-lands of Drenthe he wrote to Theo: 'For that matter, now I am here on this beautiful moor I need not tell you I have not the least desire to go to Paris and I would very seldom think about it if your letter did not lead me to do so. And I simply say this about it: if it turns out one way, I will happily go to Paris, if it turns out another way, I will happily stay here in the peat field' [335]. A few letters later, however, he regards it as inconceivable that he might possibly move to Paris. On the contrary, he attempts to persuade Theo to leave Paris and come and paint with him in Drenthe. Van Gogh: 'Come on man, come and paint with me on the moor, in the potato field, come and walk with me behind the plough and the shepherd – come and look into the fire with me – let the storm blow through you that blows over the moor. Break out of it. I do not know the future, whether it would be different or not, or whether everything would go well for us, but I simply can't say anything different. Don't seek your future in Paris, don't seek it in America, all that is eternally precisely the same. But do make the change, seek it on the moor' [339].

After Drenthe came Nuenen, and after Nuenen there was Antwerp. But then Van Gogh felt he was ready to take the great step and move to Paris. His own 'view of reality' and the techni-cal skill he had further improved during his brief stay at the Academy in Antwerp gave him the necessary self-confidence. He firmly intended to take lessons again in Paris – at Cormon's studio – in drawing after nude and classical models. Van Gogh: 'For speaking about Cormon, I imagine he would say more or less the same to me as Verlat, namely that I must draw nudes or classical statues for a year, precisely because I have always drawn from life. This requirement is not hard and fast, for I can tell you that there are those here who have been doing it for three years and are not allowed to give it up yet although they are also painting. In that year I will have to practise doing both the male and the female figure in detail and as a whole, and then I will know it, as it were, by heart. Technically speak-ing, drawing in itself is easy enough for me; I am starting to do it just as one writes, with the same ease [...] Anyone who can draw a figure from memory is much more productive than someone who does not have that ability. And through my taking this trouble to do that year of drawing, you will see one day how productive we will be. And do not think the years when I worked out of doors have been wasted. For something that is lacking in those who have never been anywhere else apart from academies and studios is precisely a view of the reality around them and the ability to find subjects' [449].

In Paris, Van Gogh proposed to go to Cormon after the summer, hence in the autumn of 1886. When still in Antwerp he writes to Theo as follows: 'I have thought a great deal about what you say about taking a studio, but I think that it would be a good thing if we looked for it together and, before we finally start living together, we should do it provisionally for a time, and if I started around April, for instance, to rent an attic until June. I myself will then be accustomed to Paris again towards the time when I go to Cormon's. And in that way I think I will stay more cheerful' [452]. He was firmly resolved to take up drawing after nude and classical models – which he had enjoyed so much in Antwerp – in Paris again, and for the time being not to start working independently 'out of doors'. Van Gogh: 'As I have already told you, there is no reason to start working out of doors again for the first year. That for the entire future it is infinitely better to draw classical and nude models in the town' [454].

Since Van Gogh had no reason to write letters to his brother when he was staying with him in Paris – apart from the times when Theo went to the Netherlands – there is little on which to base a sound chronology of the work he produced there. His contacts with other artists also offer little support for a reliable picture of his activities at that period. I see no reason to assume anything other than that Van Gogh actually carried out his plan to start working with Cormon after his first summer in Paris. It is, however, not inconceivable that he put his name down for Cormon's studio immediately after his arrival in Paris at the start of March 1886.

In a letter written in English to the artist Horace Mann Livens, with whom he had made friends in Antwerp, Van Gogh says that his time with Cormon had not fulfilled his expectations (this letter is quoted verbatim with some explanatory additions in brackets): 'I have been in Cormons studio for three or four months but did not find that so useful as I had expected it to be. It may be my fault however. Anyhow I left there too as I left Antwerp and since [then] I [have] worked alone and fancy that [ever] since I feel my own self more' [459a]. Here again, as in the case of the Antwerp period, it is difficult to decide with certainty which drawings Van Gogh made after nude and classical models in Paris. The allocation of these drawings to Antwerp and Paris therefore remains relatively arbitrary for the time being.

The above letter to Livens gives a good impression of Van Gogh's first experiences in Paris, for example, as regards contact with other artists and what an artist could expect there from the art trade as compared with Antwerp. Van Gogh continues: 'There is more chance of selling. There is also a good chance of exchanging pictures with other artists. In one word, with much energy, with a sincere personal feeling of colour in nature I would say an artist can get on here notwithstanding the many obstructions. And I intend remaining here still longer. There is much to be seen here [...] And now for what regards what I myself have been doing, I have lacked money for paying models, else I had entirely given myself to figure painting. But I have made a series of colour studies in painting, simply flowers, red poppies, blue corn flowers and myosotys, white and rose roses, yellow chrysantemums – seeking oppositions of blue with orange, red and green, yellow and violet seeking *les tons rompus et neutres* to harmonise brutal extremes. Trying to render intense colour and not a grey harmony [...] I did a dozen landscapes too, frankly green frankly blue. And so I am struggling for life and progress in art [...] And mind my dear fellow, Paris is Paris. There is but one Paris and however hard living may be here and if it became worse and harder even – the french air clears up the brain and does one good – a world of good [...] Anyone who has a solid position elsewhere let him stay where he is but for adventurers as myself I think they lose nothing in risking more. Especially as in my case I am not an adventurer by choice but by fate and feeling nowhere so much myself a stranger as in my family and country' [459a].

Besides the drawings after nude and classical models, magnificent series of townscapes have survived from the Paris period. They come partly from sketch pads Van Gogh used in Paris. The panoramic views of Paris on grey paper and a series *cat. 143 - 145* of watercolour drawings on the smooth paper on which Van Gogh also noted the only surviving self-portraits he drew *cat. 161 - 164* [F 1378 r] are examples of these. Montmartre was the base from which Van Gogh operated. It is therefore not surprising that the subject of most of the townscapes is either parts of Montmartre itself (particularly the famous windmills) or views on or from the hill. At that time, Montmartre was a hive of building activity. Van Gogh was interested both in the old characteristic picture and the urban renewals. Asnières was within walking distance of Montmartre and it was there that he sat working on the banks of the Seine in the company of Emile Bernard, among others.

139

Male Nude, Standing
Summer or autumn 1886
Pencil and charcoal on laid paper, 485 x 310 mm
F 1364c JH 1084
Amsterdam, Rijksmuseum Vincent van Gogh
(Vincent van Gogh Stichting)

140

Bust by Antonio Pollaiuolo (Plaster Cast)
Summer or Autumn 1886
Black chalk on brownish laid paper,
615 x 475 mm
SD 1701 r JH 1081
Amsterdam, Rijksmuseum Vincent van Gogh
(Vincent van Gogh Stichting)

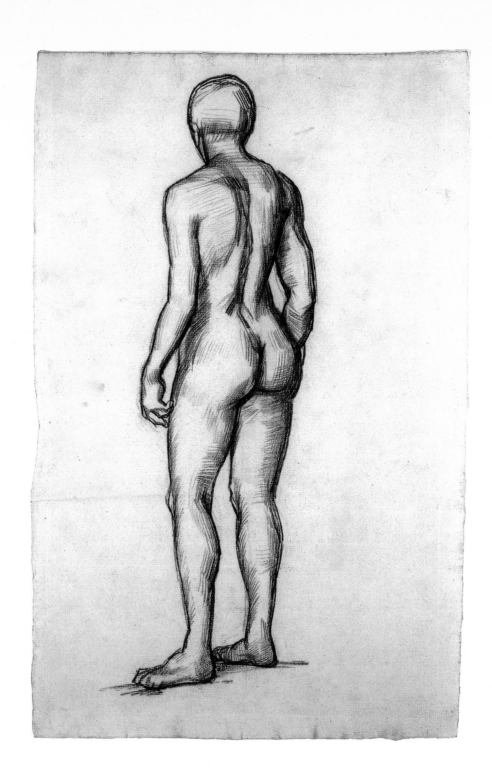

141

Male Nude, Standing
Summer or autumn 1886
Black chalk on laid paper, 476 x 306 mm
Watermark: MICHALLET
F 1364a JH 1041
Amsterdam, Rijksmuseum Vincent van Gogh
(Vincent van Gogh Stichting)

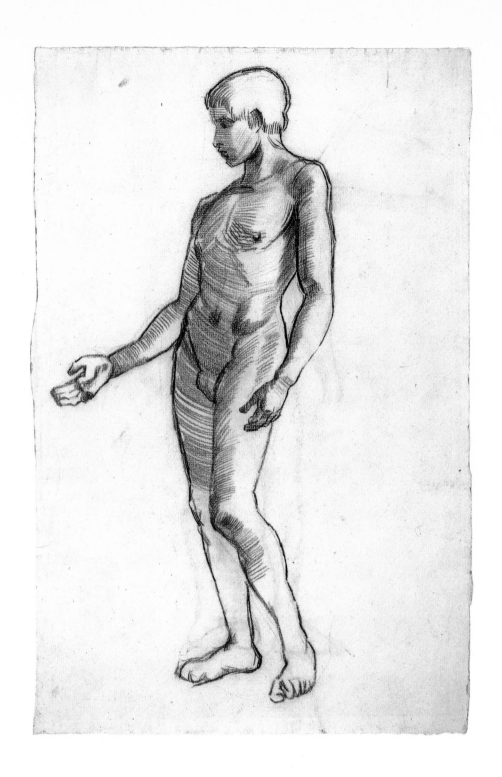

142

Male Nude, Standing
Summer or autumn 1886
Black chalk on laid paper, 477 x 313 mm
F 1364b r   JH 1046
Amsterdam, Rijksmuseum Vincent van Gogh
(Vincent van Gogh Stichting)

PARIS

143

View of Paris from Montmartre
1886
Black and white chalk on grey laid paper, 225 x 300 mm
F 1387 JH 1098
Amsterdam, Rijksmuseum Vincent van Gogh
(Vincent van Gogh Stichting)

144

View of Paris from Montmartre
1886
Black and coloured chalk on grey laid paper,
225 x 300 mm
F 1390 JH 1097
Amsterdam, Rijksmuseum Vincent van Gogh
(Vincent van Gogh Stichting)

145

View of Paris from Montmartre
1886
Black and coloured chalk on grey laid paper,
245 x 315 mm
F 1388 JH 1095
Amsterdam, Rijksmuseum Vincent van Gogh
(Vincent van Gogh Stichting)

146

Street Scene with a Woman Walking her Dog
1886
Ink and coloured chalk on wove paper, 167 x 101 mm
Annotated l.r.: De son métier elle ne faisait rien.
Le soir elle baladait son chien. La Villette
SD 1704 JH 1035 SB 4|2
Amsterdam, Rijksmuseum Vincent van Gogh
(Vincent van Gogh Stichting)

147

The Hill of Montmartre
1886
Ink and coloured chalk on wove paper, 101 x 167 mm
F 1394 JH 1181 SB 4|1
Amsterdam, Rijksmuseum Vincent van Gogh
(Vincent van Gogh Stichting)

148

Cemetery in the Rain
1886
Pencil, ink and paint on laid paper, 370 x 485 mm
F 1399a JH 1032
Otterlo, Rijksmuseum Kröller-Müller

149

Cemetery in the Rain
1886
Pencil and ink, 230 x 370 mm
F 1399 JH 1031
Vienna, Albertina

PARIS

150

The Hill of Montmartre
1886
Charcoal and chalk on laid paper, 312 x 478 mm
Watermark: PL BAS
F 1398 JH 1174
Amsterdam, Rijksmuseum Vincent van Gogh
(Vincent van Gogh Stichting)

151

The Terrace of café 'La Guinguette'
Early 1887
Pencil, ink and paint on laid paper, 380 x 520 mm
F 1407 JH 1034
Amsterdam, Rijksmuseum Vincent van Gogh
(Vincent van Gogh Stichting)

152

The Moulin de la Galette
Early 1887
Ink and black chalk on laid paper, 530 x 390 mm
F 1396a JH 1185
Washington, D.C., The Phillips Collection

153

The Moulin de Blute-Fin
Early 1887
Pencil and pastel chalk on laid paper, 400 x 540 mm
F 1396 JH 1222
Amsterdam, Rijksmuseum Vincent van Gogh
(Vincent van Gogh Stichting)

154

View from Vincent's Room in the Rue Lepic
Early 1887
Pencil and ink on laid paper, 395 x 535 mm
F 1391 JH 1220
Amsterdam, Rijksmuseum Vincent van Gogh
(Vincent van Gogh Stichting)

155

Window at the restaurant 'Chez Bataille'
Early 1887
Ink and coloured chalk on laid paper, 540 x 400 mm
Annotated and signed l.r.: La fenêtre chez Bataille Vincent 87
F 1392 JH 1218
Amsterdam, Rijksmuseum Vincent van Gogh
(Vincent van Gogh Stichting)

156

The 'Restaurant de la Sirène' in Asnières
Spring 1887
Pencil and coloured chalk on laid paper, 400 x 540 mm
F 1408 JH 1252
Amsterdam, Rijksmuseum Vincent van Gogh
(Vincent van Gogh Stichting)

157

Boulevard de Clichy
Early 1887
Pencil, ink and chalk on laid paper, 400 x 540 mm
F 1393 JH 1217
Amsterdam, Rijksmuseum Vincent van Gogh
(Vincent van Gogh Stichting)

158

Town Wall with Horse-Drawn Tram and Walkers
Summer 1887
Pencil, ink, pastel chalk and watercolour on laid paper,
395 x 535 mm
F 1400 JH 1283
Amsterdam, Rijksmuseum Vincent van Gogh
(Vincent van Gogh Stichting)

159

A Suburb of Paris, Seen from Montmartre
Summer 1887
Watercolour on laid paper, 395 x 535 mm
F 1410 JH 1286
Amsterdam, Stedelijk Museum
(Gift of the Vereniging tot het Vormen van een Openbare
Verzameling van Hedendaagse Kunst, 1949)

160

Town Wall
Summer 1887
Watercolour on laid paper, 395 x 535 mm
F 1403 JH 1281
Manchester, Whitworth Art Gallery
(University of Manchester)

161

Town Wall with Horse-Drawn Tram and Walkers
Summer 1887
Pencil, ink and watercolour on wove paper, 240 x 315 mm
F 1401 JH 1284
Amsterdam, Rijksmuseum Vincent van Gogh
(Vincent van Gogh Stichting)

162

Shelter on Montmartre, with Sunflowers
Summer 1887
Pencil, ink and watercolour on wove paper, 305 x 240 mm
Watermark: ANNONAY [...]
F 1411 JH 1305
Amsterdam, Rijksmuseum Vincent van Gogh
(Vincent van Gogh Stichting)

163

Garden Entrance on Montmartre
Summer 1887
Pencil, ink and watercolour on wove paper, 316 x 240 mm
Watermark: VIDALON – LES – ANNONAY [...]
F 1406 JH 1277
Amsterdam, Rijksmuseum Vincent van Gogh
(Vincent van Gogh Stichting)

164

Studies for a Self-Portrait
1886-87
Pencil and ink on wove paper, 317 x 246 mm
Watermark: GANSON & MONTGOLFIER VIDALON
F 1378 r JH 1197
Amsterdam, Rijksmuseum Vincent van Gogh
(Vincent van Gogh Stichting)

Arles

- 177

DRAWINGS FROM NATURE

Van Gogh's move from Paris to Arles on 20 February 1888 did not initiate immediate changes in his drawing style. In fact, it seems unlikely that he did much drawing in the early weeks of his stay, just as he had done little during his last months in Paris. While factors such as the state of his health and the inclement weather (it continued to freeze in Arles until 9 March) may account for this moratorium on drawing, a far more positive reason was his urge to transfer his vision directly into paint. Progress reports on his paintings were frequently sent to Theo and Emile Bernard, and Theo was furnished with a count of finished canvases. But not a word on drawing.

In fact, it was some seven weeks after Van Gogh's arrival that drawing was first mentioned. In a letter of 9 April, he told his - 190 brother that he had just sent off two watercolour drawings after paintings (F1469 and F1480). This letter was written at the height of his immersion in painting the orchards in blossom, which he began about 24 March and completed around 20 April. 'I must do a *tremendous* lot of drawing, because I want to make some drawings in the manner of Japanese prints [...] If there should happen to be a month or a fortnight when you were hard pressed, let me know, and I will set to work on some drawings, which will cost us less' [474].

However, references to drawings in letters come faster in late April and early May. The evidence is best presented chronologically.

Circa 21 April Van Gogh reported despatching two drawings to Theo (probably around 17 April). 'These drawings were made with a reed sharpened the way you would a goose quill; I intend to make a series of them, and hope to do better ones than the first two. It is a method that I already tried in Holland some time ago, but I hadn't such good reeds there as here' [478].

Circa 24 April Vincent had received 'bad news' from his brother; Boussod et Valadon were strongly opposed to Theo's policy of buying and showing the Impressionists, with the implication of a quarrel and even a resignation. 'As far as I'm concerned, I stopped painting at once, and went on with a series of pen drawings, of which you have had the first two, but in a smaller size [...] Since I believe it's possible to produce a work of art at less cost than one must spend on a painting, I've begun the series of pen-and-ink drawings [...] I'll send you pen drawings in a little while; I've done four already' [479].

1 May 'I have just sent you a roll of small pen-and-ink drawings, a dozen I think. By which you will see that if I have stopped painting, I haven't stopped working. You will find among them a hasty sketch on yellow paper, a lawn in the square at the entrance to the town with a building in the background [...] I'll be sure to make you a better drawing of it than the first sketch [...] [Outside the house is] the garden of the square, of which you will find two more drawings. I think I can promise you that the drawings will get better and better' [480].

Circa 7 May Theo had been in Brussels for several days. In his absence, Vincent wrote: 'there must be at least two letters that I sent to Paris, and a roll of drawings [...] There has been a good deal of mistral, so I did the dozen little drawings which I sent you. Now the weather is splendid, I have already done two big drawings and five small ones [...] I am sending these five small drawings to you in Brussels today' [483].

Among the twenty-six paintings Van Gogh was about to send to Paris was 'a little landscape with a hovel, white, red, and green, and a cypress beside it; you have the drawing of it, and I did the whole painting of it in the house. This will show you that, if you like, I can make little pictures like the Japanese prints of all the drawings' [484].

10 May '[...] the white orchard which I sent you a pen drawing of [...]' [486].

12 May 'Now I have two new studies like these [sketches in letter]: you have a drawing of one of them already, a farm by the highroad among cornfields' [487].

26 May 'He [Mourier Petersen] will have brought you two more drawings [...] I expect to draw still more [...] I must add an order for colours, though in case you'd rather not get them at once, I can do a few more drawings and it will not be time wasted [...] What is always urgent is to draw, and whether you do it directly with the brush or with something else, like the pen, you never get enough done' [490].

28 May 'Mourier will give you two more pen drawings' [492].

Circa 16 June 'Do you remember among the little drawings a wooden bridge with a washing place, and a view of the town in the distance? I have just painted that subject in a large size' [504].

These allusions provide insights into the activity of drawing, into its objectives and its techniques. We should be much the poorer without them: the more so as not a single sketchbook has survived from the Arles period.

Part of Van Gogh's reason for undertaking this series of pen-and-ink drawings was his discovery of the reed pen. Reeds grew in abundance around the canal network of Arles that another Dutchman, the engineer Van Ens, had helped to lay-out in the seventeenth century. And their quality, Van Gogh tells us, was superior to the reeds he used, briefly it must be emphasized, in Etten in June 1881. Only two drawings from *cat. 4* Etten are executed with reed (F 845 and F 846) – and then extremely cautiously and tightly. There appears to be no evidence of the reed pen's use in the rest of his Dutch period, nor in Paris.

Why the reed pen in Arles? Was it another instance of Van Gogh's passionate curiosity in the use of unusual media that had so characterized his drawing techniques in The Hague? Were there artistic precedents? We cannot be sure how much he knew first hand of Rembrandt's pen drawings. Nor can we know how aware he was of other European artists' use of the reed pen.

It is sometimes said that Van Gogh used the reed pen in a conscious attempt to imitate Japanese drawings. Yet the Japanese always used a brush, never a reed pen. What could be argued is that he thought his use of the reed pen would enable him to emulate the unerring facility and sweep of the great Japanese draughtsmen.

Should one, in any case, be searching for such prototypes and conscious influences? Ultimately, it seems far more probable that Vincent discovered the reed pen for himself. After all, he must have discovered it for himself in Etten before he was actively aware of Japanese prints.

In Arles, it became his predominant weapon – and one he continued to employ in Saint-Rémy and Auvers. So keen was he to pass on *his* discovery to others that he not only described the technique to his artist-friend Koning on two occasions, and suggested exchanging his 'first two' drawings against a painted study of Koning's, but he actually sent some reeds to Paris to enable Koning to try out the method for himself [483].

As with any new medium, Van Gogh's first attempts tended to be exploratory and rather timid, as if it were still a quill or metal pen. But in discovering its 'soul', he discovered its subtle range of expressive possibilities. Depending on the sharpening of the reed and on the amount of ink used, the impressions left on the paper could be mistaken for ordinary pen or confused with brush. One distinctive effect is the 'split' line – or tramline effect – that occurred as the ink began to run dry. Its versatility is remarkable in Van Gogh's hand, ranging from a gently evocative brush-like manner to a brutal and dense expressiveness, with inventive variability in its complex hatchings, jabs, and dots.

But, as he wrote to Koning [498a], Van Gogh used the finer, more delicate touches of the quill pen for evoking distances, particularities of buildings and sky-line.

Drawing was a necessity: he often told Theo that he must do 'a *tremendous* lot'. But not all the time; and most often in distinct phases, spells of concentrated activity between intense bouts of painting. This series of pen-and-ink drawings exemplifies this phenomenon: Van Gogh spent more than a fortnight engaged in nothing but drawing.

In addition to reasons of economy, sparked off by Theo's difficulties with Boussod et Valadon, there was the mistral. Often, that terrifyingly brutal wind made painting impossible (though, characteristically, Van Gogh refused to be intimidated by it, constructing weights to hold down his easel). In the last days of April, there was a great deal of mistral. Van Gogh also suffered 'such a fierce toothache that much against my will I had to waste time' [480]. An impending row with his landlord and his decision to rent the Yellow House from 1 May, further dissuaded him from painting.

The allusions to individual drawings in Van Gogh's April-May letters are less revealing than in later series. Summing up the references, there are four 'large' and seventeen 'small' drawings finished by 7 May.

Which are the 'small' drawings? During the actual period of execution, Van Gogh gave few descriptions, merely citing two drawings of the garden in the Place Lamartine [480]. The third reference is to an odd-one-out, a larger drawing on yellow *cat. 17* paper (F 1513), specially done to celebrate his taking of the Yellow House. Of more value are the later retrospective comments in May and June. Three in particular enable a trio of drawings to be identified – F 1499, F 1474 and F 1473. All three *cat. 16* are on identically sized wove paper measuring 255 by 347 mm. *cat. 16* The two garden drawings of the Place Lamartine can now be securely identified as F 1476 and F 1487, since they too are done *cat. 17* on similar sized paper. Around this documented nucleus of five, others can be grouped, each of them on the same paper.

For instance, around F 1499 can be placed three closely related sheets (F 1415, F 1421, and F 1474). They are fundamentally *cat. 16* quill pen drawings, heightened, so to say, by reed pen: the reed enlivens, generalises, broadens, but is by no means the substance of the drawing. But we are presented with a contradiction. All the indications in the letters suggest that Van Gogh did not begin this series of pen-and-ink drawings until mid-April. Yet this drawing of a small *mas* with a cypress (F 1499) is *cat. 16* inscribed, by the artist himself, 'Arles, Mars 88'. What an irony, the only dated drawing from Arles being put in question! Are not these four drawings, so close stylistically, likely to be the quartet mentioned as already completed by 24 April [479]? If not, and if we accept the date on the drawing, we then have to admit that four drawings already existed in March. Had Van Gogh executed them all painstakingly in quill pen *alone* in March, each one carefully plotted with his perspective frame, and then reworked them with reed pen in mid-April?

Whatever the solution, there can be no denying that these four form a clear sub-group in the series of pen-and-ink drawings. And that stylistically they must precede the others. Those that follow have much less of a quill pen base; nor do they show the use of the perspective frame. Van Gogh's own increasing ability in manipulating the reed pen led to a confident, more open articulation, apparent in F 1502, F 1473 and F 1476. One has only to compare the treatment of the trees in F 1502 with that in F 1415, or contrast the views of the Place Lamartine gardens in F 1421 and F 1476 to note the differences.

What, then, of the quartet of 'large' drawings? Van Gogh refers always to the 'first two' drawings, never once indicating the motif of either, nor their size. But one small clue is dropped in *letter* 486 – 'the white orchard which I sent you a pen drawing of'. Van Gogh did not send any 'large' drawings between *letters* 479 and 486, only the dozen 'small' (with F 1513 as a special makeweight) in *letter* 480, none of which depicts an orchard. The 'Verger de Provence' (F 1414) must therefore have been one of the 'first two' drawings reported as sent in *letter* 478. Its size is 395 x 540 mm. Its partner can now be suggested – another drawing of an orchard on identically sized paper, but this time in a vertical format. This drawing (F 1516) was also executed with the aid of the perspective frame. Knowing Van Gogh's later working methods, it seems right to assume that he would have chosen the same sized paper for these 'first two' drawings.

The relation of 'Verger de Provence' to the painting of the 'White Orchard' (F 403) can be defined. It is certainly not a drawing done after the painting, akin, that is to say, to the two watercolour copies after completed paintings (F 1469 and F 1480). The fact that Van Gogh used the perspective frame negates such an assumption. This is a drawing done from nature. Equally, however, it is not a preparatory study for the painting, but a separate sighting of the motif. There are sufficient differences between the two to support this.

The two other 'large' drawings were executed between 1 and 7 May [483]. Here, Van Gogh gives no clues to subject or size. The firmest candidate must be 'Vue d'Arles' (F 1416). This drawing, done with the perspective frame, precedes the painting (F 409) reported as finished on 12 May [487]. The relationship to the painting appears to be closer than that of the 'Verger de Provence' to the 'White Orchard'. Van Gogh admitted his compositional difficulties in making the painting. But those difficulties must first have been faced in the drawing. And the perspective frame was clearly an attempt to overcome the conflicting problems of the right-angled turns of the willows and ditches on a diagonal axis that was the essence of the motif.

The other 'large' drawing of early May is surely 'Bords du Rhône' (F 1472a). A similar mixture of quill and reed pens exists; but with a far more open sweep of town buildings, the quill is more in evidence. The state of what little foliage is visible on the quay would not deny an early May dating. And more so than in the earlier pair of identically sized orchards, the reed is now used with greater freedom displaying the first evidence in both foregrounds of the 'split' lines or 'tram' lines effect. These two drawings present two contrasting views of Arles in slightly differing formats. The 'Bords du Rhône' projects a more touristic and picturesque image, one that both illustrators (e.g. Joseph Pennell as early as September 1888) and publishers of *cartes postales* from 1900 onwards exploited.

The 'Bords du Rhône' drawing was done with violet aniline ink, highly fugitive, and inclined to end up as a faded sepia. Traces of violet are still visible where the drawing has been covered by the mount. It is also on Ingres paper with the watermark AL PL BAS. This is arguably the first Arles drawing to use this paper: Van Gogh probably acquired several sheets of it in early May. One of the most extraordinary lacunae of the Arles drawing saga (akin to the disappearance of all sketchbooks) is the lack of any reference to paper. Never once does Vincent ask Theo to send paper (an extreme contrast to his carping perfectionism about the right quality of paper in The Hague), and only once – and that during his last days in Arles – does he complain of paper being the cause of some disappointment in a drawing (F 1467).

This Ingres paper certainly dominated Van Gogh's May drawings, once the last of the 'small' pen drawings had been completed. All the half-sheets at Montmajour and Saintes-Maries were done with it. They were preceded, however, by the drawing of the Langlois Bridge (F 1470), for which Van Gogh used a *demi-feuille* measuring 300 by 470 mm, that bore the single watermark PL BAS. As with the 'Bords du Rhône', this drawing is not cited in the letters. But the return to the motif of the Langlois Bridge after a two-month lay-off, witnessed in the Cologne painting (F 571), the 'feel' of the season, and the increased economy of the drawing style, all suggest a mid-May date of execution. As such it forms a postscript to the series of pen-and-ink drawings, and an introduction to the next group.

This series of pen-and-ink drawings, deliberately undertaken as an enforced intermission between painting, have a certain thematic unity in choice of motif. Three of the four 'large' ones are inscribed: 'Verger de Provence', 'Vue d'Arles', 'Bords du Rhône'. And just one of the 'small' set is inscribed 'Arles', with the mystifying March date. Van Gogh provided his brother with a lexicon of Provencal, or, more narrowly, Arlesien, motifs. And he expected Theo to use that lexicon to be abreast of later developments.

These April-May drawings constituted an idiosyncratic guide to Arles. The monuments, Roman and Christian, were ignored. In the only view from within the walls of the town (F 1480a), Van Gogh chose a vantage-point from his top floor hotel room overloooking the roofs: an ugly chimney stack, a line of washing, a succession of tiles that recede like ploughed furrows, dominate the distanced and reduced monuments. Such a view symbolized Van Gogh's approach to Arles. Neither classical antiquity nor medieval Catholicism held any mystique for him. He preferred a humble *mas* in a field; a larger *mas* in a green cornfield; an avenue of trees in the open countryside; and, near the town, washerwomen on a canal next to the gasworks.

In that sense, these pen-and-ink drawings are comparable to the two sets of views that Van Gogh did in The Hague for his art-dealer uncle, C.M. van Gogh, in the spring of 1882. There, he shocked and upset his uncle by deliberately ignoring the historic and the picturesque, and choosing instead the gasworks, factory, railway station, and humbler dwellings of the fashionable city.

Van Gogh abandoned his use of the small format from early May until mid-July, when he began working on his sets of drawings after paintings for Bernard, Russell, and Theo. And shortly afterwards he utilized the same format in a trio of *cat. 173* drawings from nature (F 1466, F 1495, and F 1477). The last of these is another view in one of the gardens of the Place Lamartine. It continues the more deliberate and stylized treatment that can be seen in the drawings after paintings done for Theo. *cat. 171* Compare this drawing to its predecessor of late April (F 1476): in the intervening months, a concentrated change had taken place. New series of drawings had been undertaken, alternative nuclei had been created. Chronologically and stylistically, this study of the Place Lamartine garden, drawn from nature as it undoubtedly was, can only be fully grasped after the attendant developments of these other groups have been scrutinized.

fig. 27 (F 1416)
Vincent van Gogh
View of Arles with Irises in the Foreground, 1888
Providence, Museum of Art, Rhode Island School of Design
(Gift of Mrs. Murray S. Danforth)

fig. 28 (F 1480a)
Vincent van Gogh
View of Roofs and the Tower of Saint–Julien, 1888
Private Collection

The medieval abbey of Montmajour dominates the plain of the Crau, some three miles north-east of Arles. Its silhouette of ruined church, fortified tower, and massive but pillaged eighteenth century palace, rises dramatically above the former marshes of the rock-strewn soils of the Crau.

Van Gogh discovered it soon after his arrival in Arles. He wrote to Theo in early March: 'I have been for several walks in the country hereabouts but it is quite impossible to do anything in this wind. The sky is a hard blue with a great bright sun which has melted almost all the snow, but the wind is cold and so dry that it gives you gooseflesh. But all the same I have seen lots of beautiful things – a ruined abbey on a hill covered with holly, pines, and grey olives. We'll have a try at that soon, I hope' [467].

No more mention is made of the 'ruined abbey on a hill' in March or April. And it did not figure in the series of landscape drawings of Arles and its environs. Only in two drawings of early May (F 1518 and F 1518a) did the silhouette of the abbey emerge as a distant speck. It was as if Van Gogh was slowly tempting himself to come to terms with it, to get closer. He had delayed his response for three months: he had viewed it on innumerable occasions; he had walked there countless times. Silently and slowly he was summing it up, absorbing its spell, searching for a solution to capturing something of its essence. A distant view across the plain? Closer in, among its rocky slopes of 'holly, pines, and grey olives'? Selected views within the ruined abbey? Or one or more of those dominating panoramas from within its domain?

The choices must have been maturing slowly in his mind's eye, reluctant, as he was, to rush in and realise them. He was hesitant, perhaps even overawed by the massive, enigmatic ruin with its medieval connotations that were so foreign to his Northern beliefs; and resisting the obvious picturesque and romantic qualities that came too easily to the many artists and illustrators who depicted Montmajour in the nineteenth century.

Van Gogh needed a catalyst to launch him. That catalyst came in a letter from Theo of about 18 May, inviting Vincent to send some drawings to the second exhibition of the Dutch Etching Society, due to open in Amsterdam on 1 June. He responded positively on about 20 May: 'Look here, I will do my best to send you some new drawings for Dordrecht' [489]. (The confusion of Dordrecht with Amsterdam came from the letter of invitation to Theo from Jan Veth, secretary of the Society, which was sent from Dordrecht, where Veth was then living.)

For his 'new' drawings, Vincent chose Montmajour. On 26 May he was able to inform Theo: 'Today I again sent you some drawings, and I am adding another two. These are views taken from a rocky hill-slope, from which you see the country toward Crau (very good wine comes from there), the town of Arles and the country toward Fontvieille. The contrast between the wild and romantic foreground and the distant perspective, wide and still, with horizontal lines sloping into the Alpines [...] is very picturesque. The two belated drawings that I am adding now will give you an idea of the ruin that crowns the rocks' [490].

In fact, Van Gogh sent seven drawings, each on half-size Ingres paper (*demi-feuilles*, measuring 300 x 470 mm), and each bearing one part of the watermark, either AL or PL BAS. Six of the sheets have inscribed titles – 'Bruyère' (F 1493), 'Vue de la Crau' (F 1419), 'Vue prise à Montmajour' (F 1448), 'Vue d'Arles' (F 1475), 'Ruine de Montmajour' (F 1417), 'Montmajour' (F 1423) – and the seventh (F 1418) is signed. Each began with a fairly rapid compositional lay-in with pencil; Van Gogh then worked up the composition with reed pen, often creating pentimenti as he did so; and finally, for the more delicate and finer touches, especially in the backgrounds, he used a quill pen. The inscriptions and signatures were added with reed pen. *cat. 178 - 179*

In other words, he continued to work as he did in the series of drawings from nature. But one striking feature about these seven drawings is the use of violet ink. Why he made this unusual choice is not clear. Was he consciously searching for a special colour effect in reaction to sepia and black? Or had he no other ink at hand and was therefore forced to use this violet aniline ink, without realising how fugitive it was? Certainly, the first Montmajour series of drawings was not alone: in the present exhibition, two earlier drawings were done in the same violet ink (F 1472a and F 1516). *cat. 177 / cat. 175*

Ironically, chemical reaction and exposure to light have turned the violet ink to a faded sepia. Slim vestiges of violet remain at the edge of those sheets that have been covered by mounts. For example, three sheets in the Rijksmuseum Vincent van Gogh (F 1417, F 1423 and F 1493). These seven drawings are certainly the most drastically faded of all Van Gogh's French drawings. Often the ink has faded to a ghostlike veil, where even the signatures and annotations are barely decipherable. It is as if the ruin on the hill has transferred its metaphor of a noble sense of decay to the very drawings that Vincent made of it. *cat. 178*

Long pondered, the series was then executed with great speed, probably during the course of five days. Later, he referred to one of them as un *croquis hâtif*, and each bears the same hasty sketchiness. The least hasty of the group are the four panoramas, where Vincent has emphasized the clarity of light and precise reading of distant contours by a meticulous use of pencil, later strengthened with quill pen. This is especially evident in the Essen drawing, 'View of La Crau' (F 1419). By contrast, foliage, plants, rocks, fields are summarily indicated. And there is no attempt to unify the decorative articulation with a system of graphic signs. Skies are left untouched. The dot is not much in evidence. *cat. 179*

Hitherto, Van Gogh had spread his drawing activity around Arles – to the north, east, and south, with views of the Rhône within the city. These drawings of Montmajour form his first concentrated statement on one important motif. And it was a motif with a variety of possibilities. These seven drawings epitomize this variety, as if they were illustrations to an article, an implication strengthened by the titles that Van Gogh inscribed on all but one of them. In fact, he covered three main aspects. A view of the rock slopes (F 1493); two views of the abbey itself (F 1417 and F 1423); and four panoramic views – one looking toward the Rhône (F 1448), one toward Fontvieille (F 1419), one across the plain of the Crau (F 1418), and one toward Arles (F 1475). In short, he virtually circled the hill in selecting his views below.

When Vincent despatched this set of drawings to Theo on 26 May, he queried: 'But is it worth the trouble to make frames for this Dordrecht exhibition? It seems idiotic to me, and I would rather not be in it' [490]. That was enough to dissuade Theo from sending them to Amsterdam. Theo, however, decided to answer Jan Veth's request by lending from his own collection a *café-concert* drawing by Seurat which he had acquired in March, wood-engravings by Lucien Pissarro, etchings by Forain and Raffaelli, and, among several works from the gallery of Boussod et Valadon, a drawing by Degas. Vincent would have been in distinguished company.

Partly another instance of Van Gogh's equivocal attitude towards exhibiting his work – now enthusiastic, now unconcerned, now dismissive – this first Montmajour series is also a primary example of what may be called his delayed response to a motif. Van Gogh would carefully note a desirable motif, yet equally carefully resist its immediate allurements. Such was the case with Daubigny's garden in Auvers.

At Montmajour, however, this first campaign did not end with the seven half-page drawings. Having despatched them to Paris on 26 May, Vincent returned to 'the ruin on the hill' the following day. This time he armed himself with a full-page sheet of Whatman paper (490 x 620 mm). He dilated on the resulting drawing in two letters written on the same day, 29 May. First – and most revealingly – to his Dutch artist-friend Arnold Hendrick Koning (1860-1944) who was on the point of leaving Paris for Holland after having spent three months with Theo at 54 rue Lepic: '[...] I have just finished a drawing, even larger than the first two [cited as already sent in *letter* 478], of a cluster of straight pines on a rock, seen from the top of a hill. Behind this foreground a perspective of meadows, a road with poplars, and in the far distance the town. The trees very dark against the sunlit meadow [...] I did them with very thick reeds on thin Whatman paper, and in the background I worked with a quill for the finer strokes. I can recommend this method to you, for the quill strokes are more in character than those of the reed' [498a]. Then, more briefly, to Theo: 'If the roll is not too big to be accepted by the post office, you will receive another

big pen drawing, which I would very much like the Pissarros to see if they come on Sunday' [495].

This marvellously evocative drawing, now in the National Gallery, Oslo (F 1452), thus becomes one of the most fully documented of Vincent's Arles drawings. What is especially valuable in the account of its genesis and execution to Koning is the distinct functions that the artist apportions to the reed and quill pens. Nonetheless, the soft pencil used to lay-in the composition often asserts its presence – in the foreground rocks, for instance, and in the distant skyline. It is noticeable too how often Van Gogh ignores the pencil underlay with his pens, now revising a contour, now shifting the position of rock or building. *cat. 183*

In style, the Oslo drawing remains comparatively 'hasty', even though less so than the seven half-page drawings. The overall graphic rhythms are not yet systematically controlled. While Van Gogh uses dots in the meadows to simulate wheat and vines, they are much less structured than they will become. And the treatment of the sky, both in clouds and smoke, bespeaks the rapid sketching approach.

The view, so fully described to Koning, is taken from the western edge of the rocky hill, with the buildings of Montmajour at the artist's back. Part of this wide panorama is also caught in an upright drawing now in Rotterdam (F 1475), and differing sections of it in three paintings (F 391, F 465 and F 545). *fig. 29*

The Oslo drawing has a range of historical significance. It launches a sequence of large drawings done on full-size Whatman paper. It became a referential point for Van Gogh. A few days after completing it, he made a large drawing of Saintes-Maries-de-la-Mer (F 1439), which he called a pendant to the Oslo drawing [499]. This is the only occasion when speaking of his Arles drawings that he actually names pendants – something he does frequently with his paintings. Again, retrospectively, the Oslo drawing became the sixth drawing of the large Montmajour series that Van Gogh was to undertake in July: 'You have a sixth of that series from Montmajour – a group of very dark pines and the town of Arles in the background' [509]. *fig. 30*

Finally, the Oslo drawing formed part of the large collection of Van Gogh's work that was given special prominence, together with that of Gauguin, at the Danish avant-garde exhibiting society, the Frie Udstilling, in Copenhagen in 1893. There, it was bought by the National Gallery, Oslo, thus becoming the first of Van Gogh's drawings to enter a public collection.

fig. 29 (F 465)
Vincent van Gogh
Summer Evening, 1888
Winterthur, Kunstmuseum

fig. 30 (F 1439)
Vincent van Gogh
View of Saintes–Maries–de–la–Mer, 1888
Winterthur, Sammlung Oskar Reinhart 'Am Römerholz'

At intervals during his first three months in Arles, Van Gogh spoke of visiting the Mediterranean to paint seascapes. He thought of Marseilles and Martigues. But this wish, partly an artist's natural curiosity, partly the Northern European's notion of saluting the Mediterranean, partly a subconscious memory of his admiral-uncle's sea voyages there, never materialized.

It was another voyage, of more momentous import, that led to Van Gogh's only visit to the Mediterranean. In A.D. 45, the three Marys, with three companions, and their servant Sarah, landed at what came to be called Saintes-Maries-de-la-Mer and converted Provence to Christianity. In the church, relics of two Marys were preserved in a chapel over the apse. More importantly, the remains of their servant, Sarah, in the crypt became the object of an annual gipsy pilgrimage that took place on 24-25 May.

This two-day pilgrimage, with its attendant crowds, publicity, and special diligences running from Arles, clearly brought Saintes-Maries to Vincent's attention. His curiosity and desire to see the Mediterranean now had a concrete objective. Three days after the festival, he not only mentioned Saintes-Maries for the first time, but wrote explicitly to Theo: 'I expect to make an excursion to Saintes-Maries, and see the Mediterranean at last' [492, 28 May]. A day later, his plans were fixed: 'Early tomorrow I start for Saintes-Maries on the Mediterranean. I shall stay there till Saturday evening. I am taking two canvases, but I'm rather afraid it will probably be too windy to paint. You go by diligence, it is fifty kilometres from here. You cross the Camargue, grass plains where there are herds of fighting bulls and also herds of little white horses, half wild and very beautiful [495].

Having sent Theo his seven Montmajour drawings on 26 May, and having received his brother's critical comments on them in his reply of 27 May (acknowledged in *letter* 492 of 28 May), Van Gogh was anxious to continue drawing in Saintes-Maries. 'Above all, I'm taking all that is needed for drawing. I must draw a great deal, for the reason you spoke of in your last letter – things here have so much style. And I want to get my drawing more spontaneous, more exaggerated (*plus volontaire et plus exagéré)*' [495].

Van Gogh left Arles by diligence at 7am on Wednesday 30 May, arriving in Saintes-Maries at midday. He wrote one letter from Saintes-Maries on Saturday 2 June, from which two quotations are constantly taken – one describing the colour of the sea, the other describing the colour of the night sky observed on an evening walk along the shore. But this letter also contains several insights into his drawing. He intends to send some drawings by post when he returns to Arles tomorrow, he tells Theo. 'I do not think there are 100 houses in this village or this town. The principal building after the old church, an ancient fortress, is the barracks. And yet what houses – like those on our heaths and peat bogs of Drenthe, you will see some examples of them in the drawings'. He goes on: 'I am staying until tomorrow afternoon, I still have some drawings to do'. And he concludes: 'Besides half-page drawings, I have a large drawing, the pendant of the last one' [499].

During this five-day sojourn in Saintes-Maries, Van Gogh produced seven half-page (*demi-feuille*) drawings on the same Ingres paper with the same AL PL BAS watermark that he had just used for his seven views of Montmajour. Five of these are of *cabanes*, the distinctive thatched cottages of the Camargue (F 1434, F 1436, F 1437, F 1438 and F 1440); one is of the sea-shore with boats (F 1432), and one a distant view of the cemetery (F 1479). In addition, he made a large drawing of the village (F 1439), the 'pendant' of the recently completed large drawing from Montmajour (F 1452). And on the last Sunday morning, he made a breakthrough drawing (F 1428), which he described to Theo on his return to Arles: 'I am sending you by the same post some drawings of Saintes-Maries. I made the drawing of the boats very early in the morning as they were on the point of leaving, and I have the painting of it on the easel, a size 30 canvas, with more sea and sky at the right. It was before the boats cleared off. I had observed it all the other mornings, but as they leave very early I had not the time to do it [...] I have only been here a few months, but tell me this – could I, in Paris, have done the drawings of the boats *in an hour*? Even without the perspective frame, I do it now without measuring, just by letting my pen go' [500, circa 4 June].

On his return, Van Gogh sent six drawings, including that of the boats to Theo. 'I have three more drawings of cottages which I still need, and which will follow these: the cottages are rather harsh, but I have some more carefully drawn ones' [500]. The three he held back (F 1434, F 1438, and F 1440) served as working studies for two small oils painted in the Yellow House (F 419 and F 420).

Van Gogh's working procedure remained unchanged. A rapid compositional sketch in pencil preceded the reed pen: he was not yet ready to make a pure pen drawing, directly and uninhibitedly. But he chose a more conventional ink than the fugitive violet he used for his Montmajour series of drawings. Certainly, there is much less evidence of fading in these Saintes-Maries drawings. And in the more *soigné* drawings he used a quill for the finer touches and architectural details.

Theo's response to Vincent's search for a drawing style that was 'more spontaneous and exaggerated' is not recorded, even obliquely, in Van Gogh's letters. Spontaneous and exaggerated would surely apply to the two street scenes (F 1436 and F 1437), almost savagely executed in their elisions of form and shorthand attack. The street at Saintes-Maries (F 1434) is less volatile, and qualifies as one of the *soigné* group. So too does F 1440; whereas F 1438 is more transitional, caught between the two

styles. Nonetheless, it must be classed as *soigné* – thus making up the three that Van Gogh kept back for use as preparatory drawings for the studio-executed paintings.

Van Gogh's visit to the small fishing village of Saintes-Maries satisfied his long-cherished wish to see the Mediterranean. But it also had a positive and significant effect on his artistic evolution. It affected his painting: 'Now that I have seen the sea here, I'm absolutely convinced of the importance of staying in the Midi and of positively piling it on, exaggerating the colour'. Exaggerated colour characterises the two small, proto-Fauve paintings of cottages based on the drawings brought back from Saintes-Maries. As for his drawing, Van Gogh not only freed himself from his cumbersome perspective frame, but sought to heighten his own expressive skills as a draughtsman. The accelerated speed of the reed pen's passage over the paper symbolizes his sense of renewed well-being, of regained health, as well as being a palpable expression of his increased ability to handle the instrument. In early spring, he had begun using the reed cautiously, as if it were a quill or a metal pen. Now it became looser, broader, more improvisatory. It accentuated and strengthened the pencil armature; but more often it recast and restructured, searching out and emphasizing other elements in the compositional equation. Saintes-Maries helped to liberate the reed pen. Van Gogh's problem now was how to control it – something he achieved triumphantly at Montmajour in July.

'It is odd that one evening recently at Mont Majour I saw a red sunset, its rays falling on the trunks and foliage of pines growing among a jumble of rocks, colouring the trunks and foliage with orange fire, while the other pines in the distance stood out in Prussian blue against a sky of tender-green, cerulean. It was just the effect of that Claude Monet; it was superb. The white sand and the layers of white rocks under the trees took on tints of blue. What I would like to do is the panorama of which you have the first drawings. It has such breadth and then it doesn't change into grey, it remains green to the last line – that of the blue range of hills' [492, 28 May].

This is a richly layered passage, compounding Vincent's own response to a natural effect with Theo's description of a Monet painting of pine trees near Antibes. It is one of Van Gogh's unpainted pictures. But it also announces his intention to do 'the panorama of which you have the first drawings', that is, the May series of Montmajour.

On his return from Saintes-Maries on 3 June, Van Gogh was surprised by the imminence of the harvest. Once he had completed his three studio paintings of Saintes-Maries motifs (F 413, F 419 and F 420), he devoted the next fortnight to painting fig. 32 the harvest. Montmajour was unvisited; rather, he viewed it from across the Crau in two of his most marvellous drawings (F 1483, F 1484) and then painted 'La Moisson' (F 412), for him fig. 33 - 34 the touchstone, the masterpiece, of his Arles period. Montmajour was trapped from a distance, as if he had programmatically turned his back on the silhouetted town of Arles in the Oslo drawing, and looked toward the 'ruin on the hill' that had so obsessed him since his arrival in February.

But this was not to be his last word on Montmajour. The envisaged panorama could not be driven from his mind. The strange, powerful magnetism of the medieval abbey drew him into a renewed encounter.

As with the first series of May drawings, Van Gogh needed an external stimulus to launch him. Once again, Theo provided it: not with a request for drawings for an exhibition, but with the long-awaited news that Gauguin had agreed to come to Arles. Theo's letter arrived on Friday 29 June [507]. Now the brothers' problem was how to raise the money necessary to settle Gauguin's debts in Brittany and pay for his rail ticket to Arles. Van Gogh eventually found the best form that his contribution could take. After an abortive plan to spend two or three days in the Camargue with a veterinary surgeon making drawings; after painting one of the gardens in the Place Lamartine (F 428), and a view of oak trees and rocks near Montmajour (F 466); and after scraping off a large painted study of Christ in the Garden of Olives, all in the first days of July, Van Gogh finally settled on a new series of drawings of Montmajour.

In four successive letters, his progress can be followed.

Circa 5 July 'Yesterday at sunset I was on a stony heath where

fig. 31 (F 1437)
Vincent van Gogh
Saintes-Maries-de-la-Mer, 1888
Amsterdam, Rijksmuseum Vincent van Gogh
(Vincent van Gogh Stichting)

fig. 32 (F 413)
Vincent van Gogh
Boats on the Beach at Saintes-Maries-de-la-Mer, 1888
Amsterdam, Rijksmuseum Vincent van Gogh
(Vincent van Gogh Stichting)

some very small and twisted oaks grow; in the background, a ruin on the hill, and wheat in the valley [...] I brought back a study, but it is very far below what I tried to do' [508].

8 July 'I have two new large [drawings]. When there are six of them I will send them in a roll by rail [...] If the four other drawings that I have in mind are like the first two I have done, then you will have an epitome of a very beautiful corner of Provence' [505].

9 July 'I have come back from a day in Montmajour, and my friend the second lieutenant [the Zouave Milliet] was with me. We explored the old garden together, and stole some excellent figs. If it had been bigger, it would have made me think of Zola's Paradou, high reeds and vines, ivy, fig trees, olives, pomegranates with lusty flowers of the brightest orange, hundred-year-old cypresses, ash trees, and willows, rock oaks, half-broken flights of steps, ogive windows in ruins, blocks of white rock covered in lichen, and scattered fragments of crumbling walls here and there among the green. I brought back another large drawing, but not of the garden. That makes three drawings. When I have half a dozen I shall send them along'. Later in this same letter, Van Gogh added: 'I think it right to work especially at drawing just now, and to arrange to have paints and canvas in reserve for when Gauguin comes. I wish paint was as little trouble to work with as pen and paper. I often spoil a painted study for fear of wasting colour. With paper, whether it's a letter I'm writing or a drawing I'm doing, it doesn't make much difference – so many sheets of Whatman, so many drawings' [506].

Circa 13 July 'I have just sent off to you by post a roll containing five large pen drawings. You have a sixth of that series from Mont Majour – a group of very dark pines and the town of Arles in the background. Afterward I want to add a view of the whole of the ruins (you have a hurried scratch of it among the small drawings). Since I cannot help at all with money just at this moment when we are entering this combination with Gauguin, I have done all I could to show through my work that I have the plan at heart. In my opinion the two views of the Crau and of the country on the banks of the Rhône are the best things I have done in pen and ink. If Thomas should happen to want them, he cannot have them for less than 100 fr. each. Even if in that case I had to *make him a present of the three* others, as we must get some money. But we cannot give them for less. Not everyone would have the patience to get themselves devoured by mosquitoes and to struggle against the nagging malice of this constant mistral, not to mention that I have spent whole days outside with a little bread and milk, since it was too far to go back to the town every once in a while [...] Believe me I am tired out by these drawings. I began a painting as well, but there is no way of doing it with the mistral blowing [...]' [509].

Nowhere else – not even in The Hague – is a series of drawings so fully documented as these five of Montmajour. Nowhere else does Van Gogh give the feeling so palpably of

fig. 33 (F 1484)
Vincent van Gogh
The Harvest, 1888
Cambridge, Mass., Fogg Art Museum
(Bequest of Grenville L. Winthrop)

fig. 34 (F 412)
Vincent van Gogh
The Harvest, 1888
Amsterdam, Rijksmuseum Vincent van Gogh
(Vincent van Gogh Stichting)

being with him, physically present even as he battles with a variety of problems and hazards. Nowhere else does he explain his motives for choosing to draw – economic (cheaper than painting), artistic (more controlled than painting), commercial (potentially salable to the Paris art dealer Thomas, to help finance Gauguin's journey to Arles). Nowhere else does he give the sense of a unified group of drawings cohering stylistically and iconographically.

Van Gogh envisaged his programme of six drawings from the beginning. But the order of their execution can only be deduced. The most likely sequence would seem to be the two tree and rock drawings (F 1447 and not in De la Faille) reported as finished by 8 July; the view of the abbey ruins (F 1446), most probably completed on 9 July; and finally, the most securely datable, the pair of panoramic views (F 1420 and F 1424) executed between 10 and 13 July. That is, he moved from the surrounding slopes to a view of the interior, and then took up contrasting vantage-points for the two panoramas.

Inevitably, there are analogies with the May half-page series. The two trees-and-rock-on-slopes drawings, even though essentially close-ups, contain distant views – a small segment of the town of Arles in the one, part of the plateau of the Crau in the other. Each, therefore, echoes a drawing from the May series: the 'View of Arles' (F 1475) on the one hand, and the sketch of olive trees inscribed 'Bruyère' on the other (F 1493). The third July drawing has a clear prototype from the May series: F 1423. And the two panoramas have their prototypes also: the British Museum drawing (F 1424) is a more elaborated version of F 1448, while the Amsterdam view of the Crau (F 1420) includes parts of F 1419 and F 1418. And, as in the May series, there is the suspicion that Van Gogh tried to suggest a circular panorama, however incomplete, from the high vantage-point of the abbey grounds.

There is, however, a major difference in approach and technique between the May and July campaigns. Van Gogh referred to one of the May drawings (F 1423) as a *croquis hâtif*. And the entire May series could be characterized as hasty sketches, the equivalent of rapidly executed painted studies (*études*). Whereas, the July drawings are the equivalent of finished paintings (*tableaux*), exhaustively explored and carefully controlled. In May, he could have finished a drawing in less than an hour; in July, he might spend a whole day on one (see *letter 509*).

These were finished 'presentation drawings', substitute paintings, independent works of art above all. This can be seen in the three-part procedure that Van Gogh used on all five sheets of Whatman paper. Beginning with a fairly summary compositional armature in pencil, he continued with reed pen, and, for the most part, brown ink, completing the drawing with touches of quill pen and black ink for added staffage and textural emphases. Most of the work was done on the spot, but some studio retouching must have taken place, especially with

quill pen and black ink.

While Van Gogh made no specific reference to the first three drawings, he discussed at some length the two panoramic views which for him were quite simply his finest drawings in pen and ink. Indeed, much of his letter of circa 13 July is devoted to them. 'I have already said more than once how much the Camargue and the Crau, except for the difference in colour and in the limpidity of the atmosphere, make me think of the old Holland of Ruysdael's time. It seems to me that these two sites of flat countryside covered with vines and stubble fields, seen from above, will give you an idea of it [...] The fascination that these huge plains have for me is very strong, so that I felt no *weariness*, in spite of the really wearisome circumstances, mistral and mosquitoes. If a view makes you forget these little annoyances, it must have something in it. You will see, however, that there is no attempt at effect. At first sight it is like a map, a strategic plan as far as the *execution* goes. Besides, I walked there *with a painter*, and he said, 'There is something that would be boring to paint'. Yet I went fully fifty times to Mont Majour to look at this flat landscape, and was I wrong? I went for a walk there with someone else who was *not a painter*, and when I said to him, 'Look, to me that is as beautiful and as infinite as the sea', he said – and he knows the sea – 'For my part I like this *better* than the sea, because it is no less infinite, and yet you feel that it is *inhabited*'. 'What a picture I would make of it if there was not this damn wind. That is the maddening thing here, no matter where you set up your easel. And that is largely why the painted studies are not so finished as the drawings; the canvas is shaking all the time. It does not bother me when I am drawing' [509].

In his Provencal exile, Van Gogh saw these two drawings as transformed equivalents of seventeenth-century Dutch landscape *à la Ruysdael*: not the modern Dutch landscape, he insists, but the *painted* landscape of two centuries earlier. And the time he took in making the drawings denied the passing effect of an Impressionist's view. We cannot be sure of the time of day in either drawing: there are no shadows.

The drawing of the Crau (F 1420) has a timeless quality, and more than its pendant, looks 'like a map, a strategic plan as far as the execution goes'. In representing 'the flat countryside covered with vines and stubble fields seen from above', Van Gogh applied a remarkably controlled system of graphic signs. Large stabbed dots and small bunches of linear hatchings were used for the rocky foreground, curved and interlaced strokes for the foreground trees; dots were consistently applied for the stubble fields, while intermeshed strokes of brown and black ink, the latter giving a heightened textural effect, represent the vines. As in the entire series of five drawings, the sky was left untouched. Some middle-ground trees and two walking figures were added last in black ink, almost certainly in the studio. The limpidity of distant forms never ceased to delight his northerner's eye – and here they are depicted sharply with the quill pen.

This controlled system of strokes seems linked to a carefully contrived lay-out. Three near-horizontal divisions, the lower two equal in size, can be detected. The result is an essentially angular composition, strongly geometrical and gridlike. This enhanced conceptual approach clearly distinguishes the drawing from the May series.

The presence of the single-line Fontvieille railway in the British Museum drawing (F 1424) projects the spectator into the nineteenth century, thereby reducing the timeless quality of its pendant. The image is further humanized by three late (studio?) additions: the two walking figures on the road, the horse and carriage at left, and the ploughman at middle right. And while a similarly controlled and unified system of graphic signs is applied and sustained in the finest touches of the quill pen, the angular and gridlike formality of its pendant is broken by the dominating curve of the receding road, which in turn is echoed in the slower curve of the foreground descent from the hill of Montmajour.

cat. 188

There is one last presence that Van Gogh insisted upon in looking at these two drawings. Having just read Pierre Loti's *Mme. Chrysanthème*, he insisted that Japanese art should be looked at 'in a very bright room, quite bare, and open to the country. Would you like to experiment with these two drawings of the Crau and the banks of the Rhône, *which do not look Japanese*, but which really are, perhaps more so than some others? [...] Perhaps they need a reed frame, like a thin stick. Here I work in a bare room, four white walls and red paved floor. If I urge you to look at these two drawings in this way, it is because I so much want to give you a *true idea* of the simplicity of nature here' [509].

The projected sixth drawing, showing the whole ruin of Montmajour from the same vantage-point as F 1417 from the May series, was never executed. Nor did Van Gogh ever realise a painting of Montmajour. But in his two series of drawings he extracted its essence, in relative haste in May, but with supreme finality in July. Which is perhaps why he never returned there – at least to paint or draw.

Van Gogh was a reluctant watercolourist. The medium suggests ease and facility: he was constitutionally opposed to both. It was also too thin and bodiless; he sought a medium – or, more often, mixed media – that had a palpable, tangible substance.

Watercolours, therefore, form only a small part of his drawn *oeuvre*, both in his Dutch and in his French periods. In Paris, for instance, he produced only seven watercolours, all in the summer of 1887 – four of Montmartre scenes (F 1401, F 1406, F 1410, F 1411), and three for his mini-series of the Paris ramparts (F 1400, F 1402, F 1403). In Arles, his guarded scepticism about the medium is reflected in the small proportion it represents of his drawn output – just 10%. Eleven sheets exist: four are landscapes (F 1425, F 1464, F 1483, F 1484), one is a figure drawing, the 'Zouave', sent to Emile Bernard, and – the subject of the present section – six are copies after paintings.

cat. 158

These six copies do not form a contemporaneous group. They crop up from time to time over a seven month period. Given Van Gogh's cool attitude towards watercolour, this may imply a rather haphazard approach to their making. Yet such is not the case: continuities and shared characteristics are identifiable.

While references to watercolour in letters from Arles are minimal, they are nonetheless valuable. The most revealing occurs toward the end of May, when Van Gogh asks Theo to include some watercolour materials in an order for paints. And he gives his reason: 'If I have asked for some watercolours it is because I would like to make some pen drawings, to be washed afterward in flat tints like the Japanese prints' [491, 27 May]. This is exactly what happened with his four major landscape watercolours: flat washes and accents of colour were added to what was essentially a reed pen and ink drawing (F 1425, F 1464, F 1483 and, to a lesser extent, F 1484). This establishes a clear distinction between the watercolours done from nature and those made as compositional copies after paintings. With the exception of the 'Zouave', which is a case apart, the watercolour copies after paintings began with pencil or charcoal. Whenever work in pen exists, it was added last.

All but one of the six copies after paintings have some documentary support in the letters. The first two, for instance, were mentioned on 9 April. 'I have sent you sketches of the pictures which are to go to Holland. It goes without saying that the painted studies are more brilliant in colour' [474]. These two watercolours, 'Blossoming Peach Trees' (F 1469) and 'The Langlois Bridge' (F 1480), were born out of Vincent's desire to re-open business negotiations and friendships in Holland, with family (his two art-dealing uncles), erstwhile friends (Tersteeg and Breitner), and Mauve's widow. He had painted 'The Langlois Bridge' (F 397) by mid-March; two weeks later, he painted 'Pink Peach Tree in Blossom' (F 394). He planned to send the bridge to Tersteeg, with a dedication, and the orchard

cat. 189

cat. 35

fig. 35 (F 394)
Vincent van Gogh
Souvenir de Mauve, 1888
Otterlo, Rijksmuseum Kröller-Müller

fig. 36 (F 397)
Vincent van Gogh
The Bridge of Langlois, 1888
Otterlo, Rijksmuseum Kröller-Müller

to Mauve's widow, also with a dedication. To give his brother a preview of the two paintings, Vincent decided to send the two watercolours. A few days later, he resolved to make two painted copies especially for Theo, beginning with the bridge (F 571), and then moving on to the orchard (F 404).

Calling them watercolour 'copies', does not imply that they are laboriously exact replicas. That is far from the case, and was never Van Gogh's intention. For one thing, the differences in format between the paper and the painted prototypes lead inevitably to compositional changes. The format of the Langlois bridge watercolour is square, wheras the proportions of the painting are 65 x 81 cm. But Van Gogh also makes changes: for instance, in the figures of the washerwomen. And because he is working in a relatively unfamiliar medium, the colour is less 'brilliant' than in the painting.

These freely treated copies actually introduced Theo to Vincent's work from Arles. Though he had already been six weeks there, Vincent had not sent either a sketch in a letter, or any other drawings. These two watercolours have that additional claim to historical significance.

That they were done for overtly art-political reasons is emphasized by the fact that no other watercolours were produced in April or May. These two watercolours marked an isolated episode: they were more progress reports for Theo than consciously crafted works of art.

We have to wait until early June – two months later – before the next watercolour. Unfortunately, there is no letter reference to the 'Boats at Saintes-Maries' (F 1429). But it seems clear that it was done soon after the painting was finished, in that its rhythmic shapes and decorative features conform more closely to the painting (F 413) than to the preparatory drawing Van Gogh had done on the spot (F 1428). This watercolour was almost certainly the first to be done with Tasset's watercolours requested on 27 May. It probably dates from 4-5 June.

No more watercolour copies (apart from the 'Zouave') were done during the summer months. It wasn't until early September that Van Gogh felt the need to do another. Having finished his painting of the 'Night Café' (F 463) on 8 September, Vincent promised his brother a watercolour drawing to give him an idea of it. He sent off the watercolour copy (F 1463) the next day, adding another that he had made 'some time ago'. 'I shall perhaps finish by making some Japanese prints' [534, 9 September]. The same day he confirmed to his sister Wil that he had sent Theo a drawing of the 'Night Café', 'which is like a Japanese print' [W 7].

fig. 37

fig. 38

Once again, the variations from the painting are as noticable as the coincidences. Walls and effects of gaslight are simplified; the time on the clock and the shadow cast by the billiard table changed; two wall mirrors are removed; and the chairs assume exaggerated curved profiles. The overall effect is to simplify and refine the painting, both in composition and in colour. In so doing, Van Gogh approaches the use of flat tints that he was so anxious to emulate in Japanese woodblock prints. The other watercolour sent with the 'Night Café' was most probably 'The Mill' (F 1464).

cat. 191

Van Gogh finished his painting of the 'Yellow House' (F 464) toward the end of September. He sent a hasty pen sketch of it (F 1453) with a letter, telling Theo that he would send 'a better drawing than this sketch from memory' [543]. This 'better drawing' (F 1413) was eventually reported as sent in a letter of circa 9 October: 'Did you see that drawing of mine which I put in with Bernard's drawings, representing the house? You can get some idea of the colour. I have a size 30 canvas of that drawing' [548]. As with the 'Night Café', Theo might have gained an impression of the colour and the composition. But once again Vincent provided a free translation rather than a literal copy. The watercolour medium lightens the colours, so that the blue of the sky is much less intense and the greens sharper. In the slightly squarer format, there are compositional shifts and variations, especially in the lamppost at lower left and in the walking figures.

Gauguin arrived in Arles on 23 October, bringing with him 'a magnificent canvas which he has exchanged with Bernard, Breton women in a green field, white, black, green, and a note of red, and the dull flesh tints' [557]. In a further letter of mid-November Van Gogh called it *superb* [562]. More than a year later, he recalled Bernard's picture: 'I saw a picture of his of a Sunday afternoon in Brittany, Breton peasant women, children, peasants, dogs strolling about in a very green meadow; the clothes are black and red, and the women's caps white. But in this crowd there are also two ladies, the one dressed in red, the other in bottle green; they make it a very modern thing. Ask

cat. 192

Theo to show you the watercolour that I made after this picture' [W 16]. His profound admiration for Bernard's 'Breton Women and Children' led him to make this copy in watercolour (F 1422), most probably in November 1888. Another free translation resulted. Bernard's green field becomes yellow; the red and black costumes of the peasants become brown, with red and blue accents; elements are moved (the two dogs, for example); and the two foreground heads are considerably enlarged. Changes in colour, placement, and proportion and the more insistent contour all conspire to give the copy a greater integration. The idea of improving a painted composition, of ironing out the irregularities of hurried brushwork, and refining elements in the over-all lay-out, does not appear to have been deliberately practised in these copies. Yet such are the consequences in the 'Night Café' and the copy after Bernard. And these two watercolours come closest to achieving the Japanese look in the handling of the medium.

All six watercolour copies are conscious celebrations of what Van Gogh himself considered his major works. Reflections of such decisions, ephemeral message carriers though they were, these watercolours now assume the mantle of major works of art themselves – despite the reluctant watercolourist.

fig. 37 (F 463)
Vincent van Gogh
The Night Café, 1888
New Haven, Yale University Art Gallery
(Bequest of Stephen Carlton Clark)

fig. 38 (F 1463)
Vincent van Gogh
The Night Café, 1888
Private Collection

In mid-July 1888, Van Gogh took some thirty canvases from their stretchers and nailed them to his studio walls to help speed up their drying for despatch to Theo in Paris. In so doing, he was able to retouch and sign some of them. He had just finished and posted off his five large Montmajour drawings to his brother, hoping that their sale to a Paris dealer would facilitate Gauguin's arrival in Arles. And it was to evolve other ways of helping Gauguin – and the young Emile Bernard – that he began a series of drawings based on the very paintings that he had nailed up to dry.

He began with Bernard. On 15 July, he wrote: 'Perhaps you will be inclined to forgive me for not replying to your letter immediately, when you see that I am sending you a little batch of sketches along with this letter [...] Let me know whether you will consent to make sketches after your Breton studies for me. I have a batch ready to be forwarded, but before it goes off I want to do at least half-a-dozen new subjects for you, pen-and-ink sketches' [B 10].

Van Gogh's intention was not just an exchange of drawings to enable each of them to see what the other had been doing. He also planned to send Bernard's drawings on to Theo, whom, he hoped, might then buy a painting by Bernard.

On 17 July, he again wrote to Bernard: 'I have just sent you – today – nine more sketches after painted studies. In this way you will see subjects taken from the sort of scenery that inspires 'father' Cézanne, for the Crau near Aix is pretty similar to the country surrounding Tarascon or the Crau here [...] As I know how much you like Cézanne, I thought these sketches of Provence might please you; not that there is much resemblance between a drawing of mine and one by Cézanne' [B 11].

What process did Van Gogh use in selecting these fifteen drawings for Bernard? Did they reflect what he considered to be his own best works? Or did he bear in mind Bernard's own tastes and preferences? Seven of the drawings were from the harvest series, chosen as emblems of Provence with Cézannesque connotations. Two Saintes-Maries motifs show Bernard something of the Mediterranean, reminding him of discussions they had had in letters [B 6], and also recording Van Gogh's high regard for these two small canvases (F 417 and F 420). Another view of the Crau (F 1554) provided a poetic contrast to a garden in the Place Lamartine (F 1450) the last another of Van Gogh's own favourites. Tougher, more prosaic, more redolent of *la vie moderne* were two urban scenes of a canal by the gasworks (F 1444) and strollers by the Rhône (F 1507) that would surely remind Bernard of motifs in Asnières and Clichy, those northern suburbs of Paris where they had both worked in 1887. The 'cover' drawing, so to say, was the one figure piece, 'The Zouave'. Van Gogh thought of this Zouave's head as his own contribution to a painting of a brothel scene that he and Bernard would eventually collaborate on. This is why it is the only drawing that he worked up with colour, using crayon and watercolour, then adding the dedication to Bernard. (Because of the mixed media and of its essential place in the Bernard set, it is placed here and not in the 'Watercolours after Paintings' section.)

Stylistically, these fifteen drawings are uniformly consistent. Done on wove paper of identical size (one quarter that of the recently completed Montmajour sheets), they are never literal copies, more improvisatory translations, of their 'parent' paintings. Often the format differs, so that unavoidably compositions are now truncated, now enlarged, with inevitable changes of relationships and proportions. With one notable exception (F 1444), a summary pencil underdrawing establishes the composition before reed and quill pens take over. Despite appearing uncontrolled and multi-directional, the pen strokes do have a certain logic and resolved stability. Indeed, a conscious system of division exists in the representational function of hatching (very little cross-hatching), whorls and dots. Dots in particular were used with discretion: Van Gogh was well aware of Bernard's personal dislike of Signac, and his ideological opposition to Pointillism [see B 1]. The skies in these drawings contain no dots. But they are used systematically to articulate all horizontal surfaces, whether road or street, river or canal embankment paths.

Bernard received these drawings at Saint-Briac, on the north coast of Brittany. When he joined Gauguin in Pont-Aven in mid-August, Bernard had made them into an album that he showed to Gauguin. (Unfortunately, Bernard began breaking up the Album in the 1890s, and by 1906, he had sold virtually all the drawings.)

Unconsciously, it was Gauguin who provoked a further outburst of drawing after the nailed-up paintings. For some time, Van Gogh had hoped that the Australian artist, John Peter Russell (1858-1931), would buy one of Gauguin's Martinique canvases from Theo. By so doing, Russell would contribute towards paying Gauguin's debts in Pont-Aven and enable him to take the train for Arles. Vincent was greatly disappointed when Russell wrote on 22 July [501b] refusing to make the purchase. However, four days later, on 26 July, Van Gogh received a letter from Gauguin, the most optimistic to date: his health was improved, his work was going well, and he spoke of coming to Arles.

This positive news spurred Van Gogh to reconsider Russell's refusal. He described his plan to Theo on 31 July: 'I am working hard for Russell, I thought that I would do him a series of drawings after my painted studies; I believe that he will look upon them kindly, and that, at least I hope so, will bring him to make a deal [...] If we prod Russell, perhaps he will take the Gauguin that you bought [...] When I write him, sending the drawings, it will of course be to urge him to make up his mind [...] I have eight and shall do twelve' [516].

So, between 31 July and 3 August, a fortnight after completing the set of fifteen drawings for Bernard, Van Gogh did twelve drawings for Russell. In so doing, both motives and motifs changed. Once again, he considered the intended recipient, adjusting both his choice of drawings and the resulting style to suit differing preferences and prejudices. First of all, he was able to consider some recent paintings completed since his sending of the Bernard set. He chose three of them for Russell: the horizontal flower garden (F 1454), the head of the mousmé (F 1503) and the head of Roulin (F 1458). Secondly, he was less concerned than he had been with Bernard in emphasizing 'sketches of Provence' *à la Cézanne*. Instead of the seven harvest drawings sent to Bernard, Russell received only four, without the 'Sower'. Also excluded were the two river and canal views which had no relevance for Russell. Unique to Russell, however, were two drawings showing motifs after two *lost* paintings (F 1449 and F 1502a).

fig. 41
cat. 198

The twelve drawings for Russell also display stylistic characteristics distinct from the Bernard set. They are executed less hastily; as well as being more finished, they are more stylized. The major distinction lies in the prevalent use of the dot. Dots infest and overrun every sky; they also articulate background and facial modelling in two drawings of heads (F 1482a and F 1503). A decisive comparison between the Bernard and Russell sets can be made by juxtaposing the Budapest and Philadelphia drawings after the painting, 'Mas de Provence' (F 1426 and F 1427, after F 425).

cat. 196

All Van Gogh's efforts to win over Russell were in vain. Russell was then engaged in building a house and studio on Belle-Ile off the Brittany coast. He did not answer Van Gogh for over a month; and when he did, he still refused to buy Gauguin's painting of Martinique (see 536).

But Van Gogh was not yet finished with his drawings after paintings. Already, on 31 July, when telling Theo of his plan to make twelve drawings for Russell, he added: 'I hope to do these sketches after the studies for you as well. You will see that they have something of a Japanese air' [516].

And by 6 August, he asked: 'Did I tell you that I had sent the drawings to friend Russell? At the moment I am doing practically the same ones over again for you, there will likewise be twelve. You will then see better what there is in the painted studies in the way of drawing. I have already told you that I always have to fight against the mistral, which makes it absolutely impossible to be master of your stroke. That accounts for the 'haggard' look of the studies' [518].

Finally, on 8 August, he sent Theo only five, rather than the projected twelve, drawings after paintings, in the same roll as the three large Garden drawings. He explained: 'Now the harvest, the Garden, the Sower, and the two marines are sketches after painted studies. I think all these ideas are good, but the painted studies lack clearness of touch. That is another reason why I felt it necessary to draw them' [519]. Though he added that he hoped to do more, he never in fact completed the intended dozen. These five drawings must surely be taken as reflecting Van Gogh's own favourites among his paintings. Because of his constant complaint that the mistral was the principal cause of the 'haggard' look in his paintings, he deliberately chose motifs that had not been affected by it. He chose the 'Sower' (F 1441) and a Harvest scene (F 1492) – he had no need to repeat 'La Moisson' having already sent Theo a full-scale watercolour drawing of it (F 1483) – two Saintes-Maries seascapes (F 1430b and F 1431) and the 'Garden with Weeping Tree' (F 1451). Two of these were among the few paintings he singled out as worth putting on stretchers when they were finally taken to Paris by the Zouave Milliet in mid-August (F 417 and F 428).

In Theo's reduced set, the process of stylization, already a feature of the Russell drawings, is carried further. In addition to enhancing his painted studies in clearness of touch and uniformity of finish, Van Gogh improved them in placement and proportion of parts. This can be seen in the 'Sower' (F 1441) where the conception is made grander, even monumental, by the enlargement of sun, wheat, and the sower himself.

If ever proof were needed that Van Gogh was motivated by acts of will and self-determination; that he consciously adjusted his style to the specific demands of the work in hand; that he adapted motifs to motives – then these thirty-two drawings done after his own paintings from mid-July to early August clearly demonstrate it. Each group is stylistically separate and possesses its own idiosyncratic traits; each group demonstrates how Van Gogh could control and manipulate his reed and quill pens within an established formula. There are no odd-ones-out, no 'rogues'. The Bernard-Russell-Theo groups of drawings are as much conscious acts of willed stylistic decisions as are the five large Montmajour drawings that immediately preceded them.

For Theo, there was a postscript, in case he felt disappointed about receiving only five of the promised twelve drawings. On 11 August, Van Gogh began a letter to his brother with a triumphant fanfare. 'Shortly you are going to make the acquaintance of Sieur Patience Escalier, a kind of *Man with a Hoe* [a reference to Millet's painting], former Camargue peasant, now a gardener in a *mas* of the Crau. This very day I have sent you the drawing that I have made after this painting, as well as the drawing of the postman Rollin [sic]' [520].

For these two portrait drawings, Van Gogh virtually doubled the size of the sheet used for the three earlier groups, and reverted to Whatman paper. Their impact, as surrogate paintings, was further enhanced by his giving them drawn inner frames.

The 'Portrait of Patience Escalier' (F 1460) was drawn after the earlier of the two portraits Van Gogh made (F 443); the 'Portrait of Joseph Roulin' (F 1459) is based on 'the half-length with hands', now in Boston (F 432), but there are interesting

modifications. (Even in the drawing itself, pentimenti exist between the hastily indicated pencil outlines and their subsequent working over in pen.) Compared with the painting, the image has been extended on all four sides. Much more of both table and chair is shown, but the spatially complicating diagonal of the receding wall is eliminated. There are numerous minor changes and variations: the zigzag of both sleeve and coat and its crumpling effect on the buttons, the relative smallness of the right hand, and the different angle at which the POSTES cap is worn. The result is that Joseph-Etienne Roulin (1841-1903), then aged forty-seven, looks older, squatter, more vulnerable, than he appears in the Boston portrait.

More importantly, the glass on the table, absent in the painting, must surely be an explicit reference to Roulin's immoderate drinking. Images of lone drinkers abound in French illustrated periodicals of the period, as well as in the paintings of Manet (his 'Bon Bock' of 1873 could have been known to Van Gogh), Degas, Forain, Toulouse-Lautrec and Raffaelli. In the case of Roulin, Vincent admitted to Theo: 'My friend the postman [...] lives a great deal in cafés, and is certainly more or less of a drinker, and has been so all his life. But he is so much the reverse of a sot, his exaltation is so natural, so intelligent, and he argues with such sweep, in the style of Garibaldi' [550].

This portrait drawing seems to be an improved and more elaborate adaptation of the Boston painting. Van Gogh complained of Roulin's stiffness when posing. The introduction of the drinking glass imparts a more natural effect, which is sustained by the less arbitrary cut of the chair and the sitter's crumpled angularities.

cat. 199

cat. 200
cat. 201

cat. 199

fig. 42

cat. 202

This category I have called Independent Drawings: Van Gogh did not see them as such. They are akin to the group of watercolours after paintings. All the remaining groups consist of series deliberately undertaken, compact in style, comparable in intention and function, close in date. But there is surely room for a category encompassing important drawings of similar intention and purpose that are spread over months, that punctuate the artist's activity, more often than not singly. Van Gogh never saw them as a continuing series: he never linked any of them in a consecutive way, as he would often do with his paintings. They accumulated naturally, by the repetition of a working process. And the links are undeniably there, not only in the 'large' format, but in their sometimes mysterious liaisons with painting.

These mysterious liaisons take on several guises. The crux of the matter is the phenomenon of alternative recordings or 'takes' of a motif. Often, in discovering – or deciding, after long contemplation on – a new motif, Van Gogh would both draw and paint it. Can the drawing be thought of as a preparatory study, even a cartoon, for the painting? Or does it simply represent a first familiarization with the motif? Or is it in fact an entirely separate confrontation, with compositional changes, that gives it a certain parity with the related painting? The answers differ: these 'Independent Drawings' play their own variations on the theme.

cat. 203 - 210   There are fourteen of them. In chronological sequence, they are F 1439, F 1478, F 1425, F 1484, F 1483, F 1464, F 1443, F 1455, F 1456, F 1457, F 1462, F 1519, F 1468, and F 1467. Eight of them are in the present exhibition and discussion of the independent drawings will concentrate on these.

fig. 30   The drawing of the village of Saintes-Maries, dominated by
fig. 39   its church (F 1439) operates in parity with a painting (F 416). Quite clearly they are different recordings of the motif: there is a slight change in their viewpoints, while their formats – one horizontal, the other vertical – impose a more fundamental variation.

In early June, Van Gogh discovered two new motifs: a Provencal *mas*, or farmhouse, surrounded by enormous haystacks, and the plain of the Crau with the abbey of Montmajour in the background. Unfortunately, the absence from the exhibition of the three major watercolours – F 1425, F 1483, and F 1484 – precludes a detailed discussion of the subtleties of their status
fig. 34   *vis à vis* the two large paintings that evolved from Van Gogh's
fig. 40   prolonged scrutiny of each motif (F 412 and F 425). But the draw-
cat. 204   ing of the farmhouse (F 1478) partially compensates, the more so as it provides an excellent example of the close liaison that exists between the two media.

Inscribed 'Un Mas de Provence', this drawing is clearly related to the painting now in the National Gallery of Art, Washington, D.C. (F 565). It was almost certainly the first draw-

ing Van Gogh made in Arles after his return from Saintes-Maries on 3 June. Not immediately, however.

Working from drawings done in Saintes-Maries, he first completed three paintings in his studio (F 413, F 419, and F 420).   fig. 32
The latter two paintings are of especial significance for what will eventually happen in the case of the 'Mas de Provence' drawing and its related painting. In simulating the effect of an outdoor painting by working from drawings in his studio, Van Gogh did not literally follow the drawn prototype. Four kinds of changes are observable. Changes in format that lead to a cut here, an addition there. Changes of alignment in the composition done in the course of painting. Simplification of details, and a much more generalized treatment. The addition of other details – a chimney, for instance, or smoke. Each painting is a study in the almost arbitrary use of complementary colour contrasts; and each displays a profound fondness for zinc white.

A wholly comparable process occurred with the 'Mas de   cat. 204
Procence' drawing and the Washington painting. Slight differences in format enabled Van Gogh to extend the painting a little at the right and in the foreground. Alignments differ marginally: for example, the line of hills at left in relation to the building. Details are suppressed – on the facade of the farmhouse most noticeably. And some details are added – the enlargement of the tree behind the farmhouse. Cumulatively, these shifts and variations are similar to those in the Saintes-Maries pairs. But, additionally, the Washington painting not only has comparable surface qualities that belie its studio execution, but it also shows the play of complementary colour contrasts and contains the same zinc white in the path. (One has only to compare the *matière* and handling of the contemporaneous painting, 'Wheat Field' (F 564), to sense the difference between a fluid, improvised, executed-on-the-spot painting, and one that exhibits the slower deliberations of a studio painting).

The drawing of the 'Mas de Provence' was thus used directly as a working document for the Washington painting. The two do not represent separate recordings of the same motif: the observable changes are attributable to a studio working process directly comparable to that which had just operated with the Saintes-Maries pairs.

Another, but different, studio situation occurred less than a fortnight after Van Gogh had drawn and painted 'Un Mas de Provence'. A week of feverish activity painting the harvest was ended by four days of continuous rain. From 20 to 23 June, Vincent was compelled to work in his studio. He invited a Zouave soldier to pose for him. Hitherto, in Arles, he had painted only one portrait: 'The Old Arlésienne' (F 390) done during the first days of his stay.

Now, as he reported to Theo on 21 June [501] and to Bernard on 23 June [B 8], he began two paintings of the Zouave, and a drawing showing him seated (F 1443), which he found 'ugly',   cat. 203

but 'all the same, figure interests me more than landscape' [502].

Executed on full-size Whatman paper, the drawing shows a quite separate confrontation with the model than the two paintings (F 423 and F 424). Pose, costume (trousers rather than pantaloons), pipe, and arbitrarily indicated background all emphasize this. The pose has earlier analogies with drawings of almshouse men in The Hague, as well as life drawings from Antwerp. (It also has the awkward, almost brutal grace of a Degas dancer!) The directly frontal confrontation, honest and without grace, masks any pretentions at elegant presentation. But the figure was the essence, the crux of the matter: the red tiles of the studio floor are just indicated, with other summary and somewhat ambiguous shapes completing the setting. A hasty pencil armature enabled the reed pen to elaborate the decoratively exotic uniform. The touches of Chinese white are rare additions to an Arles drawing. However 'ugly' Van Gogh found the result, he nevertheless signed the drawing and despatched it to Theo on 23 June [502]. It remains Van Gogh's only drawing done directly from the model in Arles. Other figure drawings were made after completed paintings. For example, the portrait of the Zouave sent to Bernard (F 1482) *cat. 193* was drawn a month after he had finished the painting.

'I have a new drawing of a garden full of flowers, and two painted studies as well [...] There is one vertical and another horizontal of the same subject, size 30 canvases' Van Gogh announced to Theo about 19 July [512]. The two paintings, F 429 and F 430, and the drawing, horizontal in format on full- *fig. 41* size Whatman paper (F 1454), thus echo the triple relationship that Van Gogh had already set up in his studies of the Zouave. The drawing occupies a pivotal place in Van Gogh's complex stylistic evolution in the month of July, coming a week after the five large Montmajour 'substitute paintings', and between the drawings he did for Bernard and Russell. It possesses all the richly decorative range of subtle graphic signs of the Montmajour drawings, and exemplifies the three-part technical procedures that he had codified there. But there is one notable addition: the sky is now suffused with dots. Such dotted skies will eventually invade all the drawings for Russell; but the garden drawing can claim priority in its deployment of the dot.

On the one hand, these dots have a simplified abstract function, expressing Van Gogh's urge to cover the entire sheet, as if his pen had a horror of a vacuum. On the other, they can be read descriptively, simulating the intense mid-summer heat of Provence. Derivations have been sought outside Van Gogh's own self-generating impulses: in the mechanical dots of illustrated images, in Japanese prints, or in Pointillist drawings and paintings. All these were well known to Van Gogh: yet the theory of self-generation still seems more persuasive. For their use was specific; they only appear in the drawn Provencal skies of July and August – in the copies after paintings for Russell and Theo, in three large drawings of gardens, in two 'small' landscapes (F 1477 and F 1495), and, significantly, in the back- *cat. 173*

fig. 39 (F 416)
Vincent van Gogh
View of Saintes-Maries-de-la-Mer, 1888
Otterlo, Rijksmuseum Kröller–Müller

fig. 40 (F 425)
Vincent van Gogh
Hayricks, 1888
Otterlo, Rijksmuseum Kröller–Müller

fig. 42

ground of the portrait of 'Patience Escalier' (F 1460) where they potently simulate 'the full furnace of the harvest at the height of midday' [520]. After August they disappear.

This garden drawing, like that of the village of Saintes-Maries, is a clear-cut example of an independent confrontation with the motif. Its differences from the horizontal painted version (F 429) derive from a small shift in the viewing angle and the resulting cut of the composition.

Van Gogh chose not to send the drawing to Theo immediately – as he had done with the *Zouave*. Instead, he held on to it until he had completed two further drawings of Provencal gardens. These were announced in a letter of 8 August: 'I have just sent off three large drawings [...] The little cottage garden done vertically is, I think, the best of the three large ones [F 1456]. The one with the sunflowers [F 1457] is a little garden of a bathing establishment, the third garden, horizontal, is the one I made some painted studies of as well. Under the blue sky the orange, yellow, red splashes of the flowers take on an amazing brilliance, and in the limpid air there is something or other happier, more lovely than in the North [...] If the drawings I send you are too hard, it is because I have done them in such a way as to be able later on, if they're still around, to use them as guides for painting' [519].

These two garden drawings were most probably executed on 5-6 August, rather than contemporaneously with the horizontal garden drawing of circa 19 July. They are conceivably connected with the tour of the farms that Van Gogh made in the company of 'someone who knows the country [...] Oh, these farm gardens, with their lovely big red Provencal roses, and the vines and the fig trees! It is all a poem, and the eternal bright sunshine too, in spite of which the foliage remains very green' [519].

If indeed, these two drawings date from 5-6 August, they were the immediate cause of Vincent's failure to finish the twelve drawn copies after paintings for Theo. Interestingly, Van Gogh sent those five small drawings together with the three garden drawings, as if the latter compensated for the missing seven copies.

The process of refinement and stylization already observed in the copies for Russell and Theo continues in these two garden drawings. Which is why Van Gogh speaks of them being 'too hard'. They are articulated with the same attentive touches, clear, precise, and controlled.

In the letter that followed his sending of the drawings to Theo, Van Gogh speaks of having his eye on half-a-dozen subjects, 'especially that little cottage garden I sent you the drawing of yesterday' [521, 9 August]. The painting (F 578) must have been realised soon afterwards, but without benefit of the drawing at his side. This is a clear instance of separate 'takes', with inevitable diversity in viewpoint, alignments and details.

A week after sending his three garden drawings, Van Gogh reported to Theo: 'Just now I am working on a study like this

fig. 41 (F 1454)
Vincent van Gogh
A Flowering Garden, 1888
Private Collection

fig. 42 (F 1460)
Vincent van Gogh
Portrait of Patience Escalier, 1888
Cambridge, Mass., Fogg Art Museum
(Bequest of Grenville L. Winthrop)

[sketch in letter], of boats seen from the quay above, the two boats are pink tinged with violet, the water is bright green, no sky, a raw dull tricolour. A workman with a barrow is unloading sand. I also have a drawing of it' [524]. Milliet, the Zouave officer, was about to take thirty-six rolled canvases to Paris; and Van Gogh included at the last moment 'a drawing of the picture I'm working on at present – the boats with the man unloading sand' [525, 15 August].

It seems clear from this letter that the large drawing on Whatman paper preceded the painting (F 449). And there is no question of its being a preparatory study. Not only the viewpoint, but also the time of day differ, while the mistral's effects are evident in the drawing. Changes and variations occur in the figures of workmen and fishermen; while the *mise en page* is more detailed, allowing glimpses of the quay-side buildings toward the upper centre culminating in the Trinquetaille Bridge across the Rhône.

The execution is less 'hard' than in the three garden drawings. And, very apparent here, is the 'split' line effect, but accompanied by the diminishing-in-size dashes that register the receding Rhône. Final animated touches with quill pen, generally in a darker ink, repeat the three-tier progression that Van Gogh first established in his July series of Montmajour drawings.

Drawing became a subsidiary concern as, from mid-August until Gauguin's arrival in Arles on 23 October, Van Gogh devoted his energies to producing thirty size 30 canvases as a decoration for the Yellow House. Painting became paramount. The liaison with drawing virtually ceased. In fact, only one motif was shared: a view of the cafe du Forum, in the very heart of the town, a rare venture on Van Gogh's part within the town's walls.

fig. 43

In describing the painting (F 467) to his sister Wil [W 7], Van Gogh emphasized the importance of working directly on the spot at night if a painter is tackling a night scene, rather than working from a drawing in the daylight of the studio. He was

t. 208

silent about the painting to Theo; and the large drawing (F 1519) that shares the same motif was not mentioned to anyone – not even to his artist-friend, Eugene Boch when, in a letter of 3 October, Van Gogh recalled the cafe 'where we used to go' [544a].

In fact, the Place du Forum was not Vincent's side of town. And it was the more affluent Boch who enabled the two artists to visit the cafe in early September. Boch left Arles very early in the morning of 4 September; and it seems probable that Van Gogh returned to the café du Forum that day to make his large drawing.

For it must surely be a daytime drawing. How else would Van Gogh have been able to see so clearly the details of the receding buildings in the street, or pick out so distinctly the lettering on cafe and shop front – 'Buvette' and 'Coiffeur'? Such details are absent in the painting, simply because of his work-

ing at night. Also, in the drawing, the reflecting light effect from the gas-lamp is not registered: there was no need of it during the day-time.

The usual compositional differences between drawing and painting are present. The figures, for instance; the lack of the tree at right; and a slight adjustment in viewpoint, where the awning above the cafe terrace is given greater amplitude in the pictorial space, thereby obscuring the end of the street and reducing the amount of sky.

The treatment of the sky in the drawing is crucial in deciding that a day scene is represented. If one compares the compulsive, spidery horizontals, at first sight a possible evocation of a night sky, with two small letter-drawings that were done after paintings of day-time subjects (F 1453 and F 1465), the aggressive graphic convention remains the same in the skies. These three evocations of drawn skies are identical. And that of the cafe drawing, in any case, is minus the stars that are so important a feature of the painting – and which are prominently represented in another small letter-drawing (F 1515), this time after the other painted night-scene of September 1888, the view of the Rhône (F 474).

The drawing of the café du Forum, then, is separate in view, disposition, figures, and, above all, opposition of day to night. If it is datable to 4 September, then it just precedes another night-scene on which Van Gogh worked on three successive nights from 5 to 7 September – the 'Night Cafe' (F 463).

fig. 37

The rapprochement between painting and drawing ceased during Gauguin's two-month stay in Arles. Not a single original drawing by Van Gogh survives – not even a sketchbook. (That is discounting the watercolour copy after Bernard.) Nor can any drawings be traced before May 1889. Only in his very last letter from Arles, written between 3 and 6 May, does Van Gogh return to drawing. 'I am thinking again of beginning to draw more with a reed pen, which, like last year's views of Montmajour for instance, costs less and distracts my mind just as much. Today I made a drawing of that sort, which has turned out very dark and rather melancholy for one of spring, but anyhow whatever happens to me and in whatever circumstances I find myself, it's something which will keep me occupied enough and in some fashion might even make me a sort of livelihood' [590]. And later in this same letter, he goes on to describe his room, where he had hung Japanese Prints, two lithographs after Delacroix, a print of Meissonier's 'Reader', and two large reed pen drawings.

Van Gogh took these two reed pen drawings with him to Saint-Rémy on 8 May. And in sending them to Theo on about 19 June, he names them as 'Hospital at Arles' and 'Weeping Tree in the Grass', adding that they 'continued those of Montmajour of some time ago' [595].

It seems most probable that the 'very dark and rather melancholy' drawing of spring, done on 3 May, was 'Weeping Tree in the Grass' (F 1468). And that the courtyard of the

cat. 209 - 210

hospital at Arles (F 1467) was drawn a day or so later. These, then, were hung in Vincent's room during his last days in Arles, taken to Saint-Rémy, and sent off to Theo around 19 June 1889.

Both of these drawings have special relationships with paintings. In concluding the sequence of 'large' independent drawings, they also reverse the accepted processes. Instead of being done before the painting (like F 1478), instead of being done more or less contemporaneously with the painting (like F 1455 and F 1462), they were drawn after the paintings had been completed.

'Weeping Tree in the Grass' is the last of a long line of drawings and paintings whose motif was taken from a garden in the Place Lamartine (see F 428, F 468, F 1465 - after a lost painting - F 1421, F 1450 and F 1451).

Van Gogh felt it was imbued with an unintended dark melancholy. This may have been the result of his long hibernation as a draughtsman: his last reed pen drawing of the café du Forum had been made in September 1888. It was necessary to re-familiarize himself with the medium. And it was this process of re-discovery that accounts for the inhibited deliberateness and Gothic spikiness of the drawing. Otherwise, the melancholic, sombre tone has a certain appropriateness: it represented Van Gogh's farewell to his favourite Arlesien motif - one of the gardens in the Place Lamartine opposite his Yellow House.

Van Gogh described his painting of the courtyard of the hospital at Arles (F 519) in a letter of 30 April 1889: 'It is an arcaded gallery like those one finds in Arab buildings, all white-washed. In front of those galleries an antique garden with a pond in the middle, and eight flower beds, forget-me-nots, Christmas roses, anemones, ranunculus, wallflowers, daisies, and so on. And under the gallery orange trees and oleander' [W 11].

In the drawing, however, the large pots of 'orange trees and oleander' have been taken from the arcade and placed in the garden, thus confirming that it was executed several days after the painting. And the changed viewpoint further emphasizes the drawing's independent qualities. Both views were taken from the first floor of the east wing of the courtyard: in the painting, at the south-east end looking towards the north-west, in the drawing, at the north-east end looking towards the south-west. And - a delightful conceit - Van Gogh signed the drawing on the watering-can, just as he had signed the bucket in the 'Sunflower Garden' of August 1888 (F 1457).

Stylistically, the hospital drawing has something of the Northern Gothic spikiness of the 'Weeping Tree'. Descriptive particularities are realised in virile short hatchings, loosely variegated dots, and small irregular ovals. It is a large 'croquis hâtif', far from the 'hard' style of the three Provencal Gardens. In this combination of loosely structured touches and rapid working, it presages the early drawings of Saint-Rémy.

cat. 204
cat. 205

cat. 210

cat. 168
cat. 201

cat. 209

cat. 206

fig. 43 (F 467)
Vincent van Gogh
Café du Forum, 1888
Otterlo, Rijksmuseum Kröller–Müller

fig. 44 (F 519)
Vincent van Gogh
The Courtyard of the Hospital in Arles, 1889
Winterthur, Sammlung Oskar Reinhart 'Am Römerholz'

165

Path through a Field with Willows
March 1888
Pencil, pen and brown ink on wove paper, 255 x 345 mm
Annotated l.c.: Arles Mars 88
F 1499 JH 1372
Amsterdam, Rijksmuseum Vincent van Gogh
(Vincent van Gogh Stichting)

166

Meadow with Flowers
April 1888
Pencil, quill and reed pen and brown ink on wove paper,
255 x 345 mm
F 1474 JH 1407
Amsterdam, Rijksmuseum Vincent van Gogh
(Vincent van Gogh Stichting)

167

Farmhouse in the Wheat Field
April 1888
Pencil, quill and reed pen and brown ink on wove paper,
255 x 345 mm
F 1415 JH 1408
Amsterdam, Rijksmuseum Vincent van Gogh
(Vincent van Gogh Stichting)

168

Public Garden opposite the Yellow House
April 1888
Quill, reed pen and brown ink on wove paper,
255 x 345 mm
F 1421 JH 1414
Amsterdam, Rijksmuseum Vincent van Gogh
(Vincent van Gogh Stichting)

169

View of La Roubine du Roi with Washerwomen
April 1888
Pencil, quill and reed pen and brown ink on wove paper,
225 x 345 mm
F 1473 JH 1405
Munich, Staatliche Graphische Sammlung

170

The Road to Tarascon with a Man Walking
April 1888
Pencil, quill and reed pen and brown ink on wove paper,
250 x 340 mm
F 1502 JH 1492
Zurich, Kunsthaus (Graphische Sammlung)

ARLES

171

Public Garden in the Place Lamartine
April – May 1888
Pencil, quill and reed pen and brown ink on wove paper,
350 x 260 mm
F 1476 JH 1409
Private Collection

172

Public Garden in the Place Lamartine with the Yellow House
May 1888
Pencil, reed pen and brown ink on yellowish paper,
315 x 495 mm
F 1513 JH 1412
Amsterdam, Rijksmuseum Vincent van Gogh
(Vincent van Gogh Stichting)

173

Public Garden in the Place Lamartine
August 1888
Pencil, quill and reed pen with brown and black ink
on wove paper, 320 x 245 mm
F 1477 JH 1411
Amsterdam, Rijksmuseum Vincent van Gogh
(Vincent van Gogh Stichting)

174

Provencal Orchard
April 1888
Pencil, reed pen and brown ink, heightened with white
and pink on laid paper, 395 x 540 mm
Annotated and signed l.l.: Verger de Provence Vincent
F 1414 JH 1385
Amsterdam, Rijksmuseum Vincent van Gogh
(Vincent van Gogh Stichting)

175

Orchard with Arles in the Background
April 1888
Pencil, quill and reed pen with violet and black ink
on laid paper, 535 x 395 mm
F 1516   JH 1376
Glenn Falls, New York, The Hyde Collection

176

The Langlois Bridge
May 1888
Pencil, quill and reed pen with brown ink on Ingres paper,
355 x 470 mm
Watermark: PL BAS
F 1470 JH 1377
Stuttgart, Staatsgalerie (Graphische Sammlung)

177

Bank of the Rhône
April 1888
Pencil, quill and reed pen and violet ink on laid paper,
385 x 605 mm
Watermark: AL PL BAS
Signed and annotated l.l.: Bords du Rhône Vincent
F 1472a JH 1497a
Rotterdam, Museum Boymans-van Beuningen

178

Olive Trees at Montmajour
May 1888
Black chalk, reed pen and violet ink on Ingres paper,
312 x 481 mm
Watermark: PL BAS
Annotated l.c.: Bruyère
F 1493 JH 1436
Amsterdam, Rijksmuseum Vincent van Gogh
(Vincent van Gogh Stichting)

179

View of La Crau
May 1888
Pencil, quill and reed pen and brownish ink on Ingres paper,
290 x 470 mm
Watermark: PL BAS
Annotated l.l.: Vue de la Crau
F 1419 JH 1430
Essen, Museum Folkwang

181

Two Cottages in Saintes-Maries-de-la-Mer
Late May – early June 1888
Pencil, reed pen and brown ink on Ingres paper,
290 x 460 mm
Watermark: PL BAS
F 1440 JH 1451
Mr. and Mrs. Eugene Thaw

180

Street in Saintes-Maries-de-la-Mer
Late May – early June 1888
Pencil, reed pen and brown ink on Ingres paper,
305 x 470 mm
Watermark: PL BAS
F 1434 JH 1449
Private Collection, USA

182

Three Cottages in Saintes-Maries-de-la-Mer
Late May – early June 1888
Pencil, reed pen and brown ink on Ingres paper,
303 x 474 mm
Watermark: AL
F 1438 JH 1448
Amsterdam, Rijksmuseum Vincent van Gogh
(Vincent van Gogh Stichting)

ARLES

183

View of Arles from Montmajour
May 1888
Pencil, quill and reed pen and brown ink on Whatman paper,
480 x 590 mm
Watermark: J WHATMAN TURKEY MILL 1879
Signed l.l.: Vincent
F 1452 JH 1437
Oslo, Nasjonalgalleriet

184

Montmajour
July 1888
Pencil, quill and reed pen with brown and black ink
on Whatman paper, 475 x 590 mm
Watermark: J WHATMAN TURKEY MILL 1879
Signed l.r.: Vincent
F 1446 JH 1504
Amsterdam, Rijksprentenkabinet (Rijksmuseum)

185

Olive Trees: Montmajour
July 1888
Pencil, quill and reed pen with brown and black ink
on Whatman paper, 480 x 600 mm
Watermark: J WHATMAN TURKEY MILL 1879
Signed l.l.: Vincent
F o JH o
Tournai, Musée des Beaux-Arts de Tournai
(Ancienne Collection H. van Cutsem)

186

Rocks with Trees: Montmajour
July 1888
Pencil, quill and reed pen with brown and black ink
on Whatman paper, 492 x 609 mm
Watermark: J WHATMAN TURKEY MILL 1879
Signed l.r.: Vincent
F 1447 JH 1503
Amsterdam, Rijksmuseum Vincent van Gogh
(Vincent van Gogh Stichting)

187

La Crau seen from Montmajour
July 1888
Pencil, quill and reed pen with brown and black ink
on Whatman paper, 490 x 611 mm
Watermark: J WHATMAN TURKEY MILL 1879
Signed and annotated l.l.: Vincent La Crau Vue prise
à Mont Major
F 1420 JH 1501
Amsterdam, Rijksmuseum Vincent van Gogh
(Vincent van Gogh Stichting)

188

Landscape of Montmajour with Train
July 1888
Pencil, quill and reed pen with brown and black ink
on Whatman paper, 490 x 610 mm
Watermark: J WHATMAN TURKEY MILL 1879
Signed l.l.: Vincent and annotated l.r., in cartouche:
La campagne du côté des bords du Rhône
F 1424 JH 1502
London, The Trustees of the British Museum

189

Blossoming Peach Trees
April 1888
Black chalk and watercolour on Whatman paper,
454 x 306 mm
Watermark: J WHATMAN
F 1469 JH 1384
Amsterdam, Rijksmuseum Vincent van Gogh
(Vincent van Gogh Stichting)

190

The Langlois Bridge
April 1888
Pencil, pen and watercolour on Whatman paper, 300 x 300 mm
Annotated and signed l.l.: Le pont de l'Anglais à Arles Vincent
F 1480 JH 1382
Private Collection

191

The Yellow House
October 1888
Pencil, pen and brown ink, watercolour, 257 x 320 mm
Watermark: GLASLAM
F 1413 JH 1591
Amsterdam, Rijksmuseum Vincent van Gogh
(Vincent van Gogh Stichting)

192

Breton Women and Children (after Emile Bernard)
November 1888
Pencil and watercolour on Ingres paper, 475 x 620 mm
Signed l.r.: Vincent; annotated l.l.: d'après un tableau
d'E. Bernard
F 1422 JH 1654
Milan, Civica Galleria d'Arte Moderna (Raccolta Grassi)

194

Harvest in Provence
Mid-July 1888
Pencil, reed pen and brown ink on wove paper,
240 x 320 mm
F 1485 JH 1540
Berlin, DDR, Nationalgalerie der Staatlichen Museen
zu Berlin

193

The Zouave
Mid-July 1888
Pencil, reed pen and brown ink, wax crayon,
watercolour on wove paper, 300 x 230 mm
Annotated and signed u.r.: à mon cher copain
Emile Bernard Vincent
F 1482 JH 1487
New York, The Metropolitan Museum of Art
(Gift of Emanie Philips, 1962)

195

Summer Evening
Mid-July 1888
Pencil, quill and reed pen and brown ink on wove paper,
240 x 315 mm
F 1514 JH 1546
Winterthur, Kunstmuseum

196

Hayricks
Mid-July 1888
Pencil, quill and reed pen and brown ink on wove paper,
240 x 315 mm
F 1426 JH 1514
Budapest, Szépmüvészeti Múzeum

197

Hayricks
Between 31 July and 3 August 1888
Pencil, quill and reed pen and brown ink on wove paper,
240 x 310 mm
Signed l.l.: Vincent
F 1427 JH 1525
Philadelphia, The Philadelphia Museum of Art
(The Samuel S. White III and Vera White Collection)

198

Portrait of Joseph Roulin
Between 31 July and 3 August 1888
Pencil, quill and reed pen and brown ink on wove paper,
315 x 240 mm
F 1458 JH 1536
Malibu, The J. Paul Getty Museum

199

The Sower
Early August 1888
Pencil, quill and reed pen with brown and black ink
on wove paper, 245 x 320 mm
F 1441 JH 1543
Amsterdam, Rijksmuseum Vincent van Gogh
(Vincent van Gogh Stichting)

200

Garden with Weeping Tree
Early August 1888
Pencil, quill and reed pen with brown and black ink
on wove paper, 240 x 315 mm
F 1451 JH 1545
Houston, The Menil Collection

201

Fishing Boats at Saintes-Maries-de-la-Mer
Early August 1888
Pencil, quill and reed pen with brown and black ink
on wove paper, 240 x 315 mm
Signed l.r.: Vincent
F 1430b JH 1541
Brussel, Musée d'Art Moderne

202

Portrait of Joseph Roulin

August 1888

Pencil, reed pen and brown and black ink on Whatman paper,

590 x 445 mm

Watermark: J WHATMAN

F 1459 JH 1547

Los Angeles, The Los Angeles County Museum of Art

(Mr. and Mrs. George Gard De Sylva Collection)

203

Seated Zouave
June 1888
Pencil, reed pen and brown ink, heightened with white,
on Whatman paper, 520 x 660 mm
Watermark: J WHATMAN TURKEY MILL 1879
Signed l.l.: Vincent
F 1443 JH 1485
Amsterdam, Rijksmuseum Vincent van Gogh

204

Farmhouse in Provence
June 1888
Pencil, reed pen and brown ink on wove paper,
390 x 535 mm
Annotated and signed l.r.: un mas de Provence Vincent
F 1478 JH 1444
Amsterdam, Rijksprentenkabinet (Rijksmuseum)

205

Sand Boats on the Rhône
August 1888
Pencil, quill and reed pen with brown and black ink
on Whatman paper, 480 x 625 mm
Watermark: J WHATMAN TURKEY MILL 1879
F 1462 JH 1556
New York, Cooper-Hewitt Museum
(The Smithsonian Institution's National Museum of Design)

206

Garden with Sunflowers
July 1888
Pencil, quill and reed pen with brown and black ink
on Whatman paper, 607 x 492 mm
Watermark: J WHATMAN TURKEY MILL 1879
Signed l.r.: Vincent
F 1457 JH 1539
Amsterdam, Rijksmuseum Vincent van Gogh
(Vincent van Gogh Stichting)

207

A Flowering Garden
July 1888
Pencil, quill and reed pen with brown and black ink
on Whatman paper, 610 x 490 mm
Watermark: J WHATMAN TURKEY MILL 1879
Signed l.l.: Vincent
F 1456 JH 1537
Private Collection

208

Café du Forum
September 1888
Pencil, reed pen and black ink on Ingres paper,
620 x 470 mm
F 1519 JH 1579
Dallas, The Dallas Museum of Art
(The Wendy and Emery Reves Collection)

209

The Courtyard of the Hospital in Arles
May 1889
Pencil, quill and reed pen with brown and black ink
on Ingres paper, 455 x 590 mm
Watermark: AL PL BAS
Signed on the watering-can towards l.r.: Vincent
F 1467 JH 1688
Amsterdam, Rijksmuseum Vincent van Gogh
(Vincent van Gogh Stichting)

210

A Garden in the Place Lamartine
(Weeping Tree in the Grass)
Early May 1889
Black chalk, quill and reed pen with brown and black ink
on Whatman paper, 490 x 615 mm
Watermark: J WHATMAN MANUFACTURER 1888
F 1468 JH 1498
Chicago, The Art Institute
(Gift of Tiffany and Margaret Blake)

Saint-Rémy-de-Provence

1 - 226

INDEPENDENT DRAWINGS

9 - 210

When Van Gogh arrived at Saint-Rémy on 8 May 1889, he had with him two reed pen drawings, the sole survivors from more than one-hundred drawings done in Arles. He could easily have rolled them and, despite the usual objections at the post office because of their size, sent them like the rest to Theo in Paris. But he brought them to Saint-Rémy. In one sense, they marked the rebirth of his drawing activity after a prolonged hibernation period; in another, they were talismans, proof to the Director of the asylum that he was an artist, and should be allowed to practise his craft. He did not bring any paintings.

Whether Van Gogh pinned the two drawings on his wall, as he had done in Arles, or put them in a portfolio is not known. But what is sure is that he kept them with him for six weeks. When he eventually sent them to Theo around 19 June, he compared them to others recently completed. 'The drawings, 'Hospital at Arles', the 'Weeping Tree in the Grass', the 'Fields' and the 'Olive Trees' continue those of Montmajour of some time ago, others are hasty studies made in the garden' [595].

And on 2 July (not having had any response from Theo), Van Gogh sent a further roll of ten drawings to Paris. 'The drawings seem to me to have little colour this time and the too smooth paper is a little responsible for that. In fact, the weeping tree and the courtyard of the Arles hospital are more coloured, but all the same this will give you an idea of what I'm doing [in painting]' [597].

Extraordinarily enough, these two relatively short quotations are the sum total of Van Gogh's informative comments on his Saint-Rémy drawings. The rest can be summarized in a sentence. He cited two small drawings of insects, a death's-head moth (F 1523) and cicadas (F 1445), some unnamed plants [592], two of cypresses [596], and sent two unnamed drawings to Theo in December 1889 [617], and at least one other on 3 January 1890, identified in Theo's answer of 8 January as 'a superb pen drawing representing a fountain in a garden' [T 24]. A meagre harvest, compared to the richly documented Arles drawings!

And would he have said as much as he did without those two imported Arles drawings as points of contrast? They are seen to pass on the Montmajour tradition of large reed pen drawings to some current Saint-Rémy drawings, even though

these are less patiently worked out, less structured and conceptualized. Others of the garden, however, are classed as 'hasty', a term Van Gogh applied to the first series of half-page Montmajour drawings. But what is most fascinating is that the two Arles imports have 'colour', an attribute of pen-and-ink drawings never discussed in Arles itself.

Three extra-artistic factors conditioned Van Gogh's drawing activity at Saint-Rémy – the regulations of the asylum, the topography of its grounds, and, of course, the state of his health. During his one-year stay in the asylum of Saint-Paul-de-Mausole, he suffered four breakdowns, two serious and of long duration – from mid-July to late August, 1889, and from 22 February to late April 1890 – and two relatively mild, each lasting about a week in late December 1889 and late January 1890. During the three earlier crises, Van Gogh ceased to work. But during the final and the longest one – mid-February to mid-April 1890 – he did in fact paint, 'little canvases from memory - Memories of the North' [629 and 629a]. And though he doesn't actually say so himself, he must also have drawn 'Memories of the North' (F 1585 - F 1620).

Subject to the regulations of the asylum as he was, Van Gogh was denied the freedom to spend whole days out of doors exploring the countryside for motifs. Patients were only allowed outside the establishment accompanied by an attendant, and only at certain hours of the day. And during the first month of his stay, Van Gogh was confined to the large garden or park within the asylum's walls.

His pattern of work was very much dictated by the lay-out of the asylum and its grounds. Enclosed by a high perimeter wall, the asylum consisted of long, two-storey buildings which, on the men's side, were in two parts. One wing, running north-south, overlooked an enclosed wheat field. Its rooms faced east and the sunrise, with a view of the Alpilles mountains beyond the walled wheatfield. Van Gogh's room was situated in this wing. At right angles to this wing ran a second building from east to west, its main facade south and overlooking a large garden – or park, since it was dominated by enormous pines. As the asylum was far from full – Van Gogh spoke of thirty empty rooms – he was given an extra room in this wing to use as a studio. So the simple division was between bedroom and studio, sunrise and sunset, wheat field and park, unrestricted view of field and mountains and rather claustrophobic confinement in the tree-shadowed park.

Outside the walls were olive orchards, cypresses, and the Alpilles. These motifs became the main objectives of Van Gogh's extra-mural activities, and he planned to devote a series of paintings to each. Only three 'large' drawings were made of the open country (F 1542, F 1543 and F 1555).

cat. 236
cat. 224
cat. 226

Van Gogh's drawing campaign was concentrated within the walls of the asylum. In terms of large independent drawings, of which some twenty exist, this meant predominantly the park. There is only one large drawing of the enclosed wheat field (SD 1728).

cat. 225

'Since I have been here, the deserted garden, planted with large pines beneath which the grass grows tall and unkempt and mixed with various weeds, has sufficed for my work, and I have not yet gone outside' Vincent told his brother on 22 May 1889 [592], two weeks after his arrival at the asylum. And Dr. Peyron confirmed to Theo on 26 May: 'He spends the whole day drawing in the park here, but as I find him entirely tranquil I have promised to let him go out in order to find scenery outside this establishment'.

Dr. Peyron's evidence is valuable. In his letter of 22 May, Van Gogh had also told Theo: 'this month I have four size 30 canvases and two or three drawings'. These drawings, he affirms elsewhere in the letter, are of plants and the death's-head moth he had drawn the previous day (F 1523). Van Gogh began drawing around 20-21 May with the 'Study of Arum' (F 1613) - arums figure prominently in the painting he was then working on (F 609). Another plant study was of periwinkle (F 1614) – which also figures prominently in the same painting. None of the large drawings, then, was begun before 22 May. Van Gogh concluded his letter of this same date with an order for paints. While awaiting their arrival, he began seriously to draw. This first important drawing campaign lasted from 22 May until about 5 June, when Dr. Peyron allowed Van Gogh the freedom to paint outside the asylum walls. That is, he had a fortnight's intensive drawing, all of it in the park (or garden, as he called it at this stage).

It is even possible that these drawings were begun as illustrations for Theo. Theo had asked for details of life in the establishment in his letter of 21 May [T 9]. Van Gogh sent a very long and informative account of the asylum and his life there. These drawings would then illustrate what he wrote. Yet not one of them is ever mentioned at the time. Nor is there any evidence that any of them were sent to Theo in May or June. Vincent referred to (two) 'hasty studies made in the garden' in the roll of six drawings he despatched about 19 June, but these are probably the studies of plant and insect, judging from Theo's eventual response on 16 July – 'the butterfly [F 1613] and the branch of eglantine [confused with periwinkle, F 1614?] are very beautiful too; simple in colour and very beautifully drawn' [T 12].

cat. 211

Were the large studies of the garden abandoned and forgotten because of Van Gogh's excitement at being allowed to paint outdoors after 5 June? And did he ultimately prefer to send two drawings of fields and olive trees *outside* the asylum to give Theo more characteristic impressions of Provence? The brothers' silence on the garden drawings remains surprising.

Only Dr. Peyron's evidence gives a clue to the daily drawing activity that was to last a fortnight. The result was fourteen drawings, five in reed pen and ink (F 1497, F 1501, F 1505, F 1531, and F 1532), nine in mixed media with watercolour (F 1526, F 1527, F 1528, F 1529, F 1530, F 1533, F 1535, F 1536, and F 1537), of which three show the interior of the establishment. (These last, too, are uncited in the correspondance.) The series coheres stylistically and materially. Van Gogh brought his reed pens to Saint-Rémy. Additionally, he asked for small brushes to be sent in a letter that occurs in the midst of this obsession with drawing [593]. The paper he used in the majority of cases (in those sheets that have been examined) is full-size Ingres (620 by 470 mm, with variations, and with smaller dimensions in F 1531 and F 1537), watermarked AL PL BAS. Van Gogh had used this same paper for his last drawing from Arles of the hospital courtyard (F 1467).

cat. 212

cat. 215
cat. 220
cat. 209

Technically, a maximum of three stages can be isolated in the drawing process: a pencil or chalk underdrawing, then reed pen and ink (sometimes with brush), and finally (where relevant) watercolour (and gouache). One sheet displays the underdrawing extensively, with just a trace of pen added (F 1501). The Tate drawing (F 1497) carries it a stage further, with slightly more working with pen. The fiercely emphatic reed pen drawings number three – F 1531, F 1532, and F 1505 (with brush also used). The four garden drawings with watercolour and gouache (F 1533, F 1535, F 1536, and F 1537) have a very clear pen-and-ink base. They were, in fact, finished reed pen drawings; but Van Gogh decided to embellish them with watercolour and gouache. There is one certain exception to this, the Kröller-Müller sheet (F 1527), with the possibility that its companion (F 1526) shares its procedure: there, Van Gogh drew directly with brush and colour, magisterially. The three interiors of the asylum (F 1528, F 1529, and F 1530) stand apart from the rest in having no reed pen at all; instead, their colour is brushed over a chalk armature.

cat. 212

cat. 221

Stylistically, this series began cautiously (F 1497, F 1501), even using a perspective frame in the Tate Gallery drawing. This appears to be unique in the series. But the handling grew increasingly bold, with reed pen, often supported by brush, building up an animated surface pattern of decisively imparted strokes. Gone is the systematic exploitation of a limited vocabulary of graphic signs, as at Montmajour. And the dot, so much a controlling factor of midsummer Arles drawings, appears to be banished.

The *mise en page* is also varied: deep, legible spaces (F 1497, F 1501, and F 1531); close-up objects, such as a pine tree, thrust

cat. 212

dramatically across space, as in Japanese prints (F 1532); subtle tensions between surface and depth (F 1537); screenlike surfaces that vibrate (F 1527); and more traditionally handled recession, with stone steps and tree-trunks (F 1535).

There is also the question of the choice of format. Uprights and horizontals can often be paired: F 1497 and F 1501; F 1531 and F 1537; F 1532 and F 1533; F 1535 and F 1536. Whether this was haphazard or deliberate, an unconscious organic sequence or a premeditated attempt at another scheme of decoration (a minor variation on the scheme for the Yellow House), can only be guessed at. The brothers were silent.

cat. 216
In no instance can any of these drawings be connected with a painting. (The nearest is F 1532 to F 609.) Van Gogh had begun work at Saint-Rémy with a painting campaign that resulted in four large canvases of garden subjects (F 608, F 579, F 609, and F 734). His choice of motifs there was not repeated, once the fortnight of intensive drawing took over. In fact, the paintings and drawings complement each other: together, they form a marvellously rich evocation of the unkempt asylum garden.

1 - 223
Surely created as a triptych of uprights were the three gouaches of the asylum interior (F 1528, F 1529, and F 1530). All share the same size pink paper, the same chalk lay-in, the same fluid application of watercolour and gouache, and the same dull greens, ocherous yellows, and dried-blood reds. This proto-Expressionist palette is combined with boldly simplified, if not entirely flat, colour areas, heavy contours and forceful hatchings. The stark functionalism of the nineteenth-century interior is chillingly conveyed in the gloomy corridors and iron-barred windows. Yet the painter has penetrated: in the vestibule a framed painting leans against the right wall, an unframed canvas at its side. More completely, he has installed his studio: various bottles on the windowsill, with a touch of greenery and Provencal sky beyond the barred window, a table with small boxes, and on the walls, in part or in whole, four unframed canvases. Whether in two instances Van Gogh is deliberately creating the effect of paintings-within-a-painting, seems uncertain. Their connections with his own autumn canvases (such as F 640 and F 731) seem, at most, tenuous. Yet as summary landscapes of the garden outside his window, they make an ironic comment on the interior-exterior relationship.

Once outdoors after 5 June, Van Gogh still kept his drawings separate from his paintings. That deliberate process of separate 'takes', so challengingly present in Arles, no longer operates. Painting quite simply reasserts its priority. Van Gogh was launched on his summer series of wheat fields and olives, records of which, however, would steal back into the ten drawings after those paintings (see next section). Independent drawings were few: at most three, if one can be sure of the status of F 1542, which may be a drawing after a lost or destroyed painting. The two certain ones are those sent to Theo around 19 June: 'Fields' (F 1543) and 'Olive Trees' (F 1555). Unfortunately, the first of these has suffered losses at the upper

it. 236
it. 224
it. 226

right. Yet such losses cannot detract from this powerfully concentrated representation of a field with olives, backed by the Alpilles. Its realisation is spikily immediate and all-over, as if no surface should be left untouched. This contrasts with the more open, laconic strokes and pulsating rhythms of the 'Olive Trees', where even the shadows are miraculously breathed on to the sheet.

There is a postscript to this intense period of drawing in May and June: the undocumented study of the enclosed wheat-field, the only large independent drawing Van Gogh did of the motif that so preoccupied him in painting (SD 1728). cat. 225

Though it has some analogies with 'Rain' (F 650), especially in the plunging diagonal wall at left, it remains a quite separate statement. The image is dominated by field and sky, the Alpilles being little more than a distant horizontal band. All the drama is focussed on the sky: an incandescent sun, similar to that in 'Wheat Field with Rising Sun' (F 737), a painting in progress in mid-November; and a curiously-shaped, threatening storm cloud, reminiscent of the first painting Van Gogh did of the enclosed wheat field in early June (F 611).

In Provence in the 1880s, wheat was sown in mid-October. And the wheat in this drawing looks young, in a comparable state of growth to that in 'Wheat Field with Rising Sun'. This drawing, then, must date from November 1889. It can also be said to signify a considered reaction on Vincent's part to Theo's criticism of the drawings done after paintings: too abstract, too far from nature. Van Gogh sought a return to a more realistic base, both in style and subject. The strange animation and dense working of the surface in a medley of contrasting strokes, including the heavy cross-hatching used to render the deep shadow of the wall; and the rare use of white chalk to enhance the concentric expansion of the sun's rays, conspire to give this drawing the status of a surrogate painting.

DRAWINGS AFTER PAINTINGS (25 JUNE - 2 JULY 1889)

'We have had some glorious days and I have set even more canvases going, so that there are twelve size 30 canvases in prospect', Van Gogh reported to Theo on 25 June 1889. 'Two studies of cypresses of that difficult bottle-green hue [...] I will send you drawings of them with two other drawings that I have done too [...] I hope to send you some new drawings next week' [596]. True to his word, Vincent wrote on 2 July: 'In order that you have some idea of what I am doing, I am sending you some ten (une dizaine) drawings today, all from canvases I am working on. The latest one I've started is the wheat field, in which there is a little reaper and a big sun [...] The drawings seem to me to have little colour this time, and the too smooth paper is a little responsible for that [...] all the same this will give you an idea of what I am doing' [597]. And he confirmed to his sister, Wil, the same day that he had just sent Theo 'a dozen (une douzaine) drawings after canvases I am working on' [W 13].

This set of ten drawings after paintings (douzaine was a slip of the pen to Wil) differs radically from those done in Arles a year earlier. Then, Van Gogh sent drawings to three recipients – Bernard, Russell, and Theo; he had to choose from thirty paintings; he used a small format (257 by 345 mm). Now, he was working only for Theo; his choice of paintings was reduced to fourteen; and he selected paper twice the size of that used in Arles (620 by 470 mm).

Van Gogh's motives were simple, it appeared: to give Theo an up-to-date survey of his recently completed paintings. But not all of them as it turned out. He ignored all but one of the four garden paintings of May – probably because he was about to send them to Theo. His choice of the 'Sous-Bois' (F 609) reflected the very high regard he had for that picture: he would later select it for exhibition at Les XX in Brussels. He also ignored two paintings of olive trees (F 585 and F 715). That left him with nine June landscapes, images of Provencal early summer, dominated by four wheatfields, a field with poppies, olive trees with the Alpilles in the background, a starry night, and, of course, the two paintings of cypresses (F 611, F 719, fig. 45 F 717, F 617, F 581, F 712, F 612, F 613, F 620). More forcefully than the few drawings from nature despatched to Theo on 19 June, this new series would convey a truly characteristic impression of Provence.

Did Van Gogh have other motives for doing them? When he did the Arles drawings for Theo in August 1888, he wanted to improve his paintings, to clarify the touch and become master of his stroke, to remove the 'haggard' look of the paintings. The result was the most stylized, most carefully worked on, most finished of all Van Gogh's small drawings. Would these ten large drawings, by contrast, be among his most hurried improvisations?

Van Gogh complained that the drawings' lack of colour was partly due to the smooth paper he used. This was a wove paper, watermarked LATUNE ET CIE BLACONS. Yet it might be argued that he tried to exploit its limitations by varying his techniques and adjusting his style. There appears to be four variations in his use of his media. In at least three drawings – 'Trees with Ivy in the Asylum Garden' (F 1522) and the two of cypresses (F 1525 and F 1524) – Van Gogh not only began with a rapid compositional base in pencil, continuing with reed and quill pens, but he also finished with pencil, vigorously reaffirming and animating contours in parts of each drawing. In another instance (F 1494), the process is reduced to pencil and the most fluent of reed pens. In three others (F 1538, F 1540 and F 1544), finer touches of quill pen were added to the pencil and reed pen. And, in the remaining three (F 1548, F 1547, and F 1546), Van Gogh dispensed with the pencil preparation and worked directly with reed and quill pens.

These variations in technique may also reflect the actual order in which the drawings were executed. We know from Van Gogh's letter of 25 June that he had already done the two cypresses (F 1524 and F 1525) – together with two others. The 'Sous-Bois' (F 1522) must be one of these: it could be the first of the series, knowing Van Gogh's very high opinion of the painting. The fourth drawing to have been completed by 25 June could be F 1494. The remaining six, done in the week of 25 June - 2 July, divide equally: three with pencil, three without. Those without are all of wheat fields (F 1548, F 1547 and F 1546). Van Gogh began his painting of the 'Reaper' (F 617) that week, which further implies that the drawing after it belongs to this last trio. Indeed, it may be the last of all.

An interpolation here. There is one problem drawing – in terms of its status. That is 'Wild Vegetation in the Alpilles' (F 1542). It shares the same watermark of LATUNE ET CIE BLACONS (otherwise this paper was used only for the ten 'copies'.) It shares part of the motif of 'Olive Trees with Alpilles' (F 712): the 'Deux Trous' present at upper left. Like the last trio of the 'copies', it is done directly with reed pen. Is it a drawing from nature, however stylized and spatially ambiguous, or is it a drawing after a lost painting?

From this proposed sequence for the ten drawings a line of development can be suggested. Put briefly, Van Gogh began rather heavily and tonally, searching for particularities of structure and forms, and moved towards a lighter, more insubstantial expression of forms, spatially free, with pulsating rhythms dominating surfaces. There are intimations of Klimt, Toorop, Van de Velde, Matisse even. This anti-naturalistic stance was in part a distillation of Delacroix, in part a response to his concept of what Gauguin and Bernard were doing – and showing – at the café Volpini exhibition in Paris. Van Gogh felt part of their aesthetic; even if his expressions of that aesthetic were immediately distinguishable from theirs.

Theo's response to these ten drawings was one of extreme perplexity. 'The last drawings give the impression of having been made in a fury, and are a bit further removed from nature.

fig. 45 (F 620)
Vincent van Gogh
Cypresses with two Women, 1889–90
Otterlo, Rijksmuseum Kröller–Müller

fig. 46 (F 617)
Vincent van Gogh
The Mower, 1889
Otterlo, Rijksmuseum Kröller–Müller

I shall understand them better when I have seen one of these subjects in painting', he confessed on 16 July [T 12]. Vincent's mid-July breakdown prevented him reading this letter until the last week of August. He tried to defend his position in September at the time he was preparing to send Theo many of those June paintings that were the origins of the drawings. Certainly, this heightened and exalted view of the Provencal landscape, expressed in an exaggeratedly stylized, near abstract manner, was one that he abandoned in late November, when he again took up the challenge of drawing after painting.

There are two drawings, of equally large format as their July predecessors. One (F 1545), was made after the painting of 'A Corner of the Asylum Garden' (F 660), the other (F 1552) after 'Wheat Field with Rising Sun' (F 737). Though both are undocumented in the letters, they clearly must be the two drawings included in a batch of paintings sent to Theo in mid-December. 'I put in two drawings as well', was all that he said [617]. *cat. 237 - 238*

The Munich drawing has none of those pulsating, curvilinear rhythms that so dominated Van Gogh's July drawings; nor does it utilise the dot. Instead, he tried to reproduce in the drawing what he strove for in the 'parent' painting. 'There are no more impastos in the big studies. I prepare the thing with a sort of wash of essence, and then proceed with strokes or hatchings in colour with space between them. That gives atmosphere, and you use less paint' [618]. Similarly controlled hatchings dominated Van Gogh's painted series of olive trees begun in November. In the Munich drawing (F 1552), Van Gogh had to find a convincing graphic equivalent to the controlled and measured surface he had consciously evolved in his painting. His solution was a ubiquitous 'matchstick' stroke, varied slightly in length, thickness and direction. So determined was he to maintain a consistently uniform application that he even resisted the use of cross-hatching in the shadowed wall and its long cast shadow. *cat. 237*

This phenomenon of producing drawings after paintings is very much Van Gogh's own. (We don't find it in Degas, or Gauguin, or Cézanne, or Seurat: only at a certain point in his career, in Sisley, but then as a record of paintings done for himself alone, a kind of *liber studiorum*.) In one sense, it is a glorified extension of a description, or a hasty sketch, in a letter. Yet it was more: it became a complex and empirical balancing act in stylistic equivalences. The demands of conveying the essence of a painted image were pitted against the need to discover a coherent graphic vocabulary.

His solutions varied. In Arles, Van Gogh had to consider the contrasting preferences of his three recipients. In July 1889 in Saint-Rémy, he was engaged in pursuing an anti-naturalistic aesthetic; and in November 1889, he responded to a deliberately undertaken shift in his painting style.

There is a final comparison. When, in February 1890, Van Gogh partly repainted one of his two pictures of 'Cypresses' (F 621), adding two female figures, he made a drawing after the

fig. 10   restructured painting (F 1525a). It is smaller than its predecessors. But that is less significant than the fact that Van Gogh's
style shifts again. The way he handled 'that difficult bottle-
cat. 230   green hue' of the cypress in the first drawn copy of June 1889
(F 1524), employing a system of small serpentine repetitions
and variegated organic whorls, contrasts with the much more
sober presentation of the February drawing, where the flame-
like rhythms and interlaced sinuosities are virtually banished.

This was Van Gogh's last drawing after a painting. During
his few remaining months in Saint-Rémy and Auvers-sur-
Oise, the genre reverted to its origins – in letters. There, Van
Gogh did what most artists do in their letters – a very rapid
improvised sketch, often inaccurate in detail and misleading in
proportion and format, but adequate in conveying an impression. The dialectic between drawing and painting is seldom so
rich in Van Gogh's *oeuvre* than in this idiosyncratic category that
operated so comprehensively in Arles and Saint-Rémy.

211

Study of Arums
May 1889
Reed and quill pen and brown ink on wove paper,
310 x 410 mm
F 1613 JH 1703
Amsterdam, Rijksmuseum Vincent van Gogh
(Vincent van Gogh Stichting)

212

A Corner of the Asylum Garden
May 1889
Pencil, chalk, reed pen and brown ink on faded pink paper,
635 x 480 mm
Watermark: PL BAS
F 1497 JH 1852
London, The Trustees of the Tate Gallery

213

View in the Asylum Garden
May 1889
Pencil, reed and quill pen and brown ink on pink paper,
473 x 615 mm
Watermark: AL PL BAS
F 1501 JH 1739
Amsterdam, Rijksmuseum Vincent van Gogh
(Vincent van Gogh Stichting)

214

A Corner of the Asylum Garden
May 1889
Chalk, reed pen and brown ink, 455 x 605 mm
Watermark: AL PL BAS
F 1505 JH 1697
Otterlo, Rijksmuseum Kröller-Müller

215

Fountain in the Asylum Garden
May 1889
Pencil, reed and quill pen and brown ink on Ingres paper,
495 x 460 mm
F 1531 JH 1705
Amsterdam, Rijksmuseum Vincent van Gogh
(Vincent van Gogh Stichting)

216

Tree with Ivy in the Asylum Garden
May 1889
Pencil, chalk, reed pen and brown ink on Ingres paper,
617 x 473 mm
Watermark: PL BAS
F 1532 JH 1696
Amsterdam, Rijksmuseum Vincent van Gogh
(Vincent van Gogh Stichting)

217

Flowering Bushes in the Asylum Garden
May – June 1889
Watercolour and gouache on wove paper, 620 x 470 mm
F 1527 JH 1708
Otterlo, Rijksmuseum Kröller-Müller

218

Stone Steps in the Asylum Garden
May – June 1889
Pencil, black chalk, reed pen and brown ink, watercolour,
gouache on paper mounted on cardboard, 630 x 450 mm
F 1535 JH 1713
Amsterdam, Rijksmuseum Vincent van Gogh
(Vincent van Gogh Stichting)

219

Trees and Shrubs in the Asylum Garden
May – June 1889
Black chalk, reed pen and brown ink, watercolour
and gouache on Ingres paper, 470 x 620 mm
F 1533 JH 1710
Amsterdam, Rijksmuseum Vincent van Gogh
(Vincent van Gogh Stichting)

220

Stone Bench in the Asylum Garden
May – June 1889
Black chalk, reed pen and brown ink, and gouache
on Ingres paper, 374 x 617 mm
Watermark: PL BAS
F 1537 JH 1711
Amsterdam, Rijksmuseum Vincent van Gogh
(Vincent van Gogh Stichting)

221

Corridor in the Asylum
May – June 1889
Black chalk and gouache on pink Ingres paper,
650 x 490 mm
Watermark: AL PL BAS
F 1529 JH 1808
New York, The Museum of Modern Art
(Abby Aldrich Rockefeller Bequest)

222

The Vestibule of the Asylum
May – June 1889
Black chalk and gouache on pink Ingres paper,
615 x 474 mm
Watermark: AL PL BAS
F 1530 JH 1806
Amsterdam, Rijksmuseum Vincent van Gogh
(Vincent van Gogh Stichting)

223

Window of Van Gogh's Studio in the Asylum
May – June 1889
Black chalk and gouache on pink Ingres paper,
620 x 476 mm
Watermark: AL
F 1528 JH 1807
Amsterdam, Rijksmuseum Vincent van Gogh
(Vincent van Gogh Stichting)

224

Fields with Olive Trees in the Mountains
June 1889
Black chalk, reed pen and brown ink on wove paper,
499 x 650 mm
F 1543 JH 1743
Amsterdam, Rijksmuseum Vincent van Gogh
(Vincent van Gogh Stichting)

225

Wheat Field with Sun and Cloud
November 1889
Black chalk, reed pen and brown ink, heightened with
white chalk on Ingres paper, 475 x 560 mm
Watermark: AL
SD 1728 JH 1706
Otterlo, Rijksmuseum Kröller-Müller

226

Olive Trees
June 1889
Reed pen and brown ink on wove paper, 498 x 648 mm
Watermark: [...] 1889
F 1555 JH 1859
Amsterdam, Rijksmuseum Vincent van Gogh
(Vincent van Gogh Stichting)

227

Field with Poppies
June 1889
Pencil, reed pen and brown ink on cream wove paper,
480 x 640 mm
Watermark: LATUNE ET CIE BLACONS
F 1494 JH 1752
Private Collection

228

Trees with Ivy in the Asylum Garden
June 1889
Pencil, reed pen and brown ink on cream wove paper,
623 x 470 mm
Watermark: LATUNE ET CIE BLACONS
F 1522 JH 1695
Amsterdam, Rijksmuseum Vincent van Gogh
(Vincent van Gogh Stichting)

229

Wheat Field
Late June – early July 1889
Quill and reed pen and brown ink on cream wove paper,
470 x 617 mm
Watermark: LATUNE ET CIE BLACONS
F 1547 JH 1724
Amsterdam, Rijksmuseum Vincent van Gogh
(Vincent van Gogh Stichting)

230

Cypresses
June 1889
Pencil, quill and reed pen and brown ink
on cream wove paper, 625 x 465 mm
Watermark: LATUNE ET CIE BLACONS
F 1524 JH 1749
Chicago, The Art Institute (Gift of Robert Allerton)

231

Cypresses
June 1889
Pencil, quill and reed pen, brown and black ink
on white wove paper, 625 x 470 mm
Watermark: LATUNE ET CIE BLACONS
F 1525 JH 1747
New York, The Brooklyn Museum
(Frank L. Babbott and A. Augustus Healy Fund)

232

Wheat Field with Cypress
Late June – early July 1889
Pencil, quill and reed pen and brown ink
on cream wove paper, 471 x 622 mm
Watermark: LATUNE ET CIE BLACONS
F 1538 JH 1757
Amsterdam, Rijksmuseum Vincent van Gogh
(Vincent van Gogh Stichting)

233

Wheat Field
Late June – early July 1889
Quill and reed pen and brown ink on cream wove paper,
460 x 610 mm
Watermark: LATUNE ET CIE BLACONS
F 1548 JH 1726
New York, The Pierpont Morgan Library
(Gift of Mrs. Gerard B. Lambert in memory of
Gerard B. Lambert)

234

Reaper with Rising Sun
Late June – early July 1889
Quill and reed pen and brown ink on cream wove paper,
450 x 585 mm
Watermark: LATUNE ET CIE BLACONS
F 1546 JH 1754
Berlin, DDR, Nationalgalerie der Staatlichen Museen
zu Berlin

235

Olive Trees with the Alpilles in the Background
Late June – early July 1889
Pencil, quill and reed pen and brown ink
on cream wove paper, 470 x 625 mm
Watermark: LATUNE ET CIE BLACONS
F 1544 JH 1741
Berlin, DDR, Nationalgalerie der Staatlichen Museen
zu Berlin

236

Wild Vegetation in the Alpilles
Late June – early July 1889
Quill and reed pen and brown ink on cream wove paper,
471 x 623 mm
Watermark: LATUNE ET CIE BLACONS
F 1542 JH 1742
Amsterdam, Rijksmuseum Vincent van Gogh
(Vincent van Gogh Stichting)

237

Wheat Field with Rising Sun
November – December 1889
Black chalk, quill and reed pen and brown ink on toned paper,
470 x 620 mm
F 1552 JH 1863
Munich, Staatliche Graphische Sammlung

238

The Park of the Asylum at Sunset
November – December 1889
Black chalk, quill and reed pen and brown ink on toned paper,
470 x 610 mm
F 1545 JH 1851
Private Collection

Auvers-sur-Oise

9 - 240

SMALL DRAWINGS FROM NATURE

As far as is known, Van Gogh did not take any drawings to Auvers-sur-Oise on 20 May 1890. But he took four paintings, including 'Self-Portrait' (F 627) and 'L'Arlésienne' (F 540), which greatly impressed Dr. Gachet, homeopath, collector of Cézanne, Pissarro, Guillaumin, Renoir and others, and himself an etcher and painter. In Auvers-sur-Oise Van Gogh had an artist-friend, as well as a medical adviser. And there were other artists in the village. There was a tradition of artists working there, especially since Daubigny decided to build a house and studio in the village in 1861. Cézanne and Pissarro had worked there. Van Gogh would not be thought unusual. He referred to artists being there – the Frenchman Dumoulin (who had been to Japan) and a group of Americans, and he befriended others – the Australian Walpole Brooke and, from mid-June, the young Dutch painter Anton Hirschig. All, unfortunately, are now forgotten.

Auvers-sur-Oise has a very particular physiognomy. It is a long narrow village of some eight kilometres, trapped between the river and a steep escarpment, above which lies the extensive plains. Even though only twenty miles from Paris, 'Auvers is very beautiful, among other things a lot of old thatched roofs, which are getting rare' [635].

No sketchbooks survive from Arles and Saint-Rémy, but one, not completely intact, has survived from Auvers (SB 7). Additionally, Van Gogh made quick sketches *sur le motif* on a variety of different papers – different in quality, size, and colour; and he was certainly not averse to permutating his media. There is therefore enormous diversity in his sketches from nature. They are wide-ranging in subject: women working in the fields, a hasty sketch of a horse and wagon, or of a donkey, or of two young girls walking down a street. Some of these notes, taken on the wing, were used in paintings; others remained stored away. Two such pages (F 1636 and F 1615 v), one from May-June, the other from July, are included here to show something of Van Gogh's renewed responsiveness to everyday happenings; and to show something of his drawing style in more relaxed and informal moments. He was happy to be sketching without harassment or regulations, at whatever hour of the day he wished. As well as filling a sketchbook, Van Gogh made a dozen or so sheets of which many, like F 1615, have drawings on recto and verso. Such abundance makes one regret all the more those lost sketchbooks of Arles and Saint-Rémy.

INDEPENDENT DRAWINGS

cat. 241 - 248

Van Gogh said little of drawing in Auvers-sur-Oise. Twice he asked Theo to send twenty sheets of Ingres Paper. 'These I need in *any case* so as not to waste time. There is a lot to draw here' [636]. And twice he asked for Bargue's *Exercices au fusain* – urgently on 21 May, and again on 3 June, with justifications: 'I am terribly anxious to copy once more all the charcoal studies by Bargue, you know, the nude figures. I can draw the sixty sheets comparatively quickly, say within a month, so you might send a copy on approval; I will be sure not to stain or soil it. If I neglect to study proportion and the nude again, I should be badly muddled later on. Don't think this absurd or useless' [638].

Sceptical though he may well have been, Theo eventually sent this neo-classicist sub-Gérôme manual that had served Van Gogh in his early struggles to conquer the drawing of the human figure. Some sheets survive to prove it (e.g. F 1508 r and F 1609 v); and six pages in his Auvers sketchbook (SB 7).

Otherwise, there are two brief references to Van Gogh's own drawing. On 23 May: 'Just now I am very well, I am working hard, have four painted studies and two drawings. You will see a drawing of an old vineyard with the figure of a peasant woman. I intend to make a big canvas of it' [648]. On 25 May: 'I have a drawing of an old vine, of which I intend to make a size 30 canvas [...]' [637]. Just one drawing named, and one other cited: nothing more.

The drawing of the peasant woman in an old vineyard exists (F 1624). The other can be identified as 'Cottages with Thatched Roofs' (F 1640 r), since Van Gogh's first painting at Auvers-sur-Oise, made on 21 May, depicted the same motif (F 750) – 'old thatched roofs with a field of peas in flower in the foreground and some wheat, background of hills, a study which I think you will like' [636]. The projected painting of the old vineyard never materialized.

cat. 241 - 242

These two drawings form a pair, sharing the same watermarked paper, DAMBRICOURT FRERES HALLINES, and the same mixed media. They are essentially brush drawings over a pencil base, symphonies in blue-violet – and also Van Gogh's first large drawings from nature for months. The motif of cottages with thatched roofs was actually taken in a sloping field with hills beyond, as is quite apparent in the painting. In the drawing, the slope is less marked, and the hills replaced by a high screen of trees, absent in the painting. These capricious changes surely suggest that Van Gogh reworked the drawing in the studio. The swirling, rhythmic patterns, compulsively curvilinear and self-willed, are more brutally realised than anything from Saint-Rémy. Yet one aspect of his Saint-Rémy drawing convention is perpetuated in these thatched cottages. The exaggeratedly rounded roof lines – much more so than in the related painting – do not occur in French or Dutch thatched cottages. Their source lies in Van Gogh's 'Memories of the North', that series of more than thirty drawings done during his last long breakdown at Saint-Rémy, which contains his Southern adaptation of misremembered thatched cottages in Holland (e.g. F 1591 v and F 1595 v). Van Gogh's Auvers cottages are as artificially created as the blue-violet colour range and the boldly articulated linear configurations. Interestingly, he also made a drawing on the verso of the sheet (F 1640 v)of a house with chestnut trees, sober and matter-of-fact, without any added brush and colour. It too is related to a painting, 'Chestnut Tree in Flower' (F 752).

'Old Vineyard with Peasant Woman' also displays an insistent surface patterning that is riotously alive with vigorous hatchings, jabs and washes. Yet there is a firm compositional trellis, quite literally that wooden structure receding diagonally and supporting the climbing vines. The diagonal and vertical axes are echoed in the solid, four-square and oddly windowless buildings in the background. This is a more rectilinear drawing, contrasting strongly with the curvilinear emphases of its pendant.

This opening pair of Auvers drawings has no progeny, neither in their linear stylization, nor in their restricted blue-violet tonality. During his ten weeks in Auvers-sur-Oise, Van Gogh produced six more independent drawings. None is documented. And the fairly precise dating of the first pair clearly becomes difficult for the others.

cat. 244   However, one of them, 'The House of Père Pilon' (F 1638 r), must also be a May drawing. It is on the same Dambricourt Frères Hallines paper as the first pair; it shows a flowering chestnut (essentially a May phenomenon); and it relates to a *fig. 47*   painting (F 791) that was almost certainly completed in the first week of Van Gogh's stay. Drawing and painting, however, are the result of separate recordings, with slight but subtle shifts in compositional emphases that spring from changes in format and vantage point. This drawing is Van Gogh's most detailed from Auvers-sur-Oise, built up section by section, surface texture by surface texture. Even the pencil preparation is pushed fairly far; reed pen articulates discreetly rather than

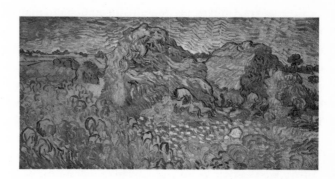

fig. 47 (F 791)
Vincent van Gogh
The House of Père Pilon, 1890
Private Collection

fig. 48 (F 809)
Vincent van Gogh
A Field with Wheat Stacks, 1890
Private Collection

smothers. It thus provides a striking contrast to the first two brush drawings.

Brush was reintroduced in the Tate Gallery drawing (F 1639), but with a wider colour range than in the blue-violet pair, one that would have been more marked before the fading of the pinks in the sky. The Oise meanders through the wide, expansive view, the only occasion Van Gogh gave such prominence to the river. Picturesque and nostalgic the view may seem, but there are two halves: the foreground fields to the line of poplars by the river, traditionally rural; beyond, modern intrusions, the suspension bridge, inaugurated in December 1889, and a large factory chimney.

The remaining quartet of drawings divides into two of farms and two of fields. The two farms (F 1653 and F 1642) share a compositional lay-out of foreground fields receding towards a middle ground of clustered buildings. And in each, a peasant is at work – added as an afterthought in the Louvre drawing. The labours of the field figure in several of Van Gogh's smaller drawings (cf F 1615 v). In the Louvre drawing, the traditional working of reed pen over a pencil in-lay remains. In the Chicago sheet, however, Van Gogh has introduced a wide range of mixed media that gives additional texture and colour. Graphic marks respond to the various kinds of growth. Shapes are densely organic, like the jigsaw effect in the foreground, and the snake-like orthogonals. Neither drawing has any equivalent in a painting.

By contrast, the two drawings of fields (F 1643 and F 1641), do have painted analogies. These are to be found among the sequence of double-square paintings. The haystacks of the Whitworth drawing have their counterpart in F 809; the sheaves of the Amsterdam drawing in F 771. Both drawings must date from July 1890. Drawn on the vast expanse of the Auvers plain above the village, they are about the complex interaction of textures and space, about those seemingly limitless vistas so typical of the landscape of the Ile de France. They are also about absence: no peasants, no evidence of any labour, no implements, just two lonely crows in the Whitworth drawing. They are about simplicity of statement, economy of placement, and spareness of touch. The pen strokes are like gentle gestural repeats.

Drawing in Auvers-sur-Oise did not have its clearly demarcated phases, as it did in Arles and Saint-Rémy. In just seventy days, and with painting by far Van Gogh's primary means of expression, it could not be other than an occasional activity. Yet in these independent sheets there is sufficient diversity in technique, selection of motif, *mise en page*, and relationship to paintings to render them some of Van Gogh's most challenging, most puzzling, most magnificent drawings.

t. 245

t. 243
t. 246

t. 239

- 248

fig. 48

239

Harvesting
July 1890
Black and blue chalk on Ingres paper, 239 x 311 mm
Watermark: MBM
F 1615 v JH 2085
Amsterdam, Rijksmuseum Vincent van Gogh
(Vincent van Gogh Stichting)

240

Houses at Auvers with Peasant Woman Walking
May – June 1890
Pencil and black chalk on Ingres paper, 446 x 277 mm
Watermark: HALLINES
F 1636 JH 2079
Amsterdam, Rijksmuseum Vincent van Gogh
(Vincent van Gogh Stichting)

241

Cottages with Thatched Roofs
May 1890
Pencil, brush, watercolour, and gouache on laid paper,
450 x 545 mm
Watermark: DAMBRICOURT FRERES HALLINES
F 1640 r JH 1986
Amsterdam, Rijksmuseum Vincent van Gogh
(Vincent van Gogh Stichting)

242

Old Vineyard with Peasant Woman
May 1890
Pencil, brush, watercolour, and gouache on laid paper,
435 x 540 mm
Watermark: DAMBRICOURT FRERES HALLINES
F 1624 JH 1985
Amsterdam, Rijksmuseum Vincent van Gogh
(Vincent van Gogh Stichting)

243

The Farm of Père Eloi
June 1890
Pencil, reed pen and brown ink on Ingres paper,
470 x 615 mm
F 1653 JH 1993
Paris, Musée du Louvre

244

The House of Père Pilon
May 1890
Pencil, reed pen and brown ink on laid paper,
445 x 550 mm
Watermark: DAMBRICOURT FRERES HALLINES
F 1638 r JH 1996
Amsterdam, Rijksmuseum Vincent van Gogh
(Vincent van Gogh Stichting)

245

Landscape with Bridge across the Oise
June 1890
Pencil, brush and gouache on pink Ingres paper,
475 x 630 mm
Watermark: AL PL BAS
F 1639 JH 2023
London, The Trustees of the Tate Gallery

246

Farmhouse in a Field
July 1890
Black and white chalks, blue pastel, reed pen and brown ink
on faded blue-grey laid paper, 470 x 625 mm
Watermark: MBM
F 1642 JH 1994
Chicago, The Art Institute (Bequest of Kate L. Brewster)

247

Haystacks
July 1890
Black chalk, reed pen and brown ink on Ingres paper,
465 x 610 mm
Watermark: ED&CIE PL BAS
F 1643 JH 2119
Manchester, Whitworth Art Gallery
(University of Manchester)

248

Sheaves
July 1890
Black chalk, reed pen and brown ink, brush and grey wash
on blue-grey laid paper, 474 x 630 mm
Watermark: MBM MBM
F 1641 JH 1484
Amsterdam, Rijksmuseum Vincent van Gogh
(Vincent van Gogh Stichting)

Literature

DE LA FAILLE

In 1928 J.-B. de la Faille was the first person to publish a classification of the work of Vincent van Gogh. The F numbers introduced by him are still in use today.

> J.-B. de la Faille, *l'Oeuvre de Vincent van Gogh, Catalogue raisonné*, 4 vols., Brussels 1928 (vols. I-II: paintings, vols. III-IV: drawings, watercolours and lithographs)
> J.-B. de la Faille, *Vincent van Gogh*, Paris 1939 (Hyperion, revised edition only including paintings)
> J.-B. de la Faille, *The Works of Vincent van Gogh. His Paintings and Drawings*, revised, augmented and annotated edition, Amsterdam 1970 (paintings and drawings in separate parts; based on notes left by De la Faille, who died in 1959, and further supplemented and corrected by a committee under the chairmanship of A.M. Hammacher)

ADDITIONS TO DE LA FAILLE

To obtain the fullest possible impression of the drawn *oeuvre* of Van Gogh the publications containing additions to the 1970 edition of his works by De la Faille are listed below.

> *Verzamelde Brieven van Vincent van Gogh*, published and annotated by his sister-in-law J. van Gogh–Bonger; with further additions by Ir. V.W. van Gogh, Amsterdam & Antwerp (1953-54) 1973; English edition: *The Complete Letters of Vincent van Gogh*, 3 vols., Greenwich, Conn. (1958) 1978 (letter sketches)
> Jan Hulsker, *Van Gogh door Van Gogh. De brieven als commentaar op zijn werk*, Amsterdam 1973 (letter sketches and separate sketches sent by Van Gogh with his letters)
> Ken Wilkie, 'Yes! It's an original', *Holland Herald* 2 (1973) 8, pp. 10-13 (drawing of Van Gogh's London lodgings)
> Han van Crimpen, 'Drawings by Vincent, not included in De la Faille', *Vincent. Bulletin of the Rijksmuseum Vincent van Gogh* 3 (1974) 3, pp. 2-5 ('A Barn' and 'Two Nude Figures')
> Martha Op de Coul, 'The Entrance to the 'Bank van Leening' (Pawnshop)', *Vincent. Bulletin of the Rijksmuseum Vincent van Gogh* 4 (1975) 2, pp. 28-30 (JH 126. A more detailed treatment can be found in: Martha Op de Coul, 'Toegang van de 'Bank van Leening' door Vincent van Gogh', *Oud Holland* 90 (1976), pp. 65-68)

> Jan Hulsker, *Van Gogh en zijn weg. Al zijn tekeningen en schilderijen in hun samenhang en ontwikkeling*, Amsterdam 1977, (6th expanded and updated edition 1989); English/American edition: *The Complete Van Gogh. Paintings. Drawings. Sketches*, Oxford/New York 1980 (drawings and paintings combined in chronological order; additions and omissions)
> Martha Op de Coul, 'Een mannenfiguur, in 1882 door Vincent van Gogh getekend', *Oud Holland* 97 (1983), pp. 196-200 ('Male Figure')
> *Impressionist and Modern Drawings and Watercolours*, London (Sotheby's) 27 June 1984 (pp. 8-9, no. 303: 'Paysan', 'Paysan, étude de forche')
> Johannes van der Wolk, *De Schetsboeken van Vincent van Gogh*, [Amsterdam] 1986; English/American edition: *The Seven Sketchbooks of Vincent van Gogh*, New York/London 1987 (fig. 17-19, SB 1: Nuenen, SB 2: Nuenen, Antwerp, Paris, SB 3: Antwerp, SB 4: Paris, SB 5: Paris, SB 6: (Antwerp and) Paris, SB 7: Auvers-sur-Oise)
> Ronald Pickvance, exhibition catalogue *Van Gogh in Arles*, New York (The Metropolitan Museum of Art) 1984; French edition: *Van Gogh à Arles*, Lausanne 1985 (p. 111: 'Olive Trees: Montmajour')
> Brooks Johnson (ed.), exhibition catalogue. *Hampton Road Collects*, Norfolk, Virginia (The Chrysler Museum) 1984 (p. 72: 'The Dutch Coalminer')
> *Impressionist and Modern Watercolours and Drawings*, London (Christie's) 24 June 1986 (pp. 10-11: 'Paysanne agenouillée devant une cabane')

GENERAL PUBLICATIONS ON DRAWINGS

In this section the general publications containing information on drawings are arranged according to their year of publication. The list is incomplete. Every effort has been made to include most of the literature specifically concerned with drawings, with particular emphasis on the publications dating from 1970 onwards.

> *Vincent van Gogh. 100 Teekeningen uit de Verzameling Hidde Nijland in het Museum te Dordrecht*, Amsterdam 1905
> J. Cohen-Gosschalk, 'Vincent van Gogh', *Zeitschrift für Bildende Kunst* 43 (1908) 9, pp. 225-235
> H.P. Bremmer, *Vincent van Gogh. Inleidende Beschouwingen*, Amsterdam 1911

H.P. Bremmer, *Vincent van Gogh. Reproducties naar zijn Werken in de Verzameling van Mevr. H. Kröller-Müller*, The Hague 1919

Julius Meier-Graefe, *Vincent van Gogh der Zeichner*, Berlin 1928

J.-B. de la Faille, *Les Faux Van Gogh*, 1930

René Huyghe, *Les Dessins de Van Gogh*, Paris 1936

W. Münsterberger, *Vincent van Gogh, teekeningen, studies, schetsen*, Bussum 1947

G.F. Hartlaub, *Vincent van Gogh. Rohrfederzeichnungen (Meister der Graphik)*, Hamburg 1948

Otto Höver, *Vincent van Gogh als Zeichner*, Emmendingen 1948

Bruno Kern, *Vincent van Gogh. Handzeichnungen und Lithographien*, Zurich 1948

Gabriel White, 'De tekeningen van Vincent van Gogh', *Internationale Echo van Ideeën en Gebeurtenissen uit Alle Landen* 3 (1948) 26, pp. 189-197

A.M. Hammacher, *Van Gogh (Les Grands Maîtres du Dessin)*, Milan 1953

Herbert Ashmodi, *Vincent van Gogh. Sonne und Erde. Zeichnungen*, Feldafing Obb. 1954

Douglas Cooper, *Zeichnungen und Aquarelle von Vincent van Gogh*, Basel 1954; English edition: *Drawings and Watercolours*, New York 1955

Leopold Zahn, *Vincent van Gogh. Landschaftzeichnungen*, Baden-Baden 1955

W. Jos de Gruyter, *Tekeningen van Vincent van Gogh*, s.l. 1962

Stephen Longstreet, *The Drawings of Van Gogh (Master Draughtsman series)*, Alhambra, Calif. 1963

Jérôme Peignot, 'Van Gogh. Le feu sacré pour le dessin', *La Connaissance des Arts* (January 1966), pp. 32-39

Nicholas Wadley, *The Drawings of Van Gogh*, London, New York, Sydney, Toronto 1969

Claude Marks, *From the Sketchbooks of the Great Artists*, New York 1972

Claude Mettra, *l'Univers de Van Gogh (Les Carnets de Dessins)*, Paris 1972

Ronald Pickvance, exhibition catalogue *English Influences on Vincent van Gogh*, Nottingham (University Art Gallery) etc. 1974-75

Charles Scott Chetham, *The Role of Vincent van Gogh's Copies in the Development of his Art*, (Outstanding Dissertations in the Fine Arts), New York/London 1976

Evert van Uitert, *Vincent van Gogh tekeningen*, Bentveld & Aerdenhout 1977; German edition: *Vincent van Gogh. Zeichnungen*, Cologne 1977; English edition: *Van Gogh. Drawings*, London 1979

Danièle Boone, *Van Gogh. Dessins*, s.l. 1980

A.M. Hammacher, *A detailed catalogue of the paintings and drawings by Vincent van Gogh in the collection of the Kröller-Müller National Museum*, Otterlo (Rijksmuseum Kröller-Müller) (1959) 1980

Hope B. Werness, exhibition catalogue *Vincent van Gogh. The Influence of Nineteenth Century Illustrations*, Tallahassee, Florida (The University Fine Arts Gallery, Florida State University) 1980

Carol Zemel, *The Formation of a Legend: Van Gogh Criticism, 1890-1920*, Ann Harbor 1980

Miloslava Neumannová, *Van Gogh, aquarelles, gouaches et dessins*, Paris 1987; German edition: *Vincent van Gogh. Zeichnungen*, Hanau 1987

Evert van Uitert & Michael Hoyle (eds.), *The Rijksmuseum Vincent van Gogh*, Amsterdam 1987

PUBLICATIONS ON DRAWINGS BY PLACE OF ORIGIN

This section presents an overview of the publications on Van Gogh's drawings, arranged in sequence of the places where he lived. Articles and books which do not deal exclusively with drawings are only included if they contain relevant information on drawings. Annual reports and 'picture books' have been disregarded. The emphasis is on more recent literature.

Juvenilia

J.G. van Gelder, 'Vincents Begin', *De Tafelronde* II (1955) pp. 8-9; English version: 'The Beginnings of Vincent's Art', in: *A detailed catalogue with full documentation of 272 works by Vincent van Gogh belonging to the collection of the State Museum Kröller-Müller, Otterlo* (Rijksmuseum Kröller-Müller) 1959, pp. xv-xx (pictorial themes from his early drawings return in his later work)

Anna Szymanska, *Unbekannte Jugendzeichnungen Vincent van Goghs und das Schaffen des Künstlers in den Jahren 1870-1880*, Berlin 1967 (three sketchbooks for Betsy Tersteeg)

H.F.J.M. van den Eerenbeemt, 'The unknown Vincent van Gogh, 1866-1868; (1) The Secondary State School at Tilburg', *Vincent. Bulletin of the Rijksmuseum Vincent van Gogh* 2 (1972) 1, pp. 2-12 (JUV XIIa)

H.F.J.M. van den Eerenbeemt, 'The unknown Vincent van Gogh 1866-1868; (2) The drawing master Huysmans', *Vincent. Bulletin of the Rijksmuseum Vincent van Gogh* 2 (1973) 2, pp. 2-10 (JUV VIII)

H.F.J.M. van den Eerenbeemt, *De onbekende Vincent van Gogh. Leren en tekenen in Tilburg, 1866-1868*, Tilburg 1972 (contains the same information as the two above-mentioned articles by Van den Eerenbeemt)

Borinage

H.L.C. Jaffé, 'Vincent van Gogh bei den Bergleuten im Borinage', *Der Anschnitt* 14 (1962) 3, pp. 19-25 (biographical notes)

The Dutch Period

Walther Vanbeselaere, *De Hollandsche periode (1880-1885) in het werk van Vincent van Gogh (1853-1890)*, Antwerp/Amsterdam 1937 (first some biographical details from each period, followed by a catalogue of works and a discussion)

Paul Nizon, *Die Anfänge Vincent van Goghs: der Zeichnungsstil der holländischen Zeit*, dissertation Bern, 1960 (artistic form and philosophy of life)

Jaap W. Brouwer, 'Van Rappard and Van Gogh', in: Jaap W. Brouwer et al., exhibition catalogue *Anthon van Rappard, Companion & Correspondent of Vincent van Gogh. His Life & All his Works*, Amsterdam (Vincent van Gogh

Museum) 1974, pp. 29-39 (F 68, F 845, F 874 v, F 1115
and works by Van Rappard)

Josef Giesen, 'Vincent van Gogh. Frühe Zeichnungen',
Die Kunst 90 (1978) 5, pp. 289-296.

Griselda Pollock, exhibition catalogue *Vincent van Gogh in*
zijn Hollandse jaren. Kijk op stad en land door Van Gogh en zijn
tijdgenoten 1870-1890, Amsterdam (Rijksmuseum
Vincent van Gogh) 1980-81

Etten

L. Gans, 'Twee onbekende tekeningen uit Van Gogh's
Hollandse Periode', *Museumjournaal* 7 (1961-62) 2,
pp. 33-34 (SD 1674 and SD 1677)

Bulletin Museum Boymans-van Beuningen 16 (1965) 1, pp. 20-21
(F 902a)

Lili Jampoller, 'Gardner with Pruning Knife', *Vincent.*
Bulletin of the Rijksmuseum Vincent van Gogh 1 (1971) 3,
pp. 13-14 (F 895)

Evert van Uitert (ed.) et al., exhibition catalogue
Van Gogh in Brabant. Schilderijen en Tekeningen uit Etten en
Nuenen, 's-Hertogenbosch (Noordbrabants Museum)
1987-88

The Hague

E. Haverkamp Begemann, 'Vroege Tekeningen van
Breitner en Van Gogh', *Bulletin Museum Boymans*
Rotterdam 1 (1950) 4, pp. 58-61 (a comparison of F 1025
with a study by Breitner)

Margrit de Sablonière, 'Sien', *De Tafelronde* (1955),
pp. 54-65 (a biographical study on Sien Hoornik)

H.L.C. Jaffé, 'Een onbekende aquarel van Vincent van
Gogh', *Museumjournaal* 2 (1956), pp. 5-6 (F 946 r)

V.W. van Gogh, 'Bij de tekening en de litho de de
Koffiedrinker. Van Gogh publicaties (1)',
Museumjournaal 13 (1968) 1, pp. 42-45 (F 1657 and
SD 1682)

H.L.C. Jaffé, 'Vincent van Gogh en G.H. Breitner. Een
parallel?' in: *Miscellanea Joseph Duverger*, Ghent 1968, I,
pp. 384-387 (a comparison of F 970 with Breitner's
'Distributing the Soup')

Martha Op de Coul, 'Een onbekend Haags stadsgezicht
van Vincent van Gogh', *Museumjournaal* 14 (1969) 1,
pp. 42-44 (SD 1679)

Jan Hulsker, 'The Houses where Van Gogh lived in
The Hague', *Vincent. Bulletin of the Rijksmuseum Vincent van*
Gogh 1 (1970) 1, pp. 2-13 (drawings made from his
studio and the immediate vicinity)

Jan Hulsker, 'Van Gogh's studio in The Hague
identified', *Vincent. Bulletin of the Rijksmuseum Vincent van*
Gogh 1 (1971) 2, pp. 2-5 (F 915)

Jan Hulsker, 'Van Gogh's dramatic years in The Hague',
Vincent. Bulletin of the Rijksmuseum Vincent van Gogh 1
(1971) 2, pp. 6-21

Jan Hulsker, 'Van Gogh's family and the public soup
kitchen', *Vincent. Bulletin of the Rijksmuseum Vincent van*
Gogh 2 (1973) 2, pp. 12-15 (F 1020)

W.J.A. Visser, 'Vincent van Gogh en 's-Gravenhage',
Jaarboek Die Haghe (1973), pp. 1-125 (identification and
localisation of many drawings made in The Hague)

Jan Hulsker, 'A new extensive study of Van Gogh's stay
in The Hague', *Vincent. Bulletin of the Rijksmuseum Vincent*
van Gogh 3 (1974) 2, pp. 29-32 (discussion of the
W.J.A. Visser article of 1973)

W.J.A. Visser, 'The Florist's Garden of Van de Putte on
the Schenkweg', *Vincent. Bulletin of the Rijksmuseum*
Vincent van Gogh 3 (1974) 4, pp. 8-11 (F 923 and F 930)

Jan Hulsker, 'Van Gogh's first and only Commission as
an Artist', *Vincent. Bulletin of the Rijksmuseum Vincent van*
Gogh 4 (1976) 4, pp. 5-19 (drawings commissioned by
C.M. van Gogh)

Griselda Pollock, 'Stark Encounters: Modern Life and
Urban Work in Van Gogh's Drawings of The Hague
1881-3', *Art History* 6 (1983) 3, pp. 330-358

Anneke Landheer, 'Een hoekje in het Van Stolkpark',
Van Stolkpark Koerier 10 (1987) 38, p. 1, 4 (F 922a)

Carol Zemel, 'Sorrowing women, rescuing men.
Van Gogh's images of women and family', *Art*
History 10 (1987) 3, pp. 351-368 (69 drawings of Sien
Hoornik and her family)

Roland Dorn, 'Een tekenaar onder schilders: Vincent
van Gogh in Den Haag, 1881-1883', in: exhibition
catalogue *De Haagse School. De collectie van het Haags*
Gemeentemuseum, The Hague (Haags
Gemeentemuseum) 1988, pp. 56-80; German edition:
exhibition catalogue *Die Haager Schule. Meisterwerke der*
holländischen Werke aus Haags Gemeentemuseum, Mannheim
(Kunsthalle Mannheim) 1987-88, pp. 56-80 (Van
Gogh's drawing activities and his relationships with
fellow artists in The Hague)

Drenthe

Mark Edo Tralbaut, *Vincent van Gogh in Drenthe*, Assen 1959

Nuenen

Jack P.G. van den Hoek, 'Twee Schetsen van Vincent van
Gogh', *Brabants Heem* 1 (1979), pp. 9-12 (JH 640 and
JH 606)

Bogomila Welsh-Ovcharov, *Van Gogh. The Vicarage at*
Nuenen (Art Gallery of Ontario Masterpiece
Exhibition Series 1), Toronto 1984 (F 1343)

Ton de Brouwer, *Van Gogh en Nuenen*, Venlo 1984

Carol Zemel, 'The 'Spook' in the machine: Van Gogh's
pictures of weavers in Brabant', *The Art Bulletin* 67
(1985) 1, pp. 123-137; Dutch, abridged version:
'Het 'Spook' in de Machine. Van Goghs Schilderijen
van Wevers in Brabant', in Evert van Uitert, (ed.) et
al., exhibition catalogue *Van Gogh in Brabant. Schilderijen*
en Tekeningen uit Etten en Nuenen, 's- Hertogenbosch
(Noordbrabants Museum) 1987-88, pp. 47-58
(an iconographical study of the weaver as a theme)

Johannes van der Wolk, *De Schetsboeken van Vincent van*
Gogh, [Amsterdam] 1986; English/American edition:
The Seven Sketchbooks of Vincent van Gogh, New York/
London 1987 (SB 1: Nuenen, SB 2: Nuenen, Antwerp
and Paris)

Evert van Uitert, (ed.) et al., exhibition catalogue
Van Gogh in Brabant. Schilderijen en Tekeningen uit Etten en
Nuenen, 's-Hertogenbosch (Noordbrabants Museum)
1987-88

Griselda Pollock, 'Van Gogh and the poor Slaves: Images of rural labour as modern art', *Art History* 11 (1988) 3, pp. 406-432 (detail studies and drawings thematically related to 'The Potato Eaters')

Antwerp

Mark Edo Tralbaut, *Vincent van Gogh in zijn Antwerpsche Periode*, Amsterdam 1948

Mark Edo Tralbaut, '1. Het Steen', *Het Cahier – De Nevelvlek* (1955) pp. 8-14 (F 1350 and F 1351)

Mark Edo Tralbaut, '2. De Grote Markt', *Het Cahier – De Nevelvlek* (1955) pp. 15-16 (F 1352)

Mark Edo Tralbaut, *Van Gogh te Antwerpen*, Antwerp 1958

Johannes van der Wolk, *De Schetsboeken van Vincent van Gogh*, [Amsterdam] 1986; English/American edition: *The Seven Sketchbooks of Vincent van Gogh*, New York/London 1987 (SB 2: Nuenen, Antwerp and Paris, SB 3: Antwerp, SB 6: (Antwerp and) Paris)

Paris

Fritz Novotny, 'Die Zeichnungen van Goghs in der Albertina', *Albertina Studien* 1 (1963), pp. 15-20 (the relationship between F 1399 and the burial scene in Emile Zola's 'L'Oeuvre')

Bogomila Welsh–Ovcharov, *Vincent van Gogh. His Paris Period, 1886-1888*, Utrecht-The Hague 1976.

Bogomila Welsh-Ovcharov, exhibition catalogue *Vincent van Gogh and the Birth of Cloisonism*, Toronto-Amsterdam (Art Gallery of Ontario-Rijksmuseum Vincent van Gogh) 1981

Johannes van der Wolk, *De Schetsboeken van Vincent van Gogh*, [Amsterdam] 1986; English/American edition: *The Seven Sketchbooks of Vincent van Gogh*, New York/London 1987 (SB 2: Nuenen, Antwerp and Paris, SB 4: Paris, SB 6: (Antwerp and) Paris)

Richard Thomson, 'Van Gogh in Paris: The Fortifications Drawings of 1887', *Jong Holland* 3 (1987) 3, pp. 14-25 (drawings of the Paris fortifications)

Bogomila Welsh–Ovcharov, exhibition catalogue *Van Gogh à Paris*, Paris (Musée d'Orsay) 1988

Pierre Richard, 'Vincent van Gogh's Montmartre', *Jong Holland* 4 (1988) 1, pp. 16-21 (F 1406 and F 1407)

Arles

Paul Fierens, 'Un dessin de Vincent van Gogh', *Bulletin Koninklijke Musea voor Schone Kunsten Brussels* pp. 40-47 (F 1430b)

Fritz Novotny, 'Van Gogh's teekeningen van het 'Straatje te Saintes-Maries', *Maandblad voor Beeldende Kunsten* 12 (1936), pp. 370-380 (F 1434 and F 1435)

Henry Thannhauser, 'Van Gogh and John Russell: Some unknown Letters and Drawings', *The Burlington Magazine* 73 (1938) 426, pp. 95-104 (F 1430a, F 1482a, F 1502a, F 1507a and the sketch in letter 501a)

Fritz Novotny, 'Reflections on a Drawing by Van Gogh', *The Art Bulletin* 35 (1953) 1, pp. 35-43 (F 1500)

Christian Carroy, 'Een panoramalandschap van Van Gogh', *Bulletin van het Rijksmuseum* 4 (1962), pp. 139-142 (F 1420 and F 1446)

Fritz Novotny, 'Die Zeichnungen van Goghs in der Albertina', *Albertina Studien* 1 (1963), pp. 15-20 (F 1518a)

Annet Tellegen–Hoogendoorn, 'Geen panoramalandschap bij van Gogh', *Bulletin van het Rijksmuseum* 2 (1964), pp. 57-61 (F 1420 and F 1446)

Mark W. Roskill, 'Van Gogh's 'Blue Cart' and his Creative Process', *Oud Holland* 81 (1966) 1, pp. 3-19 (F 1483- 1486)

E. Langui, 'Vincent van Gogh (1853-1890) Marine-1888', *Openbaar Kunstbezit in Vlaanderen* (1967), pp. 17a-b (F 1430b)

Annet Tellegen, 'Vincent van Gogh en Montmajour', *Bulletin Museum Boymans-van Beuningen* 18 (1967) 1, pp. 16-33

Mark W. Roskill, 'Van Gogh's exchanges of work with Emile Bernard in 1888', *Oud Holland* 86 (1971) 2-3, pp. 142-179 (Appendix A: a checklist of drawings made in Arles in 1888. Appendix B: a discussion of three early publications on the 1888 drawings)

Charles W. Millard, 'A Chronology for Van Gogh's Drawings of 1888', *Master Drawings* 12 (1974) 2, pp. 156-165

Jan Hulsker, 'The Intriguing Drawings of Arles', *Vincent. Bulletin of the Rijksmuseum Vincent van Gogh* 3 (1974) 4, pp. 24-32

Lucien Stoenesco, *Les dessins de Van Gogh pendant la période Arlésienne*, 2 vols., Mémoire de Maîtrise, Université de Paris-iv, Institut d'Art et d'Archéologie, October 1980 (artistic development and the relation to Japanese drawings)

John A. Walker, 'Van Gogh's Drawings of La Crau from Mont Majour', *Master Drawings* 20 (1982) 4, pp. 380-385

Ronald Pickvance, exhibition catalogue *Van Gogh in Arles*, New York (The Metropolitan Museum of Art) 1984; French edition: *Van Gogh en Arles*, Lausanne 1985

Ronald Pickvance, exhibition catalogue *Van Gogh et Arles. Exposition du centenaire*, Arles (Ancien Hôpital Van Gogh) 1989

Saint-Rémy-de-Provence

Ronald Pickvance, exhibition catalogue *Van Gogh in Saint- Rémy and Auvers*, New York (The Metropolitan Museum of Art), 1986-87

Auvers-sur-Oise

Margrit de Sablonière, 'Een onbekende schets van Vincent van Gogh', *Het Cahier – De Nevelvlek* 1955, pp. 30-31, 46-47 (F 1654 v)

Het Cahier – De Nevelvlek 1955, p. 10 (SD 1730 and SD 1732)

Johannes van der Wolk, *De Schetsboeken van Vincent van Gogh*, [Amsterdam] 1986; English/American edition, *The Seven Sketchbooks of Vincent van Gogh*, New York/London 1987 (SB 7: Auvers-sur-Oise)

Ronald Pickvance, exhibition catalogue *Van Gogh in Saint-Rémy and Auvers*, New York (The Metropolitan Museum of Art), 1986-87

Alain Mothe, *Vincent van Gogh à Auvers-sur-Oise*, Paris 1987

Index

Numbers

F/SD/JUV
The F, SD and JUV numbers refer to the corresponding numbers in: J.-B. de la Faille, *The Works of Vincent van Gogh. His Paintings and Drawings*, revised, augmented and annotated edition, Amsterdam 1970

JH
The JH numbers refer to the corresponding numbers in: Jan Hulsker, *The Complete Van Gogh. Paintings. Drawings. Sketches*, Oxford/New York 1980

SB
The SB numbers refer to the corresponding numbers in: Johannes van der Wolk, *The Seven Sketchbooks of Vincent van Gogh*, New York/London 1987

[ ]
The [numbers] refer to the corresponding numbers in: *The Complete Letters of Vincent van Gogh*, 3 vols., Greenwich, Conn. (1958) 1978

GAC
The GAC numbers refer to the corresponding numbers in: Douglas Cooper, *Paul Gauguin: 45 Lettres à Vincent, Théo et Jo van Gogh. Collection Rijksmuseum Vincent van Gogh, Amsterdam*, The Hague & Lausanne 1983

Colophon

Editor
Johannes van der Wolk

Translation
J.W. Watson, M.A./Trait d'Union, Eindhoven
(the articles by Johannes van der Wolk and E.B.F. Pey)

Typography
Walter Nikkels, Dordrecht & Düsseldorf

General Coordination
Marisa Inzaghi
Antonella Minetto

Typesetting
Drukkerij Mart. Spruijt bv, Amsterdam

Technical Production
Elemond Impianti Industriali, Milan
Carlo Mion
Angelo Mombelli
Luigi Colombo

Photo credits
All photos have been provided by the museums or the owners of the works. The colour photographs of the drawings in the Rijksmuseum Vincent van Gogh and the Rijksmuseum Kröller-Müller were taken by Tom Haartsen.

ISBN 88-242-0023-0

Printed in Italy by Arnoldo Mondadori Editore, S.p.A.

This book is printed on 'Pordenone' 120 gsm, from Cordenons Paper Mills, Cordenons, Pordenone, Italy.